WALKING THE DENVER-BOULDER REGION

by Darcy & Robert Folzenlogen

WILLOW PRESS
Littleton, Colorado

ISBN: 0-9620685-3-5
Library of Congress Catalog Card Number: 91-68587

Published by Willow Press
            6053 S. Platte Canyon Rd.
            Littleton, Colorado 80123
Printed by Otto Zimmerman & Son Company, Inc.,
            Newport, Kentucky
Typesetting by Debbie Metz, Mass Marketing, Inc.,
            Cincinnati, Ohio

Photos by Authors
Maps adapted from those provided by the U.S. Geologic
   Survey, the Colorado Division of Parks & Recreation,
   Denver Parks & Recreation Department, City of Boulder
   Open Space, Boulder County Open Space, Jefferson
   County Open Space and other areas covered in this guide.

For Sarah, Zach and Ally

ACKNOWLEDGEMENTS

Our sincere thanks to the many Park Rangers, Secretaries, Librarians, Ministers, and Historians who provided background information for this guide. The following groups and individuals deserve special mention for their contributions to our research:

Ann Armstrong, Interpretive Aid, Boulder Mountain Park Rangers
Boulder County Parks & Open Space Department
Boulder Parks and Recreation Department
Britt-Inger Bryant, Office of Public Relations, University of Denver
City of Boulder Open Space Department
Bonnie Clements, Manager, Depot Arts Center, Littleton
Colorado Division of Parks & Outdoor Recreation, Colorado
    Department of Natural Resources
Colorado Division of Wildlife, Colorado Department of Natural Resources
Colorado History Museum
Denver Botanic Gardens
Denver Museum of Natural History
Denver Parks & Recreation Department
Denver Public Library
Denver Zoological Foundation
Four Mile Historic Park
Jane Gardner, Arvada Historical Society
Historic Denver Inc.
Jefferson County Open Space Department
Roy W. Jones, Secretary, Highlands Lodge No. 86, A.F. & A.M.
Littleton Historical Museum
Doris McGowan, Guest Relations, Adolph Coors Brewing Company
Paul Millette, Archivist, Iliff School of Theology, Morrison Town Hall
Ellen Rice, Aurora Parks & Recreation Department
Jeff Shoemaker, Director, Platte River Greenway Foundation
Rich Smith, Chief Ranger, City of Boulder Open Space Department
Judith Trent, Executive Director, Historic Boulder Inc.
Lynn Tyler, Park Superintendent, South District, Denver Parks &
    Recreation Department
University of Colorado
Sean Warren, Seasonal Ranger, South Platte Park
Brent Wheeler, Ranger & Historian, City of Boulder Open Space
    Department
U.S. Geological Survey

We also wish to thank Debbie Metz, at Mass Marketing Inc., and Jan Jolley, at Otto Zimmerman & Son Company Inc., for their creative and technical assistance.

Finally, our thanks to Sarah, Zach & Ally for their company, patience and moral support!

— *Darcy & Robert Folzenlogen*

CONTENTS

INTRODUCTION

Avid walkers are often naturalists at heart and true naturalists understand that human activity has a profound impact on the character and health of our natural environment. In that spirit, this guide offers over 100 day hikes and urban walks within 1 hour of Metro Denver-Boulder, chosen to illustrate the geologic, topographic, floral, faunal and historic features of Colorado's Front Range.

Spaced from the rolling Piedmont to the alpine tundra, the routes were selected to appeal to families, visitors, naturalists, history buffs and weekend hikers. Throughout the guide, emphasis is placed on the natural and cultural history of the region and on our responsibility to protect what remains of that heritage.

Trail Data

For each walk or hike in this guide the following information is provided:

Route Distance - Unless otherwise stated, this is the roundtrip distance, in miles, from your starting point. The walks in this book range for .5 to 14 miles but the great majority are in the 2 to 5 mile range.

Difficulty - The walks and hikes are rated within the context of those included in this guide. Easy hikes can be achieved by persons in average condition who are acclimated to the Metro Area's altitude. Strenuous hikes should only be attempted by fit and experienced hikers who are also acclimated to the higher elevations of the Front Range. Moderate hikes obviously fall between these two parameters.

Walking Time - Given in hours, this provides the range of time that the average walker will need to cover the trail's course, including time for brief reststops along the way. It does not include time for picnics, shopping or other diversions enroute.

Elevation - Provided in feet above sea level, this is the range of elevation covered by the trail. The lowest elevation is not always the starting point and the highest elevation is not always the destination. Furthermore, topography along the route may cause far more elevation change than is apparent from the range listed. One should thus rely on the difficulty rating rather than the elevation range to assess the potential challenge of any given hike.

1

Life Zones of the Front Range

The walks and hikes in this guide are grouped into the three geographic regions that characterize the Front Range:

The Colorado Piedmont - This is the rolling countryside along the eastern base of the Front Range, dissected from the western High Plains by the South Platte River and its many tributaries. While early explorers, such as Zebulon Pike and Major Stephen Long, derided eastern Colorado as the "Great American Desert," later settlers and, of course, the native Indians, found that the Piedmont was rich in flora and fauna.

Today, the great majority of Coloradans live on the Piedmont which stretches from the Pike's Peak region to the Wyoming and Nebraska borders. Elevations range from 4000 feet in northeastern Colorado to 5800 feet along the base of the foothills. Natural woodlands, consisting of cottonwoods, willows and hackberry are "riparian," occurring along the River and its feeder streams. Before the arrival of white settlers, native shortgrass prairie covered most of the Piedmont where semi-arid conditions and periodic wildfires retarded the invasion of forest.

White-tailed and mule deer, coyotes, red fox, prairie dogs and thirteen-lined ground squirrels are typical residents of the Colorado Piedmont. Hawks, falcons, great-blue herons, meadowlarks, magpies, flickers and grassland sparrows are among the characteristic birds. Numerous lakes and reservoirs, essentially all man-made, attract waterfowl, shorebirds, egrets, ibis, cormorants and white pelicans, especially during spring and fall migrations. Of course, much of the Piedmont is now covered by irrigated farmlands, roads, city buildings and suburban sprawl.

The Foothills - Though the distinction between foothills and mountains is subjective in many areas, we have chosen elevations from 5800 to 8500 feet to represent the foothills. This corresponds to the following two life zones of the Front Range.

Foothill Shrublands - Stretching from the base of the foothills to almost 8000 feet on south-facing slopes, this zone is characterized by dry, rocky soil, scattered junipers, mountain mahogany, skunkbrush, Gambel oak and yucca-studded grasslands. Resident mammals include rock squirrels, deer mice, chipmunks, mule deer and mountain lions; bighorn sheep are found in a few of the lower foothill canyons. Rufous-sided and green-tailed towhees, rock wrens, scrub jays and golden eagles typify the bird population.

Transition Zone - Also called Montane Forest or the Yellow-Pine Zone, this mixed woodland stretches from 6500 feet to almost 9000 feet on sunny slopes. Open ponderosa pine woodlands, often called ponderosa parklands, cover the sun-scorched, south-facing hillsides while dense forests of Douglas fir, pine and blue spruce cloak the shaded, north-facing slopes. Abert's squirrels, chipmunks, porcupines, mule deer and black bear characterize the mammal population. Resident birds include nuthatches, hairy woodpeckers, Williamson's sapsuckers, western bluebirds, broad-tailed hummingbirds, Steller's jays and blue grouse.

The High Country - This is the popular name for the subalpine forest and the alpine tundra which, combined, stretch from the upper reaches of the Transition Zone to over 14,000 feet.

The Subalpine Forest is characterized by lodgepole pine, Engelmann spruce and quaking aspen, giving way to limber and bristlecone pines near timberline. These rich woodlands are home to pine martens, red squirrels, Clark's nutcrackers, gray jays, mountain chickadees and three-toed wood-peckers. Elk, mule deer, golden-mantled ground squirrels and mountain bluebirds may be spotted on high country meadows.

Timberline occurs at about 11,500 feet along Colorado's Front Range. Excessive cold, high winds and lack of moisture prevent tree growth above this natural barrier. Yet, the alpine tundra is inhabited by a surprising variety of plants and animals. Pikas, yellow-bellied marmots, white-tailed ptarmigan, water pipits, rosy finches, mountain goats and bighorn sheep are among the resident fauna. Alpine wildflowers provide a spectacular display from mid July through August.

Hiking Season

Walking and hiking are certainly excellent forms of exercise and recreation throughout the year. Each season has its special rewards for those who venture into our open spaces. A snow-laden forest offers a peaceful escape during the winter months and resident mammals are generally more active and conspicuous at that time of year. Crisp autumn days are especially appealing to most hikers and, in late September, the golden glow of aspen draws many flat-landers to the High Country. Spring ushers in the season of wildflowers which peak in June across the foothills but not until late July on the alpine meadows of the Front Range.

For any given trail, the hiking season is limited by three factors: snowfall, sun exposure and elevation. Assuming proper footwear, urban walks and hikes across the Piedmont are accessible throughout the year. On the other hand, trails that cross shaded slopes of the higher mountains may be covered by snow for more than 10 months of the year. Conversely, sunny areas in the High Country may have longer open seasons than shaded slopes in the foothills.

In general, hiking trails below 8000 feet are likely to be passable throughout the year, excluding mid winter and for several days after heavy spring snowfalls. Trails above 9000 feet are usually snowed-in from late October through mid June. Unless you're an experienced hiker with proper backcountry gear, limit your High Country excursions to the months of July, August and September.

Safety Considerations

Those who venture into our open spaces and wilderness areas should be familiar with the safety recommendations discussed below. These points are not raised to scare visitors from our wild areas; rather, they are included to advise hikers how to avoid the potential dangers that are inherent to the environment and climate of Colorado's Front Range.

Hiking Companion - While many of us crave the peace and solitude of mountain wilderness, an unexpected fall or injury can be fatal, especially during the colder months. Even in summer, temperatures may drop below freezing on the higher slopes. A hiking companion, old enough to go for help, is thus strongly advised.

Adequate Food & Water - Though our mountain streams are usually clear and inviting, they may harbor infectious agents or heavy metals from nearby mines. It is best to carry in your own water or, if necessary, boil it for several minutes before consumption. High-calorie food rations will help to appease your tired muscles and are essential to combat hypothermia should you become lost or trapped by the weather.

Altitude Sickness - Mild headaches and transient nausea are common when visitors from lower elevations arrive in Colorado; these symptoms usually abate within 12-24 hours. A more serious form of altitude sickness can strike anyone — even fit and acclimated hikers, especially above 10,000 feet. Shortness of breath, resulting from fluid accumulation in the lungs (pulmonary edema) and mental confusion, resulting from brain swelling (cerebral edema) and lowered blood oxygen, are the primary symptoms. This condition can be fatal; prompt descent to lower altitude is the most important therapy but medical attention should be sought as soon as possible.

Hypothermia - Lowered body temperature can be fatal but is almost always preventable. Wind and moisture add to the chilling effect of low temperatures and a water-proof parka should be carried on any of the longer hikes. Layered clothing, preferably of wool or synthetic materials, will allow for adjustment to changing conditions through the day. Some type of cap will diminish heat loss through the scalp and high-energy snacks will replenish heat from within. Hikers should watch for signs of hypothermia in their companions; shivering is an early-warning sign which should be heeded by adding clothing, ingesting food and turning back. Later symptoms include lethargy, cyanosis and mental confusion.

Sun Exposure - Many a skier and high country hiker has had his or her vacation disrupted by a bad sunburn. Remember that the rarefied air of Colorado, especially in the higher mountains, permits far more ultra-violet light to reach your skin. Protective eyewear and a high quality sunscreen (#15 or greater) are strongly advised.

Weather Conditions - Mountain weather is notoriously fickle and conditions in the High Country cannot be predicted from the Front Range cities. Other factors remaining equal, air temperature drops 3 degrees for every 1000 foot gain in elevation. In addition, high winds are common in the foothills and mountains, augmenting the chilling effect of the colder temperatures. Thunderstorms develop rapidly above the Continental Divide and are especially common from April through mid July; they are best avoided by hiking early in the day or by planning your High Country excursions for late summer.

Snakes - Poisonous snakes in our region (rattlesnakes) are most likely to be encountered in rocky areas of the Piedmont or lower foothills. Those who remain on designated trails rarely see these reptiles or, if they do, spot them from a safe distance. Persons bitten by rattlesnakes are usually climbing in off-trail areas, or under the influence of alcohol or bravado, attempt to confront the snake.

Bears - Most naturalists believe that grizzlies have been extirpated from Colorado, though a few sightings have been reported in the remote San Juan Mountains. Those who hike in the foothills and mountains of the Front Range may encounter black bears; the following advice is offered by wildlife officials.

1. Hike during daylight hours and make some noise along the trail to warn bears of your approach; be extra cautious near streams and when traversing thick brush.

2. Never attempt to feed or harass bears; keep a safe distance and back away slowly if one is spotted; avoid direct eye contact and speak in a non-threatening tone while retreating.

3. Don't run away and don't panic if the bear approaches or stands upright; he is more likely to be curious than aggressive.

4. Always stay away from cubs and never come between a sow and her offspring; this would invite an attack.

Mountain Lions - A series of mild winters, a burgeoning deer population and human encroachment on lion territory have all combined to produce an increase in human-lion encounters along the Front Range. The following recommendations come from the Colorado Division of Wildlife.

1. Never hike after dark and make some noise along the trail to warn lions of your approach.

2. If a lion is encountered, do not run or make quick movements; back away slowly, talk calmly and avoid direct eye contact; don't crouch or turn your back on the lion.

3. Never approach a lion.

4. If attacked by a lion, fight back!

Trail Ethics

When traveling through our open spaces, *"Take only photos and leave only footprints."* Native flora and fauna should be left undisturbed. Private lands should be respected and gates should always be closed after crossing fenced boundaries.

Be sure to stay on designated trails and do not take short-cuts between switchbacks; such behavior enhances erosion and harms native vegetation. Dogs, if permitted in the area, should be kept on a leash; free-roaming dogs harass wildlife and often disturb other hikers.

Finally, after enjoying our open spaces, contribute time and/or money to the organizations in Appendix II. These vital groups work to protect what remains of our dwindling wildlife habitat.

— *Darcy & Robert Folzenlogen*

KEY TO MAPS

Roads:	————————————————
Parking Areas:	(road with P markers)
Foot Trails:	– – – – – – – – –
Paved Trails:	— – — – — – — –
Railroads:	+–+–+–+–+–+–+–+
Lakes/Streams:	(lake and stream symbol)
Marshes:	(marsh symbol)
Forest/Woodland:	(forest symbol)
Rock Wall/Cliffs:	(cliff symbol)
Summits/Ridgetops:	(summit and ridgetop symbols)
Elevation (in feet):	☼ 8530 △ 7235

LOCATION OF WALKS & HIKES

1. Boulder Valley Ranch
2. The Foothills Trail
3. Boulder/Mapleton Hill
4. University of Colorado/University Hill
5. Sawhill Ponds Nature Preserve
6. East Boulder Trail/Teller Farm/White Rocks
7. Doudy Draw/Greenbelt Plateau
8. Rock Creek Farm
9. Barr Lake State Park
10. Standley Lake
11. Golden
12. Olde Town Arvada
13. Hayden/Green Mountain Park
14. Crown Hill Park & Nature Preserve
15. Sloan's Lake
16. Potter Highlands Historic District
17. South Platte Greenway
18. Lower Downtown/Auraria/Larimer St.
19. Civic Center/Capitol Hill/Quality Hill
20. Cheesman Park Area
21. Curtis Park Historic District
22. City Park/Park Hill
23. Four Mile Historic Park
24. Montclair Historic District
25. Aurora Environmental Park
26. Bear Creek Lake Park/Morrison
27. Washington Park/Country Club Historic District
28. University of Denver/University Park
29. Cherry Creek State Recreation Area
30. Littleton
31. Highline Canal
32. Chatfield State Recreation Area
33. Castlewood Canyon State Park
34. Bald Mountain Scenic Area
35. Mount Sanitas
36. Betasso Preserve
37. Gregory Canyon/Saddle Rock Trail
38. Green Mountain/West Ridge Trail
39. Walker Ranch
40. Eldorado Canyon State Park
41. Mesa Trail/Shadow Canyon
42. Golden Gate Canyon State Park
43. White Ranch Park
44. Central City
45. Idaho Springs
46. Beaver Brook Trail
47. Jefferson County Conference & Nature Center
48. Matthews/Winters Park - Red Rocks - Hogback Park
49. Lair O' The Bear Park
50. Mount Falcon Park
51. Elk Meadow Park/Bergen Peak
52. Alderfer/Three Sisters Park
53. Meyer Ranch Park
54. Reynolds Park
55. Waterton Canyon
56. Roxborough State Park
57. Indian Peaks Wilderness
58. East Portal/Crater Lakes
59. St. Mary's Glacier
60. The Continental Divide/Berthoud Pass
61. Georgetown
62. Chicago Lakes Trail
63. Chief Mountain
64. Abyss Lake Trail
65. Three-Mile Trail
66. Tanglewood Trail
67. Ben Tyler Trail
68. Devil's Head

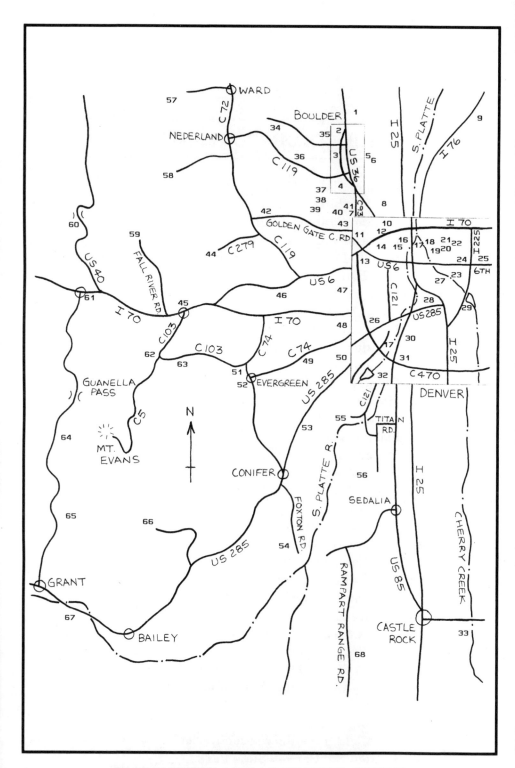

WALK/HIKE AREAS IN THIS GUIDE

9

I. THE COLORADO PIEDMONT

1. Boulder Valley Ranch
2. The Foothills Trail
3. Boulder/Mapleton Hill
4. University of Colorado/University Hill
5. Sawhill Ponds Nature Preserve
6. East Boulder Trail/Teller Farm/White Rocks
7. Doudy Draw/Greenbelt Plateau
8. Rock Creek Farm
9. Barr Lake State Park
10. Standley Lake
11. Golden
12. Olde Town Arvada
13. Hayden/Green Mountain Park
14. Crown Hill Park & Nature Preserve
15. Sloan's Lake
16. Potter Highlands Historic District
17. South Platte Greenway
18. Lower Downtown/Auraria/Larimer St.
19. Civic Center/Capitol Hill/Quality Hill
20. Cheesman Park Area
21. Curtis Park Historic District
22. City Park/Park Hill
23. Four Mile Historic Park
24. Montclair Historic District
25. Aurora Environmental Park
26. Bear Creek Lake Park/Morrison
27. Washington Park/Country Club Historic District
28. University of Denver/University Park
29. Cherry Creek State Recreation Area
30. Littleton
31. Highline Canal
32. Chatfield State Recreation Area
33. Castlewood Canyon State Park

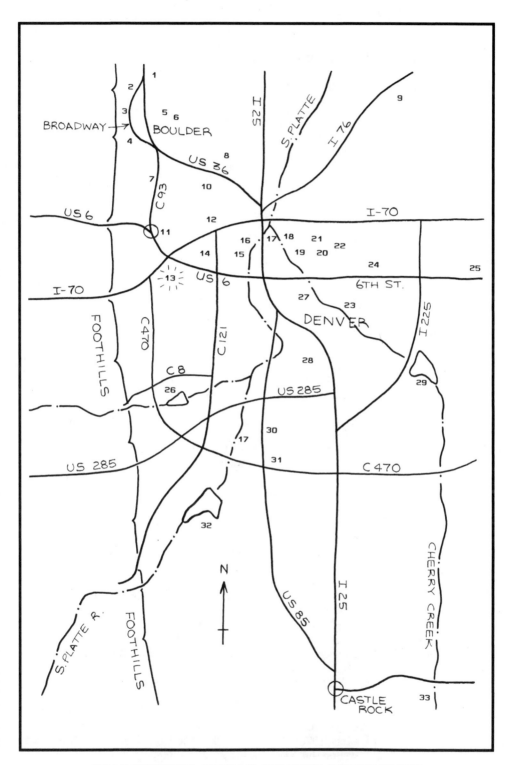

WALK/HIKE AREAS ON THE PIEDMONT

1 BOULDER VALLEY RANCH

Distance: 3.4 miles
Difficulty: Easy
Walking Time: 2-2.5 hrs.
Elevation: 5350-5560 ft.

If you enjoy open spaces and broad vistas, plan a visit to Boulder Valley Ranch, just north of Boulder. Formerly the site of a large cattle ranch and a smelter plant, the area is now protected within the City of Boulder Open Space system. Part of the land is still leased as a horse ranch and boarding facility.

A network of trails take you onto the central mesa and through the adjacent valleys. Routes atop the mesa (average elevation 5500 ft.) yield sweeping views of the Boulder basin, the Front Range foothills and the rural countryside north of the city.

Directions:

From Boulder, drive north on U.S. 36 (28th St.). Proceed one mile beyond the intersection of U.S. 36 and Broadway (Colorado 7) and turn right (east) on Longhorn Road. A parking area will be one mile ahead, on your right.

Route:

From the lot, walk to the south and then cut over to the **Pinto Trail (PT; see map).** This trail leads to the south and climbs onto the mesa via a series of stairways, crossing several drainages. Once atop the plateau it intersects the **Eagle Trail (ET)**; turn right and then bear left onto the **Mesa Reservoir Loop (MRL).**

This trail circles the old reservoir which has been dry since the early 1970s. Previously filled by water from the Silver Lake Ditch, the depression is now protected as vital wildlife habitat. Curving to the south side of the mesa the route yields a broad view of the Boulder basin, backed by Green Mountain, Bear Peak and South Boulder Peak.

Continue around the old reservoir, descending a bit as you turn northward. Cross over the **Degge Trail (DT)** and continue up through the valley to a multi-trail intersection. Bypass the **Hidden Valley Trail (HVT)** and angle to the east on the **Eagle Trail (ET)** which follows high ground across the mesa. Bypass the **Old Mill Trail (OMT)** but detour onto the **Mesa Reservoir Loop (MRL)** for a short excursion along the north edge of the basin. A sign describes local efforts to protect this unique habitat for wild residents of the Piedmont.

Switch back to the **Eagle Trail**, hiking along the northern rim of the mesa. A sweeping view of rural Boulder County unfolds to the north and east; Haystack Mountain (5588 ft.) pokes above the rolling landscape to the NNE. The **Eagle Trail** soon descends from the mesa and intersects the **Sage Trail (ST)**. Angle to the northwest on this wide path which parallels Farmer's Ditch. Cottonwoods and thickets along the canal offer a welcome retreat for raptors, songbirds and a variety of mammals that hunt or forage on the semi-arid grasslands.

Follow the **Sage Trail** back to the parking area, completing a hike of 3.4 miles.

*The central mesa yields broad views
of the Piedmont and foothills.*

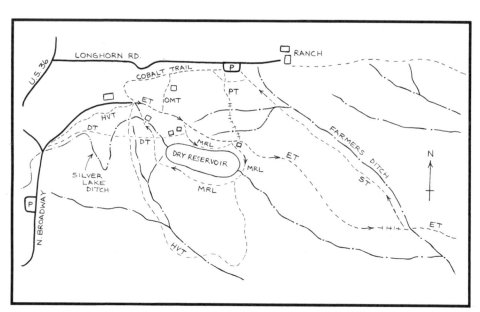

BOULDER VALLEY RANCH

2   THE FOOTHILLS TRAIL

Distance: 4.6 miles roundtrip
Difficulty: Easy
Walking Time: 2.5-3.5 hrs.
Elevation: 5520-5680 ft.

A popular route for walkers, joggers and mountain bikers, the **Foothills Trail** begins at Wonderland Lake, near the northern edge of Boulder. Covering a distance of 1.8 miles, the trail undulates across the Colorado Piedmont near the base of the foothills, crossing scrub grassland along most of its route. Yuccas and wildflowers produce a colorful display during the warmer months and the path yields sweeping views of the Boulder Valley and the nearby foothills.

Directions:
Parking areas will be found at either end of the Foothills Trail. We suggest using the **Foothills Trailhead** lot on N. Broadway. From Boulder, head north on Broadway or on U.S. 36 (28th St.). These streets merge at the northern edge of the city; just beyond the junction turn right on N. Broadway and proceed .25 mile to the Trailhead lot, on your left (see map).

Route:
From the **Foothills Trailhead**, hike to the west, crossing under U.S. 36 via a tunnel. The trail snakes westward, crossing the abandoned **Silver Lake Ditch**, and gradually climbs toward the base of the foothills.
Bear left at the first trail junction, crossing a drainage and passing through a gate. A short but steep climb brings you to another trail intersection; bear left again, crossing through an area of scattered ponderosa pines. Views now extend eastward across the Piedmont and southward to highlands beyond the Boulder basin. A gradual descent is followed by a detour to the east, skirting the edge of a horse pasture.
The **Foothills Trail** crosses Lee Hill Road and then angles to the southwest, soon crossing Fourmile Canyon Creek. Bear left at the next intersection where other trails lead off to the west, providing access to **Fourmile Canyon** (see map). The path now makes a beeline to the south, crossing semi-arid grassland that characterizes the western edge of the Upper Sonoran Zone. Jogging to the west of a residential area, the **Foothills Trail** soon descends into the basin of **Wonderland Lake** and intersects a trail that circles this scenic wetland.
Make your way around the Lake, paralleling the **Silver Lake Ditch** above its northern and western shores. The **Foothills Nature Center (NC)**, on Broadway, is operated by a private, non-profit organization; the city of Boulder owns the facilities and Open Space programs are often held at the Center.
Having circled the Lake via interconnecting trails and walkways, retrace your route to the **Foothills Trailhead**, completing a hike of 4.6 miles.

Approaching the basin of Wonderland Lake.

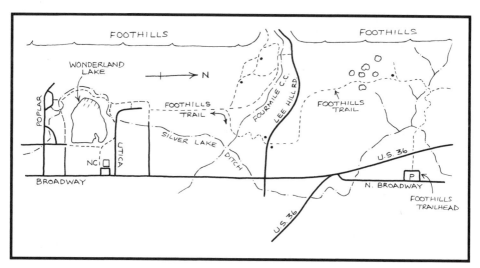

THE FOOTHILLS TRAIL

3 BOULDER/MAPLETON HILL

Distance: 3.6 miles
Difficulty: Easy
Walking Time: 3-4 hrs.
Elevation: 5340-5480 ft.

The first white settlement in Boulder County was informally established by Captain Thomas Aikens and his cohorts in October, 1858. Entering the Boulder Valley from Fort St. Vrain, on the South Platte, the party was exploring the area for gold which had been discovered along Cherry Creek earlier in the year.

Still part of the Nebraska Territory, the Valley proved to be fit for agriculture and, one month after the gold strike at "Gold Hill," the Boulder City Town Company was formed in February, 1859. Farming, grain milling, gold mining, lumber production and coal mining brought economic prosperity to the region. Boulder County was created with the birth of the Colorado Territory, in February, 1861, and the town of Boulder, founded in 1871, was eventually incorporated in 1878.

Boulder's continued vitality was assured when railroads reached the city, in 1873, and with the opening of the University of Colorado, in 1877. Later economic boosts occurred with the opening of Rocky Flats, in 1951, with completion of the Denver-Boulder Turnpike, in 1952, and with the dedication of the National Center for Atmospheric Research on Table Mesa in 1960. A 3.6 mile walk, described below, takes you through the older section of downtown Boulder and through the adjacent residential community of Mapleton Hill.

Directions:
Proceed to downtown Boulder and park in the lot at Broadway and Spruce (or in the near vicinity).

Route:
Walk toward the west on Spruce St. The **Soule-Coates House (1)**, at 1123 Spruce,

was built in 1877; it was purchased by Edwin Coates in 1898, then the Postmaster of Boulder. The house at **1105 Spruce (2)**, circa 1894, was the home of Lucius Paddock, hailed by many as the Dean of Colorado journalism. In the next block is the **Squires-Tourtellot House (3)**; built by Frederick Squires and Jonathan Tourtellot, in 1865, it was the first permanent residence in Boulder. The land holdings of these two lumber and mining barons became the first addition to the City of Boulder in 1870.

Head south on 10th St. and then east on Pearl. The **Buckingham Building (4)** dates from 1899. Cross 11th St. and enter the **Pearl St. Mall**, which was dedicated on August 6, 1977. Lined with shops and cafes, the 4-block Mall is the site of art shows, festivals and other cultural events throughout the year. The **National State Bank (5)**, circa 1899, is the oldest business still operating in Boulder; its forerunner was the Buckingham Brothers' Bank, founded in 1874. The **Boulder County Courthouse (6)** was constructed in 1933 using sandstone blocks from the old Switzerland Trail Railroad bridge supports. Across 14th St. is the historic **Boulder Theater (7)** which originally opened as an opera house in 1906. Under the guidance of Robert Boller, a Kansas City architect, the structure was remodeled and expanded for use as a film theater in 1935, re-opening on January 9, 1936. Closed down through much of the 1980s, the Boulder Theater is once again the site of concerts, receptions, stage productions and film festivals.

Continue east on Pearl St., passing the **Odd Fellows Hall (8)**, circa 1899, turn left on 16th st. and then left (west) on Spruce. The **Allen-Faus House (9)**, now an interior design center, dates from 1874. The **First United Methodist Church of Boulder (10)** was constructed in 1891; a new sanctuary was added in 1960. At 13th and Spruce is the **Boulderado Hotel (11)**

The Squires-Tourtellot House

Scene along the Pearl St. Mall

which opened in 1907 and was publicly owned until 1940; among its celebrated guests were Bat Masterson and Clarence Darrow.

Turn right on Broadway and then east on Pine St. The **First Congregational Church (12)**, English Gothic in style, was completed in 1906; it sits near the site of Boulder's first church which was built by the Congregationalists in 1870. A bell from the original structure rests along the north side of the Church. The **Trinity Lutheran Church (13)** was built in 1929; a large addition was completed in 1969 and a thorough renovation occurred in 1988. The **First Baptist Church of Boulder (14)** was erected in 1926; the congregation was established in 1872.

Across 13th St. is the **Boulder Victoria (15)**, a Bed & Breakfast that occupies the historic Dwight-Nicholson House. The original one-story house, as well as the carriage house, were built in the mid 1870s. Colonel Nicholson renovated the house and added a second story in 1895.

At the next intersection is **St. John Episcopal Church (16)**, completed in 1905; the tower was added in 1921. The **Temple House (17)**, built in 1882, was thoroughly restored in 1971. Further along is the **Austin House (18)**, circa 1875, built by Eugene Austin who served as Boulder's mayor from 1887-1891.

Turn left on 16th St. passing the **Carriage House (19)** for the Austin House, now remodeled into a residence and studio. Proceed west on Mapleton Avenue to the **Sacred Heart of Jesus Catholic Church (20)**; this parish, founded by the Benedictine Fathers in 1877, is home to the only Catholic school in Boulder. Across 13th St. is the **First Church of Christ Scientist (21)**, built from 1926-1931; the congregation organized in 1902.

Another block brings you to the edge of the **Mapleton Hill Addition**, platted by the Boulder Land & Improvement Company in 1888; it has since remained Boulder's most prestigious neighborhood. The **Grill Mansion (22)**, built in 1904, served as a mortuary from 1926 into the early 1970s.

The **McInnes Mansion (23)**, at 1020 Mapleton, also dates from 1904. Constructed by a local banker and lumber baron, the home includes a third-floor ballroom. At 933 Mapleton is the **Patton House (24)**, circa 1900; Judge Patton served as the first President of the Boulder County Bar Association.

Mapleton Elementary School (25) first opened in September, 1889; additions were approved in 1951 and 1974. Across from the school, at **811 Mapleton Ave. (26)**, is the former home of Boulder's first kindergarten, established by Faye Curtin in 1921; classes were moved to Mapleton School in 1938.

Turn left on 8th St. and then right on Highland Ave. The **Moorhead House (27)**, circa 1903, was the home of James Moorhead who served as Colorado's Secretary of State. The **McHarg House (28)**, at 725 Highland, is reminiscent of the Deep South plantations. The house at **603 Highland (29)**, built in 1890, served as the Hermosa Vista Nursing Home from 1939-1966.

Return to Mapleton Avenue and turn west along this tree-lined boulevard. The house at **430 Mapleton (30)** was built by Robert Duncan, a mining engineer, in 1892; Duncan also constructed Boulder's first street car line, which ran between downtown and the Chautauqua (see next chapter).

Turn left on 4th St. and then left on Pine St. The unique **Lewis-Cobb House (31)** dates from 1903. Proceed to 6th St. where the **Dodge House (32)** sits on the southwest corner; built in 1895, it was the home of Dr. Horace O. Dodge, first President of the Boulder Medical Society. Across Pine St. is the former **home (33) of Walter Buckingham**; he and his brother founded the Buckingham Brothers' Bank in 1874, now the National State Bank.

Head south on 6th St. and then east on Spruce. The frame house at **723 Spruce (34)** dates from the mid 1870s; it was the home of J. Alden Smith, named Colorado Territorial Geologist in 1872. Cut over to Pine St. via 8th St. The **McKenzie House (35)** was built by banker and mining

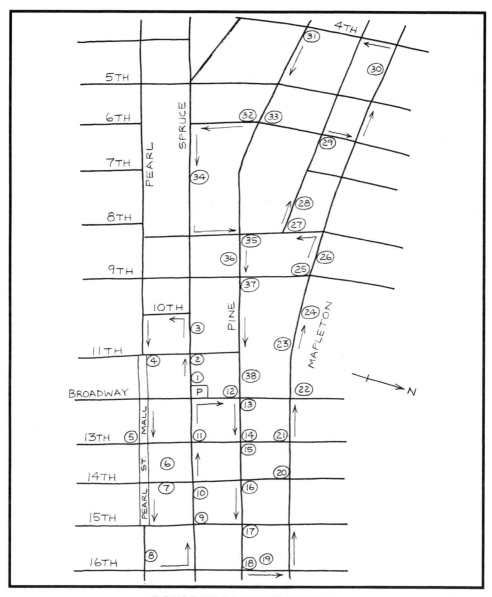

BOULDER/MAPLETON HILL

executive Neil McKenzie in 1890. The house at **820 Pine (36)**, circa 1892, was the home of Dr. William Casey, Boulder's Superintendent of Schools from 1892 to 1934. The **Earhart-Degge House (37)**, built in 1879, offers a fine example of Federal Style architecture, common throughout older sections of Boulder.

Continue east to Broadway, passing the **Carnegie Branch Library for Local History (38)**. Constructed in 1906 and funded by an Andrew Carnegie grant, the building's Greek-Temple Style was inspired by Boulder's reputation as the "Athens of the West." Originally the home of Boulder's Public Library, it became a center for Local History in 1983.

Turn right on Broadway and return to your car, completing a 3.6 mile tour of old Boulder and Mapleton Hill.

4   UNIVERSITY OF COLORADO/UNIVERSITY HILL

Distance: 4 miles
Difficulty: Easy
Walking Time: 2.5-3.0 hrs.
Elevation: 5400-5720 ft.

Once called the "Athens of the West," Boulder has been committed to education since the Valley was first settled. The first schoolhouse in Colorado (then Jefferson Territory) was erected at what is now 15th and Walnut Sts. in 1860. The original log structure was replaced by the Central School, a stone and brick building that occupied the site from 1872 until it was razed in 1972.

Efforts to establish the University of Colorado began to gel when the Board of Trustees was appointed in 1870 and accelerated when the Territorial Legislature authorized funding in 1874. Officially founded in 1876, the University opened a College Preparatory School in that year, followed by a full academic schedule in September, 1877.

Searching for a site to establish its summer retreat, the Texas Teachers Association chose the Boulder Valley in 1897 and "Texado Park," a 75-acre hillside south of the city, was designated for the Chautauqua. Educational programs at the retreat included music and art courses, drama study, philosophy and exploration of social issues. Physical education was also important and a "Climbers' Club" was soon organized.

The Texas-Colorado Chautauqua became the Colorado Chautauqua Association in 1900 and the grounds and facilities were designated an Historic District in 1978. A four mile walk, described below, takes you across the oldest section of the University of Colorado (The Norlin Quadrangle Historic District), up through the University Hill neighborhood to the Chautauqua and back to the University again.

Directions:
From U.S. 36 in south Boulder, exit onto Baseline Road and head west. Proceed to Broadway and turn right. Watch for the East Euclid Avenue entrance to the University and park in the visitors lot (see map).

Route:
Walk northwestward, paralleling Broadway on a paved bike path. Pass the **University Memorial Center (1)** and stop in at the **University of Colorado Museum (2)**. Open 9 AM-5 PM, M-F, 9 AM-4 PM on Saturday and 10 AM-4 PM on Sunday, the Museum house exhibits illustrating the natural history of the Rocky Mountain region; admission is free. After your visit, cut northward between the Museum and the **Denison Building (3)** and then turn right between the **Hellems Building (4)** and the **University Theatre (5)**. Hellems, named for the former Dean of Liberal Arts and Olympic fencer (1896) Dr. Fred B. R. Hellems, opened in 1921. The University Theatre, dating from 1902, was originally the main library on campus; it was converted to a performing arts theatre in 1940, one of many WPA projects along the Front Range. The **Ekeley Chemical Laboratories (6)**, erected in sections from 1898 through 1975, is named for Dr. John B. Ekeley who chaired the Chemistry Department for 35 years. At the east end of the **Norlin Quadrangle** is the **Norlin Library (7)**, completed in 1939. Both the Library and the Quadrangle are named for University President George Norlin, originally a Professor of Greek Literature and director of the Athletics Department, who guided the University for 22 years.

Begin a clockwise tour of the Norlin Quadrangle which is surrounded by the oldest and most historic buildings on campus; indeed, the **Norlin Quadrangle Historic District** was placed on the National Register of Historic Places in 1980. The **Guggenheim Building (8)**, donated to the University by Senator Simon Guggenheim,

Old Main

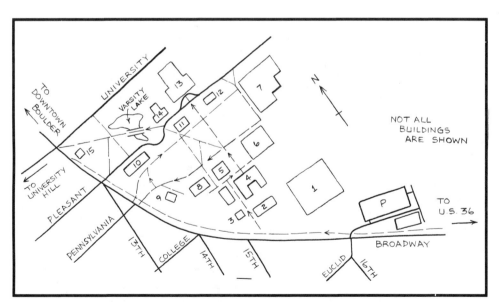

NORLIN QUADRANGLE HISTORIC DISTRICT

served as the School of Law for more than 50 years; it is now the Geography center. **Cottage No. 1 (9)**, completed in 1884, was the original women's dormitory on campus. Across the Quadrangle are the **Hale Science Building (10)**, which opened in 1895, and **Old Main (11)**, the first University building. Completed in 1876, Old Main housed classrooms, administrative offices, a chapel and living space for the President, the janitor and their families.

East of Old Main is **Woodbury (12)**, circa 1890, originally used as a men's dorm; it served as a makeshift hospital during the influenza epidemic of 1918-19. Cut northward to **Macky Auditorium (13)**, named for banker Andrew J. Macky who donated funds for its construction; unfortunately, Macky's will was contested and construction of the Auditorium, which began in 1909, took 13 years to complete. **McKenna Hall (14)**, originally a women's dorm, exemplifies the rural Italian style of architecture that is common throughout the University; Charles Z. Klauder designed this building and several others on campus.

Angle northwestward to University Avenue, crossing Varsity Lake. The **Koenig Alumni Center (15)** dates from 1883 when its original structure served as residence for the University President and his family. Cross Broadway and walk to the west along University Ave., entering **University Hill**. This residential district developed soon after the University of Colorado opened, creating nearby housing for professors and administrators.

Proceed 5 blocks and turn left (south) on 9th St. At Pleasant Ave., detour through **Pioneer Cemetery**; established in 1870, this was the first permanent cemetery in Boulder and many of the city's founding fathers (and mothers) are buried here. Continue southward along 9th St. to **"The Castle" (16)**, the many-angled creation of brick mason B. Franklin Gregg, completed in 1906. Turn right (west) on Aurora Ave. and proceed to 7th St. The **Rea House (17)**, built in 1898, was one of the first homes on University Hill. The **Coulson-Nixon House (18)**, constructed for Dr. David

Coulson, a local dentist, was the childhood home of astronaut Scott Carpenter. Further north, at 963 7th St., is the **Muenzinger House (19)**, circa 1930; this was originally the home of Karl Muenzinger, a German immigrant and Professor of Psychology at the University.

Cut over to 6th St. (see map) and ascend southward. **Cascade Manor (20)**, now a cluster of townhomes, was originally built as a dance hall for University students (1925). The **Fraser House (21)**, at 6th & Baseline, was built in 1917 by George Fraser, a miner and stone mason from Nova Scotia; a newer addition has since altered the home.

Turn eastward on Baseline and then ascend into the grounds of the **Chautauqua** (see map). Pass the Ranger cottage (R) and turn east on Clematis St. Frame cottages began to replace the Chautauqua's "tent city" during its second summer (1899). Circle past the **Dining Hall (22)** which was built in 1898; the wrap-around porch was added in 1901. At the top of the hill are the **Auditorium (24)**, the **Community House (23)**, circa 1918, and the **Administration Building (25)**, completed in 1900. The Auditorium, which dates from 1898, is listed on the National Register of Historic Places.

Descend down a long driveway that leads to 12th St. (see map) and turn left on Baseline Rd. Walk one block and turn right (north) on 11th St. The **David Holmes House (26)** was built in 1922; this Spanish-style house was used by a sorority from 1930-1934 after which it was repurchased by its architect and original owner. The **H. Reginald Platts House (27)**, at 750 11th St., dates from 1927; its tile roof and brick/stone facade are common features throughout University Hill. The **George-Paddock House (28)**, at 845 11th St., was constructed in 1909 for Dr. Russell George, a native of Ontario and Chairman of the Geology Department at the University of Colorado.

Turn right on Aurora and then left on 12th St. The **Harbeck-Bergheim House (29)**, now home to the **Boulder Historical Society Museum**, was built in 1899. This

The Chautauqua Administration Building

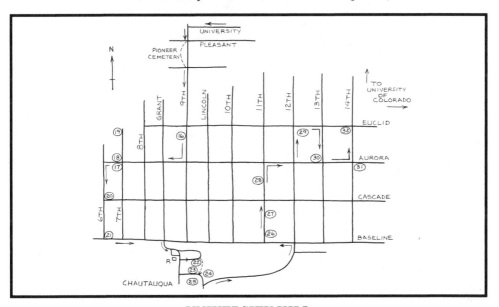

UNIVERSITY HILL

large, stone house, with its Dutch-style doorway and leaded glass windows, stood vacant for 30 years before it was sold to the City of Boulder in 1969. At 13th & Aurora is the **Derham House (30)**; this Gothic-style home was built in 1905 for Dr. Mico Derham, Dean of the University Summer Program and Chairman of the Classics Department.

One block east is **St. Thomas Aquinas Chapel (31)** which has served the com-munity since 1950. Walk northward along 14th St. to the **McNutt-Downing House (32)** which dates from 1892; the home was later purchased by Roderick Downing, a railroad and highway engineer who taught at the University and spearheaded efforts to build the Denver-Boulder Turnpike.

Return to the University via either 14th St. or Euclid Avenue, completing a 4-mile tour of Colorado's most renowned academic enclave.

5   SAWHILL PONDS NATURE PRESERVE

Distance: 1-2 miles
Difficulty: Easy
Walking Time: 2 hrs.
Elevation: 5120-5140 ft.

If we are to succeed in the protection of threatened and endangered species, we must devote ourselves primarily to the preservation of natural habitat. While guarding our untouched wilderness areas is of prime importance, the reclamation of damaged lands has become crucial to the overall effort.

Sawhill Ponds, in eastern Boulder County, provides an excellent example of what can be done with previously disrupted landscape. Once a series of gravel pits along the Boulder Creek floodplain, the preserve is now home to a diverse population of wildlife. Managed by the City of Boulder Open Space Department, the pits have been converted to a network of ponds and marshes, interspersed with grassy meadows and stands of cottonwood.

Birdwatchers flock to Sawhill Ponds in spring and fall to witness the seasonal migration of waterfowl, shorebirds, ospreys, egrets and songbirds. Great blue herons, kingfishers, great horned owls and kestrels can be found at the preserve throughout the year. Among the summer residents are green-backed herons, American bitterns, black-crowned night herons, soras and spotted sandpipers. Sawhill's mammal population includes red fox, raccoons, mule deer, muskrats and beaver.

Directions:
From the intersection of 28th St. (U.S. 36) and Valmont Road, in Boulder, proceed east on Valmont. Drive just over 4 miles and turn left (north) on 75th St. Cross the railroad tracks and turn left onto the entry road for the Sawhill Ponds preserve.

Route:
Interconnecting trails, many of which run atop earthen dikes, provide access to the restored wetlands. Educational plaques are spaced throughout the preserve, introducing the visitor to nature's handiwork. As illustrated on the map, walking tours of Sawhill Ponds can follow many potential routes with distances generally ranging from 1-2 miles. Whatever your route, plan to walk quietly, pause frequently and enjoy the many creatures that make their home at the preserve.

Early spring at the Ponds.

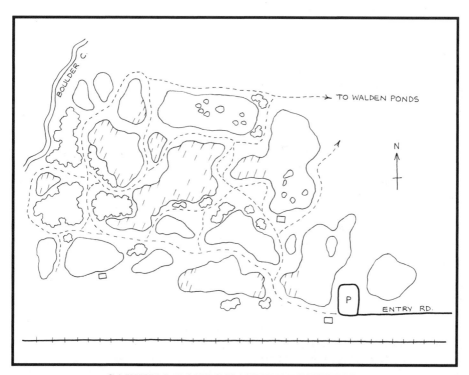

BOULDER C.

→ TO WALDEN PONDS

N

P

ENTRY RD.

SAWHILL PONDS NATURE PRESERVE

6   EAST BOULDER TRAIL/TELLER FARM/WHITE ROCKS

East Boulder/Teller Farm Trail
  Distance: 4.6 miles roundtrip
  Difficulty: Easy
  Walking Time: 2.5-3.0 hrs.
  Elevation: 5110-5210 ft.

East Boulder/White Rocks Trail
  Distance: 3.5 miles roundtrip
  Difficulty: Easy
  Walking Time: 2-2.5 hrs.
  Elevation: 5060-5200 ft.

The **East Boulder Trail**, which leads through the agricultural region of eastern Boulder County, offers an excellent avenue for hiking, birdwatching and nature study. The Trail begins at Teller Farm, a City of Boulder Open Space preserve, winds northward into the Boulder Creek Valley and then climbs onto the southern flank of Gun Barrel Hill. Several trailheads are spaced along its route and day hikes can be varied accordingly. The trail section between Arapahoe and Valmont Roads is called the **East Boulder/Teller Farm Trail**; that portion from Valmont Road northward and eastward to 95th St. is designated the **East Boulder/White Rocks Trail**.

Directions:

Proceed to U.S. 36 (28th St.) in Boulder. To reach the **South Teller Farm Trailhead (T1)**, drive east on Arapahoe Road, proceed 5 miles and turn left on the entry road to Teller Farm; this is 1 mile east of 75th St.

To reach the **North Teller Farm Trailhead (T2)**, drive east on Valmont Road from U.S. 36. The parking lot will be 6 miles ahead, on your right; this is 2 miles east of 75th St.

The **White Rocks Trailhead (T3)** is on the west side of 95th St., approximately 1.5 miles north of Valmont Road (see map).

Routes:

There are several potential day hikes along the **East Boulder Trail**. We suggest the following routes, both of which originate and end at the **North Teller Farm Trailhead (T2)** on Valmont Road (see map).

East Boulder/Teller Farm Trail (4.6 miles roundtrip). From the **North Teller Farm Trailhead (T2)**, walk to the south, cross through a gate and proceed along a wide path that skirts the western end of Teller Lake #5. The trail crosses a lakeside marsh, winds past old farm structures and turns eastward. Angling to the south along a grove of cottonwoods, the trail crosses Leyner Cottonwood Ditch and then follows this irrigation canal to the southwest. The open croplands of Teller Farm are now leased from the City of Boulder and are used primarily for alfalfa production. Smooth brome grass is the dominant vegetation on the non-irrigated fields.

After paralleling the ditch for ½ mile the trail angles to the south, passes a residential area and curves to the west just north of Teller Lake. A picnic area at the **South Teller Farm Trailhead (T1)** offers a shady spot for lunch before returning to your car via the same route.

East Boulder/White Rocks Trail (3.5 miles roundtrip). From the **North Teller Farm Trailhead (T2)**, walk to the west along Valmont Road for .2 mile to a small lot and private drive north of the road. The **East Boulder/White Rocks Trail** leads northward from this lot, paralleling Dry Creek. Cutting away from the stream and its riparian woodland, the trail crosses the Union Pacific Railroad and then curves to the east of a broad, shallow lake; herons, egrets and other water birds are often spotted here during the warmer months. Migrant waterfowl may be abundant on the lake in spring and fall.

The trail crosses Boulder Creek and then climbs onto the southern flank of Gun

Scene along the East Boulder/White Rocks Trail.

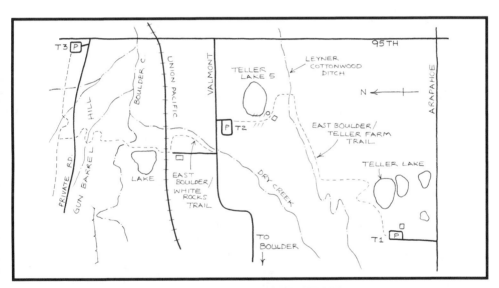

THE EAST BOULDER TRAIL

Barrel Hill, a broad ridge underlain with late Cretaceous sandstone. This "white rock" forms spectacular cliffs along the north wall of the Boulder Creek Valley and is exposed along stream beds all across the ridge. Climb to the crest of the hill for a sweeping view that extends across the rolling Piedmont, along the Boulder Valley and westward to the Front Range. The majestic Indian Peaks, 35 miles distant, rise above the foothills.

Return to the North Teller Farm Trailhead via the same route, completing a roundtrip hike of 3.5 miles.

7 DOUDY DRAW/GREENBELT PLATEAU

Distance: 7 miles
Difficulty: Easy
Walking Time: 3-4 hrs.
Elevation: 5720-6100 ft.

Flatirons Vista Trailhead, along Colorado 93, yields access to a 7-mile loop hike across the rolling Piedmont south of Boulder. The route utilizes sections of three trails within the City of Boulder Open Space system and offers sweeping views of the Front Range foothills, from Coal Creek Canyon to the Ft. Collins area. Hawks, golden eagles and falcons hunt across the broad grasslands. The mixed-grass habitat is characterized by blue grama, western wheatgrass, green needlegrass and a host of introduced species. Yuccas, skunkbrush and open woodlands of ponderosa pine add to the floral diversity. Even scattered remnants of tallgrass prairie are found along some of the drainages. Wildflowers, including pasque-flowers, sand lilies, wild iris and golden banner adorn the grasslands from early spring through late summer. Resident mammals include mule deer, coyote, red fox and badgers. Watch for Abert's squirrels, great horned owls, flickers and Steller's jays in the pine woodland along Doudy Draw.

Directions:

Flatirons Vista Trailhead is on the west side of Colorado 93, 2.2 miles south of the junction with Colorado 170; this is approximately 3.5 miles south of Boulder or 11.5 miles north of Golden.

Route:

From the **Flatirons Vista Trailhead** the **Doudy Draw Trail (DDT)** leads westward across an open grassland. The Front Range foothills, adorned with the "flatiron" rock formations, loom in the distance. The flatirons are part of the Fountain Formation,

dating back to the Pennsylvanian Period of the late Paleozoic Era (approximately 300 million years ago). Composed of sediments washed down from the ancestral Rockies, the rocks were originally horizontal and were tilted into their present position as the modern Rockies pushed skyward, 70 million years ago.

Approaching Doudy Draw the trail enters an open forest of ponderosa pine. Watch for mule deer resting beneath the trees during the colder months. Curving to the south the trail begins a long descent into Doudy Draw; ahead of you is Coal Creek Peak (8484 ft.) and across the valley to the west is the rugged mouth of Eldorado Canyon.

Angling back to the north the trail completes its descent to Doudy Draw. Thickets along the east wall of the valley provide ideal habitat for blue grouse during the warmer months. Leading northward the Doudy Draw Trail crosses and then recrosses the creek before intersecting the **Community Ditch Trail (CDT)**. From this intersection a paved path continues northward to Colorado 170.

Turn right along the Community Ditch and wind toward the northeast above an eroded grassland. Though you have the sensation of climbing, the water in the ditch is paradoxically flowing in your direction. Views of Greater Boulder unfold as you approach Colorado 93.

Cross the highway and continue eastward on the **Greenbelt Plateau Trail (GPT)**. The trail climbs eastward and then southward through an open ponderosa pine woodland. Nearing the summit of the ridge you are treated to a sweeping view of the Boulder Valley, backed by the Front Range foothills. The National Center for Atmospheric Research sits atop Table Mesa at the base of Green Mountain.

If you're hiking at dawn or dusk, watch for coyotes that often hunt along the drainages that incise the eastern edge of the

Eldorado Canyon from the Community Ditch Trail.

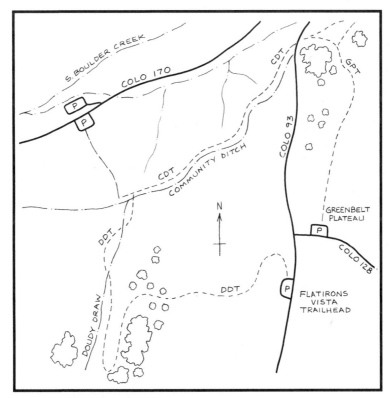

DOUDY DRAW/GREENBELT PLATEAU

plateau. Horned larks, occasionally joined by flocks of longspurs are common along the trail during the colder months. The route leads southward across the windswept grassland, terminating at the **Green-** **belt Plateau Trailhead** on Colorado 128 near its junction with Colorado 93. A short walk southward along Colorado 93 takes you back to the **Flatirons Vista Trailhead** (see map).

8 ROCK CREEK FARM

Distance: 3.4 miles
Difficulty: Easy
Walking Time: 2 hrs.
Elevation: 5240-5280 ft.

Wildlife watchers will thoroughly enjoy a visit to Rock Creek Farm. Acquired by Boulder County Open Space to preserve a piece of the County's agricultural heritage, most of the Farm's 994 acres are leased to private concerns for crop production and livestock grazing and are thus closed to the public. However, a 3.5-mile network of earthen trails provides access to the varied natural habitats that characterize the preserve.

Much of the route crosses open grasslands and pastures where black-tailed prairie dogs have established extensive colonies. Ever wary of the hawks, kestrels and prairie falcons that hunt across this open country, the prairie dogs forage near their burrows, ready to dive below when danger approaches. Among their other nemeses are red fox and coyotes.

Stearns Lake, a 25-acre pond just east of 104th St., attracts herons, cormorants and grebes during the warmer months and is a magnet for waterfowl during the spring and fall migrations. Muskrats are often spotted along the marshy shallows. South of the Lake, drainage channels and meandering tributaries of Rock Creek offer greenbelts for wildlife through the drier grasslands. Cottonwoods, willows and a variety of shrubs line the waterways, providing choice habitat for great horned owls, magpies, kingfishers, raccoons and numerous songbirds.

Directions:

From U.S. 36 between Denver and Boulder, take the Broomfield/Lafayette Exit and head north on U.S. 287. Drive 2.5 miles to Dillon Rd. and turn left (west). Parking areas are located on Dillon Rd. and on 104th St., as illustrated on the map.

Route:

From the small lot on the south side of Dillon Rd., walk toward the southwest on a trail that parallels a double fence line and crosses an open grassland, pitted with prairie dog burrows. Watch for kestrels and prairie falcons that often perch on fenceposts between hunting forays. Red-tailed hawks soar overhead throughout the year, joined by Swainson's hawks in summer and northern rough-legged hawks in winter. Meadowlarks are abundant on the grassland from April to November.

About .5 mile from the trailhead the route angles to the right, yielding a broad view of the Front Range along the western horizon. Turning south again, the trail descends to the basin of Stearns Lake, crosses an irrigation ditch, splits into parallel paths and follows the eastern shoreline. Take the upper trail (nearest the shore) which offers a constant view across the open waters and into the lakeshore marshes. Soras and bitterns may be spotted among the cattails in spring and late summer and, as mentioned above, muskrats are often found along the shallows. Herons, teal, killdeer and snipe may flush as you hike above the wetland.

Halfway along the southern shore the upper and lower trails merge. Cut back to the east along the lower route and then angle to the southeast, soon crossing a stream bed (see map). Cross a dirt road and continue southward, passing over a second creek and then paralleling its course to the west. This is perhaps the best stretch of riparian habitat within the preserve.

Upon reaching the trail intersection, turn right, walk a short distance and continue northward along 104th St. to the Park's primary access lot. Re-enter the preserve, backtracking along the lakeshore and returning to the Dillon Rd. lot via your initial entry route.

Stearns Lake reflects a summer sky.

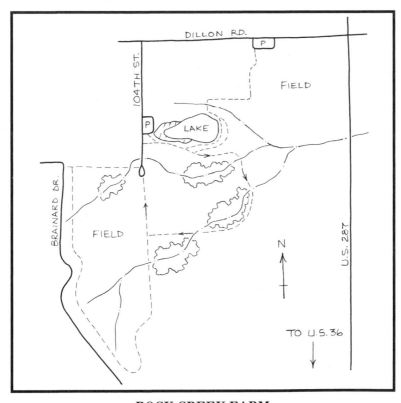

ROCK CREEK FARM

9 BARR LAKE STATE PARK

Lake Loop
  Distance: 9 miles
  Difficulty: Easy
  Walking Time: 5-6 hrs.
  Elevation: 5100 ft.

Nature Center to Gazebo
  Distance: 3 miles roundtrip
  Difficulty: Easy
  Walking Time: 1.5-2.0 hrs.
  Elevation: 5100 ft.

Climbing north out of Stapleton Airport, many a passenger has surely been struck by the shimmering waters of Barr Lake. Rimmed by marsh and woodlands, the 1937-acre reservoir stands out in sharp contrast to the semi-arid plains of eastern Adams County. So too are avian travelers drawn to this blue and green oasis as they wend their way along the Front Range corridor.

A vast array of birdlife can be found at Barr Lake; indeed, more species have been documented here than at any other location in Colorado. Perhaps best known for its nesting pair of bald eagles and its summer population of western grebes and white pelicans, Barr Lake State Park harbors a tremendous diversity of birdlife during any season. Mixed flocks of waterfowl, loons, grebes, gulls and phalaropes gather on the open waters during spring and fall migrations. Shorebirds are often abundant in late summer as mudflats expand along the shrinking reservoir. Herons, egrets, white pelicans, cormorants and western grebes are among the summer residents while winter visitors include bald eagles, rough-legged hawks, short-eared owls and longspurs. Great horned owls, kestrels, red-tailed hawks, flickers and magpies are found at the Park throughout the year. In addition to its large bird population, Barr Lake is home to mule and white-tailed deer, coyotes, red fox, muskrats, thirteen-lined ground squirrels, raccoons and other small mammals.

Directions:
From Denver, drive north on I-25 and exit onto I-76 toward Ft. Morgan. Proceed 16 miles and exit onto Bromley Lane (Exit #22). Turn right (east), drive almost 1 mile and turn right (south) on Picadilly Rd. Proceed to the Park entrance, on your right. Park at the **Nature Center (NC)**, near the southeast shore of the Lake, which houses Park offices, educational exhibits and a small bookstore. Plan a visit to the Center before or after your hike.

Route:
A 9-mile earthen path encircles Barr Lake and is easily accessed from either parking lot. Birding is generally best along the southern and eastern shores where the Denver & Hudson Canal parallels the trail and where side trails lead down to blinds and boardwalks (see map). A **gazebo (G)**, reached by a long, elevated boardwalk, is a popular destination for day hikes (3 miles roundtrip from the Nature Center) and offers a fine view of the lake. Barr Lake's **heronry (H)** is easily viewed from the gazebo; in recent years a pair of bald eagles have nested near the northeast tip of the heronry island (**E**).

Sections of the trail can be boggy during the spring and insect repellant is highly recommended from May through September. Birding is most productive during the early morning and late daylight hours and resident mammals are best observed at dusk.

The gazebo boardwalk.

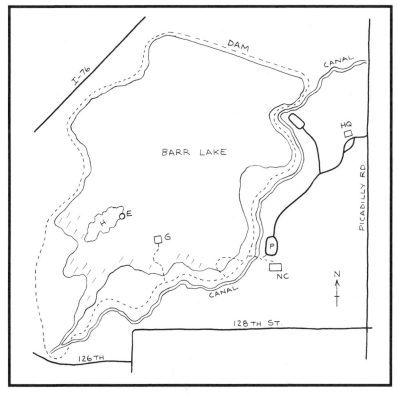

BARR LAKE STATE PARK

10 STANDLEY LAKE

East Loop Hike
  Distance: 2.2 miles
  Difficulty: Easy
  Walking Time: 1-1.5 hrs.
  Elevation: 5510-5590 ft.

West Loop Hike
  Distance: 1.8 miles
  Difficulty: Easy
  Walking Time: 1-1.5 hrs.
  Elevation: 5510-5590 ft.

Colorado's fabulous climate notwithstanding, many of us still yearn for an occasional escape to the seashore. Unfortunately, the closest ocean is more than 1000 miles from the semi-arid world of the Front Range.

While several large reservoirs are spaced throughout the Metro area, few offer a setting reminiscent of coastal areas. Mudflats, marshes, campgrounds, rock dams, parking lots and suburban homes line many of the lakes. An exception to this pattern is the south shore of Standley Lake where Jefferson County Open Space preserves a natural grassland and where a sandy beach stretches for two miles from the western to the southern inlets.

Strolling near the shore on a blustery, north-wind day, the feel of the ocean comes easily. Whitecaps lash the shoreline while gulls tilt and soar above the turbulent water. Were it not for the barks of prairie dogs and the majestic wall of mountains to the west, one could easily forget that he or she was on the edge of the High Plains.

Directions:
From Denver, head west on I-70. Take the Wadsworth Avenue Exit and drive north for 3.7 miles. Turn west on 80th Avenue and proceed 1.4 miles to Kipling. Turn right (north) on Kipling and drive .7 mile to W. 86th Parkway. Turn left (west) and proceed 1.1 mile to a parking area on the right side of the road.

Routes:
A 4-mile, double-loop hike can be achieved from the parking area. Those desiring a shorter hike can choose either loop.

East Loop (2.2 miles). From the parking lot, walk to the north, cross the irrigation canal and turn right (east). Just past the trees, turn left and descend to the lakeshore above a deep ravine (see map). The trail loop curves eastward paralleling the beach and crossing an open grassland where meadowlarks and western kingbirds feast on insects during the warmer months. Bypass the first cutoff and continue east to the south inlet of Standley Lake.

To complete the loop, climb southward along an access trail (see map) and then bear right (west) onto a jeep path that runs across the wall of the basin. This trail takes you back to the parking area and provides a different perspective on the Lke and its surrounding countryside.

West Loop (1.8 miles). Though a bit shorter than the East Loop, this hike crosses more varied terrain and is likely to be of more interest to naturalists. From the parking lot, walk to the north, cross the irrigation canal and then turn left (west) on a trail that parallels the canal. A half mile from the lot you will reach a bridge that provides access to the area for an adjacent residential community. South of the canal and extending to either side of the access trail is a large prairie dog town.

Continue along the canal which curves to the north and then back to the west. Cottonwoods thrive along the ditch, providing choice habitat for flickers, great horned owls and numerous songbirds. Crossing above a deep ravine the trail forks; bear

A lone cottonwood clings to the shore.

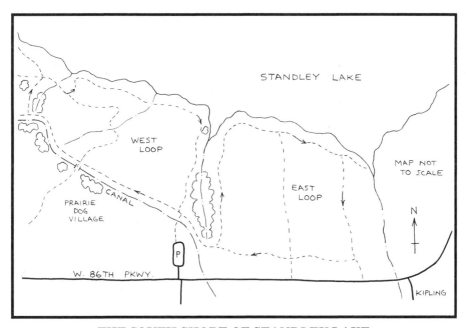

STANDLEY LAKE

WEST
LOOP

EAST
LOOP

MAP NOT
TO SCALE

CANAL

PRAIRIE
DOG
VILLAGE

N

P

W. 86TH PKWY.

KIPLING

THE SOUTH SHORE OF STANDLEY LAKE

right and descend into the Standley Lake basin. A huge prairie dog village, perhaps the largest in our region, spreads west of the Lake and extends along part of the southern shore.

Turn eastward, cross a creek bed and then descend further to the beach. The primary loop continues to the east along the lakeshore and then ascends to the parking lot above a deep ravine.

11 GOLDEN

Distance: 2 miles
Difficulty: Easy
Walking Time: 2 hrs.
Elevation: 5650-5780 ft.

Nestled below South Table Mountain at the mouth of Clear Creek Canyon, Golden was founded by the Boston Company in 1859 and was named for Thomas Golden, a local miner. Now best known as the home of the Adolph Coors Brewery and the Colorado School of Mines, Golden served as the first capital of the Colorado Territory, from 1861 to 1867.

A 2-mile walk takes you through this historic city and across the attractive campus of the Colorado School of Mines.

Directions:

From Denver, follow U.S. 6 to Golden. Turn right on 19th St. and then left (north) on Washington Avenue (Golden's "Main St."). Leave your car along the edge of **Parfet Park**, on the southeast corner of 10th & Washington.

Route:

Just north of the Park is the **Gertrude Bell Middle School (1)** which opened as Golden Junior High School in 1963. Walk south along Washington Ave. and turn east on a paved walkway that parallels Clear Creek (see map). Upon reaching Ford Avenue, the **Adolph Coors Brewery (2)** looms straight ahead. Founded by Adolph Coors, a native of Prussia, in 1880, the brewery switched to food and "near-beer" production during the 17 years of prohibition. With repeal of the Volstead Act, in 1933, brewing resumed and the company soon became one of the largest and most innovative breweries in the world.

Circle to the left, crossing Clear Creek and curving through **Vancouver Park**. The **Burgess House (3)**, built by Thomas Burgess in 1866, originally served as a boarding house for railroad workers. Now owned by Coors Brewing Company, the former hotel still serves as an apartment house.

Turn south on Ford Ave. and proceed to 12th St. where the **Guy Hill School (4)**, circa 1876, sits on the northwest corner. Walk westward along 12th St.; on the northwest corner of 12th and Washington is the **Golden Mercantile Building (5)**, former meeting place of the Territorial Legislature. Further along is the **Astor House Museum (6)**, the oldest stone hotel west of the Mississippi.

Continue westward into the 12th St. Historic District. The brick house at **1018 12th St. (7)** was built by George West, one of Golden's founders, in 1872. On the southeast corner of 12th & Maple is a **two-story house (8)** first occupied by Captain George Kimball, a Civil War veteran, in 1874.

Turn left on Maple and then left on 13th, passing the **Steinhauer Fieldhouse (9)**. The Gothic-style **Episcopal Church (10)** dates from 1867. Across Arapahoe St. is the **Armory Building (11)**, circa 1913, the largest cobblestone building in the United States. Walk south along Arapahoe and turn right on 14th St. **Stratton Hall (12)** is a math and social studies center for the Colorado School of Mines.

Turn left on Illinois St., passing the **Arthur Lakes Library (13)**. **Guggenheim Hall (14)**, the Administration Building, overlooks the **campus mall (15)**, backed by the rugged mesa of South Table Mountain. The **Colorado School of Mines**, first organized as Jarvis College in 1869, was officially established in 1874. It is the oldest public university in Colorado and the second oldest mining school in the U.S. **Berthoud Hall (16)** houses the geology labs and offices.

Turn east along 16th St., passing the **Jefferson County Courthouse (17)**, and then turn left (north) on Washington Ave. The **Foothills Art Center (18)**, which opened in September, 1968, occupies the

The Astor House Hotel

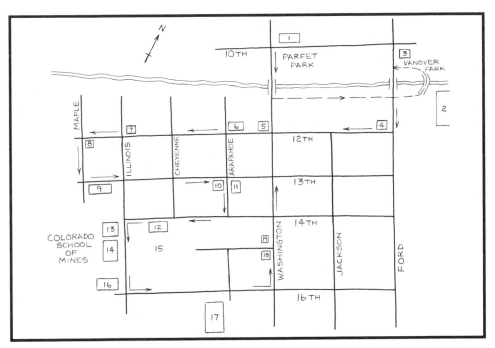

GOLDEN

former First Presbyterian Church of Golden, erected in 1872. The Center expanded in 1983, adding Foothills II in the adjacent Victorian house; the addition is home to a Gift Gallery that displays the artwork of Colorado residents. Another fine **Victorian home (19)**, dating from the 1880s, overlooks Golden from the northwest corner of 15th and Washington.

Descend northward along Washington Avenue, passing through Golden's central business district, and return to Parfet Park.

12 OLDE TOWN ARVADA

Distance: 1.5 miles
Difficulty: Easy
Walking Time: 1-1.5 hrs.
Elevation: 5315-5340 ft.

In June of 1850 a group of men, led by the Russell brothers from Georgia, were travelling northward along the Front Range, on their way to the Oregon Trail and thence to the gold fields of California. While camping in present-day Arvada, Lewis Ralston found nuggets of gold in a creek that now bears his name. Despite this discovery, the party pushed on to California but returned to Colorado in 1858; it was then that the Russell brothers founded Auraria near the confluence of Cherry Creek and the South Platte River.

"Ralston's Point" was established in 1860, just north and west of the Clear Creek-Ralston Creek junction, and Ralston Township became a division of Jefferson County in 1863. The local population began to blossom when the Central Colorado Railroad reached the area in 1870 and a plat was filed for the town of Arvada by Benjamin and Mary Wadsworth; they named the town for Mary's brother, Hiram Arvada Haskin. The town's post office was opened in the Wadsworth home and, by 1882, Arvada's first schoolhouse was built.

In an effort to preserve the cultural heritage of their community the Arvada Historical Society was organized in August, 1972, and the original townsite, now designated Olde Town Arvada, was targeted for prime attention. The following 1.5 mile walk takes you through the central core of Olde Town Arvada and back to the turn of the Century.

Directions:

From Denver, head west on I-70 and take the Wadsworth Blvd. Exit. Drive north on Wadsworth for approximately 1.3 miles to Ralston Road. Turn left (west), proceed 4 blocks and turn left on Yukon St.; a public parking lot will be noted on your left (see map).

Route:

Walk to the south on Yukon. The **Russell House (1)**, built in 1899, was placed on the National Register of Historic Places in 1963.

Turn east along Grandview Ave. At Old Wadsworth is the **Davis Block (2)**, circa 1916, and the **First National Bank of Arvada (3)**, organized in 1904; the bank building itself was constructed in 1896. Walk south along Old Wadsworth to the **Arvada Flour Mill (4)**, built by E. E. Benjamin in 1925. Listed on the National Register of Historic Places in 1975 and opened as a museum in 1980, the mill is now managed by the Arvada Historical Society; for tour information, call 431-1261.

Return to Grandview Ave. and head east. The current **music store (5)** was originally William Graves' blacksmith shop, one of Arvada's first businesses. A chain of antique shops lead to Webster Avenue where the **Grandview Grille (6)** occupies the old grocery store. Next door is the **Rose Tea Room & Gift Shop (7)**, formerly Black's Print Shop (1890s), and, east of the Tea Room, a group of shops fill the vacated site of the **Arvada Creamery (8)**. The frame house at **7401 Grandview (9)**, now a law office, dates from 1890. Across the street is the **Arvada Garden Club Park (10)**, dedicated in 1941, and, at Grandview and Upham, the former **site of Benjamin and Mary Wadsworth's home (11)** is now occupied by a restaurant.

Several fine **Victorian homes** will be noted along Grandview Avenue **(12 & 13)**, some of which enjoy sweeping views of the Clear Creek Valley to the south. Turn left on Reed St. and then left again on Ralston Road. The frame, **cottage-like homes** on your left **(14)** date from early 1900s.

Re-cross Wadsworth Blvd. and continue westward. The **Arvada Lodge (15)** was

The Arvada Flour Mill

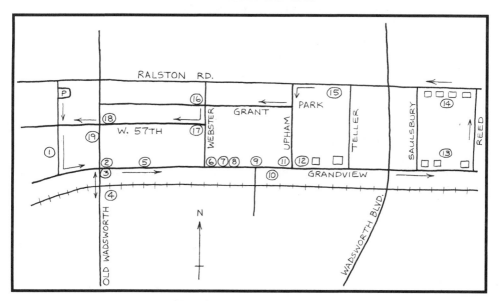

OLDE TOWNE ARVADA

completed in 1948, providing a new home for Masonic groups that formerly met in the First National Bank building. West of the Lodge is **McIlvoy Park**, one of Arvada's first public parks. Turn left on Upham and then right on Grant Place. The **Shrine of St. Anne Church (16)**, with its attractive bell tower, tile roof and brick/ tile facade, was built in 1920; a new addition was completed in 1962.

Turn south on Webster and then west on 57th St. The **Arvada Central Baptist Church (17)**, originally a Methodist Church, was built in 1909; Benjamin Wadsworth was reportedly killed in an accident while delivering the stained glass windows in a horse-drawn wagon. Continue west on 57th St., passing **Olde Town Square (18)**, the site of seasonal events. The **Festival Playhouse (19)**, formerly the Clear Creek Valley Grange, has served the community since 1873.

Turn north along Old Wadsworth Avenue for a stroll through the central business district and return to the Yukon St. lot via Ralston Road.

13 HAYDEN/GREEN MOUNTAIN PARK

Distance: 3.5 miles
Difficulty: Moderate
Walking Time: 3-3.5 hrs.
Elevation: 6040-6855 ft.

Like a massive loaf of grass-covered rock, **Green Mountain** rises above the gateway to the Colorado Rockies. Geologically, the mountain is a mound of Tertiary sediments (part of the Denver Formation) which eroded from the eastern flank of the modern Rocky Mountains and were carved from the adjacent Piedmont by the drainages of Clear Creek, to the north, and Bear Creek to the south. Underlying the Tertiary gravels and sandstones are late-Cretaceous rocks that were deposited along shallow seas before the mountains rose.

Suburban development is gradually climbing onto the east side of Green Mountain but the western face is preserved within Hayden/Green Mountain Park, a component of Jefferson County's Open Space system. An extensive network of trails is accessed from lots along Rooney Road and on Colorado 26, west and south of the mountain, respectively. Home to a wide variety of Upper Sonoran species, mule deer, coyotes, prairie falcons and scrub jays are often encountered during a visit to the Park. Much of the mountain is covered by open grasslands, studded with yuccas; scrub oak, mountain mahogany, junipers and ponderosa pine cluster along the drainages.

Directions:

Take U.S. 6 west from Denver. Nearing the foothills, turn left (west) on U.S. 40. Proceed .5 mile and turn left (south) on Rooney Road. Drive 2 miles to the Park's access lot, on the left side of the road.

Route:

A maze of trails stretch across the western and southern slopes of Green Mountain; we suggest the following 3.5 mile day hike.

From the Rooney Road lot, follow the wide path that leads across C-470. Cross the paved bike path and follow the **jeep road (A)** that curves to the north and winds up the west face of Green Mountain. Half way up, the path enters a sheltered ravine where mule deer often escape the summer sun and the frigid winds of winter.

Climbing higher, the **jeep road** loops around the upper reaches of a drainage channel, makes a long curve to the north and levels out atop a side ridge of the mountain. Your effort is rewarded by a sweeping view of the Front Range foothills, backed by the higher peaks of the Mt. Evans massif. Red Rocks park nestles beneath the east flank of Mt. Morrison, just west of the Hogback.

Hike toward the southeast and watch for a faint **spur trail (B)** that leads up to the summit of Green Mountain (6855 ft.). After taking in the view, return to the **jeep road** and proceed out to the transmission tower (T) atop the southeast ridge of Green Mountain. From there you have a broad view of Metro Denver and the Colorado Piedmont, extending southward to the mesas and buttes of the Castle rock region.

For your return trip, backtrack along the **jeep road (A)** and take the third **trail (C)** on your left (see map). This trail circles beneath the summit of Green Mountain and intersects a **trail (D)** that makes a long, occasionally steep descent toward the southwest. Nearing the base of the mountain the trail enters a shaded ravine and intersects several other routes. Curve back to the north along a **trail (E)** that hugs the base of Green Mountain, passes several rock formations and eventually returns to the **jeep road.** Cross C-470 to the parking lot, completing a hike of 3.5 miles.

Looking west to Mt. Morrison from the summit of Green Mt.

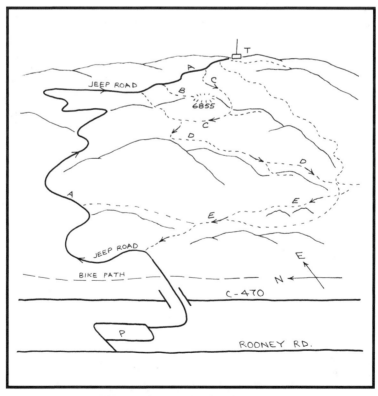

THE WEST FACE OF GREEN MT.

14 CROWN HILL PARK & NATURE PRESERVE

Distance: 1.8 miles
Difficulty: Easy
Walking Time: 1-1.5 hrs.
Elevation: 5560-5570 ft.

An easy stroll through Crown Hill Park offers a pleasant mix of exercise, mountain scenery and wildlife watching. Established in 1981 through the combined efforts of Lakewood, Wheatridge and Jefferson County Open Space, the Park provides an excellent example of what dedicated conservationists can do with limited space to protect our dwindling wildlife habitat.

Crown Hill Park covers 168 acres atop a high ridge west of Denver. The Preserve surrounds two natural lakes which attract migrant waterfowl in spring and fall and provide a vital oasis for urban wildlife throughout the year. In recognition of the Park's crucial role as a wetland preserve, the northwest section was set aside as a wildlife sanctuary. This refuge, officially dedicated on Earth Day, 1990, is closed to the public from March through June to afford added protection for nesting species.

Directions:

Follow U.S. 6 west from downtown Denver and Exit onto Kipling St. Turn right (north) and drive 2 miles to 26th St. Turn right (east) and proceed .4 mile to the second parking area, on your left.

Route:

Crown Hill Park is accessed by 6.5 miles of paved and earthen paths. The following route yields a 1.8 mile walk and crosses through the more interesting sections of the Preserve.

Walk down to the south shore of Crown Hill Lake and turn right along the 1.2 mile hike/bike path that loops around the lake. A popular avenue for walkers, joggers and cyclists, the path can be congested on

weekends. A sweeping view of the Front Range unfolds to the west and Crown Hill Cemetery's Tower of Memories rises east of the Park. The Tower, a regional landmark, was constructed in the 1920s and was recently listed on the National Register of Historic Places.

Circle around to the north shore of Crown Hill Lake, bypass the first cutoff and proceed to the second side trail that exits the loop near a gazebo (G). Turn right onto the paved path and then angle northwest on an earthen trail that leads into the wildlife sanctuary. Be sure to close the gate behind you, thereby protecting resident wildlife from stray dogs.

Bypass cutoff trails and loop around Shallow Lake which is ringed by a cattail marsh. Red-winged and yellow-headed blackbirds, night herons, wood ducks, teal and great blue herons utilize the marsh during the warmer months. Watch for painted turtles and frogs along the shores of the pond. Year-round residents of the wildlife sanctuary include mule deer, fox squirrels, skunks, red fox, Canada geese, flickers and kestrels. Realizing that the cattail marsh would gradually invade the open waters of Shallow Lake, refuge managers have intervened to ensure a diversity of habitat; marsh vegetation is periodically cut back to extend the life of the pond.

Complete the sanctuary loop near the gazebo (see map) and return to the paved trail along the lakeshore. The larger lake attracts fishermen who angle for bass, sunfish, bluegill, catfish and other species. Waterfowl and gulls will be found on the lake throughout the year; Canada geese and ring-billed gulls are especially numerous during the colder months and ducks peak in number and variety during the spring and fall migrations.

After completing the loop walk around Crown Hill Lake, return to the parking area for a total route of 1.8 miles.

Winter grips the Shallow Lake refuge.

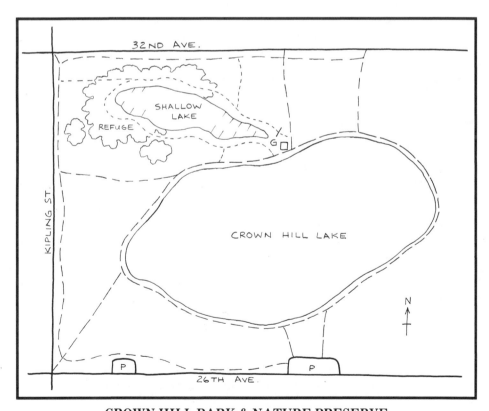

CROWN HILL PARK & NATURE PRESERVE

15 SLOAN'S LAKE

Distance: 2.7 miles
Difficulty: Easy
Walking Time: 1.5-2.0 hrs.
Elevation: 5310 ft.

Sloan's Lake, a few miles west of downtown Denver, has a fascinating history. Its origin reportedly dates from 1861 when Thomas Sloan, a local farmer, drilled a new well and awoke the next day to find a broad lake filling much of the basin that stretched eastward from his property; his well shaft had apparently drained a subterranean aquifer.

The 200 acre lake blocked the former route of the Georgetown stage line but soon became a recreation spot for early Denverites. Sloan himself built an ice house along the shore but moved on to Pueblo in 1872. Noting the Lake's popularity, the Grandview Hotel (located at present-day 17th and Federal) constructed a canal to the Lake and ran a steamer, "The City of Denver," to provide cruises for guests and local residents.

In 1890, Adam Goff, a German immigrant, opened Sloan's Lake Resort on the northwest shore, offering rental boats and a lakeside pavilion for parties. The Manhattan Beach Company took over the resort in 1891, greatly expanding the facilities. Amusement rides, a small zoo, a theater and a broad beach of California sand were among the attractions. Most of the resort burned down on December 26, 1908, possibly at the hands of an arsonist. Luna Park opened one year later but, by 1914, shut down due to dwindling attendance.

The city of Denver acquired much of the land around the Lake during the 1930s and Sloan's Lake Park has since become a popular destination for fishermen, joggers, picnickers and water skiers. A 2.7 mile walk takes you around this urban oasis and offers some of the most pleasing vistas in Metro Denver.

Directions:
From I-25, just west of downtown Denver, take the 17th St. Exit and drive west for approximately 1 mile to the Lake. Park in one of the lots along the south shore (see map).

Route:
Follow the paved hike/bike path for a 2.7 mile stroll around Sloan's Lake. **St. Anthony Hospital (1)**, founded by the Sisters of St. Francis in 1892, was originally a medical care center for Union Pacific Railroad workers. It is now operated by the largest private nonprofit health care corporation in Colorado. At the southwest end of the Lake is the **Submariner's Memorial (2)**, dedicated to the U.S.S. Grayling, Colorado's memorial sub, which was lost at sea near the Phillipines in 1943.

Cross the inlet stream and walk northward along the west shore. The skyscrapers of Denver rise to the east, framed by the greenbelts that surround the Lake. Curving eastward, the path crosses through the former **site of Manhattan Beach (3)**, currently disrupted by dredging operations. Once completed, this area will be graded, planted and returned to use as soccer fields and picnic grounds.

Proceed eastward along the north shore of Sloan's Lake, passing a **shallow inlet (4)** where gulls, ducks and geese congregate to feast on handouts. Despite signs discouraging this misguided generosity, visitors continue to feed the waterfowl, creating unnatural flock concentration and setting the stage for fatal disease.

Overlooking the east shore of Sloan's Lake is **Lake Junior High School (5)**, completed in 1926. This attractive building, of Tudor style with Byzantine influence, was designed by Burnham Hoyt, a native of the Highlands neighborhood. Continue southward and then westward, returning to your car and completing a 2.7 mile walk.

A view from the east shore

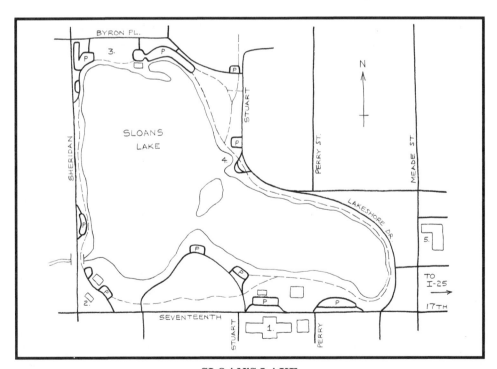

SLOAN'S LAKE

16 POTTER HIGHLANDS HISTORIC DISTRICT

Distance: 2.3 miles
Difficulty: Easy
Walking Time: 2 hrs.
Elevation: 5310-5370 ft.

As the pioneer towns of Denver City and Auraria grew along the banks of Cherry Creek, the first "brown cloud" began to appear across the South Platte Valley. To escape the thickening pall of dust and wood smoke, some of the more wealthy citizens began to relocate in the "Highland" area, north and west of the River. Going one step further, Dr. William Bell and General William J. Palmer, regional developers and businessmen, established the community of Highland Park. Planned to resemble a Scottish village, the original 288 acres straddled what is now Federal Blvd., between 29th and 38th. By 1875, the Village of Highlands was incorporated; this included Highland Park and was bounded by the current streets of Lowell, 38th, Zuni and Colfax. In 1890, the Village expanded westward to Sheridan.

Potter Highlands Historic District preserves a piece of Highland Park. A 2.3 mile tour of this appealing neighborhood takes you back to the first days of Front Range suburbia.

Directions:
From downtown Denver, follow Speer Blvd. northwest to Federal Blvd. Turn right (north) on Federal, proceed 1 block and turn left, parking along the edge of Highland Park (see map); this small plot of open space joined the Denver Park system in 1899.

Route:
Proceed to the northeast corner of the Park where the **Roger W. Woodbury Branch of the Denver Public Library (1)** has served the community since 1912. Named for the founder of the D.P.L., it was one of the four original branch libraries.

Cross Federal Blvd. and walk northward. The **Highlands Masonic Temple (2)**, built in 1905, is the home of Highlands Lodge No. 86, which was chartered in September, 1891.

Turn right on 36th Ave. where two, nicely restored Victorian homes face the Temple. Proceed 1 block and turn left on Eliot St. The **Sadie Brodie House (3)**, at 3631 Eliot, circa 1880s, was first owned by Col. Daniel Sayer, a Civil War Veteran, an attorney, a police magistrate and a mining baron. Further along, the west side of the **3700 block (4)** harbors a fine collection of restored Victorian homes.

Walk to the east along 37th Ave. An interesting mix of late 19th and early 20th Century homes are found along this block. The **John Monat House (5)** was built by a lumber executive. Turn right (south) along Alcott St. The west side of the **3400 block (6)** is especially attractive. The **Hugh MacKay House (7)**, constructed with Castle Rock granite in 1891, has been designated a Denver Landmark. MacKay was a Scottish engineer who was locally involved with mining and dam construction.

Turn right on 34th and then left on Bryant St., two nicely restored blocks. Walk east on 33rd to Zuni, which is the east boundary of Potter Highlands Historic District. The **Weir Building (8)**, a fine Victorian Commercial structure, originally housed several shops, a theater, offices and a dance hall. Looking east along 32nd Ave. you will see **All Saints Church (9)**; built in 1890, the Church's Episcopal congregation was organized in 1874.

Walk westward along 32nd which is lined with restored Victorian storefronts and then turn right on Bryant St. The **James Fisher House (10)**, at 3227 Bryant, was built in 1892. The attractive frame house at **33rd and Bryant (11)** was built by **Frank Arbuckle** in 1885; Arbuckle was president of the Beaver Brook Water Company which supplied water to the

The Sadie Brodie House

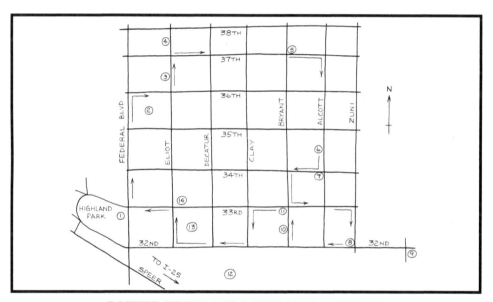

POTTER HIGHLANDS HISTORIC DISTRICT

Highlands area.

Turn left on 33rd, left on Clay and then right on 32nd Ave. **North High School (12)**, completed in 1911, occupies the property between 32nd and Speer Blvd.; one of the school's more famous alumni was Golda Meir (1913-1914). The **Gardens of St. Elizabeth (13)**, an elderly care center operated by the Sisters of St. Francis, the former site of the Oakes Homes; built in 1894 by the Reverend Frederick Oakes, the facility was the second TB sanitarium in the U.S. The original chapel still stands and has been designated a Denver Landmark. One block north is **The Lennox Guest Home (14)**, formerly known as the Adams Memorial Home; built in 1902, this beautiful structure, with its open, sunny verandahs, was part of the Oakes Home Sanitarium. Family owned for the last 25 years, the Lennox has served as a retirement center since 1947.

Return to Highland Park via 33rd Ave., completing a 2.3 mile walk.

17 SOUTH PLATTE GREENWAY

Gates-Crescent Park to Downtown	Bowles Ave. to Nature Center
Distance: 2.6 miles roundtrip	Distance: 4.6 miles roundtrip
Difficulty: Easy	Difficulty: Easy
Walking Time: 2 hrs.	Walking Time: 2.5-3.5 hrs.
Elevation: 5180-5200 ft.	Elevation: 5310-5350 ft.

Bowles Ave. to C-470
Distance: 8 miles roundtrip
Difficulty: Easy
Walking Time: 4-6 hrs.
Elevation: 5310-5370 ft.

Lifeline of the Front Range, the South Platte River exits Waterton Canyon, enters Chatfield Reservoir and then flows northward through Metro Denver. The River and its tributaries drain the east slope of the Front Range and have carved the Colorado Piedmont from the westernmost reaches of the High Plains.

By 1970 much of the South Platte Valley had become a ribbon of flotsam, industrial debris and commercial sprawl. Environmentalists began to push for a greenbelt along the course of the River and, in 1974, a mayoral committee was formed to spearhead the effort. From these beginnings the Platte River Greenway Foundation was spawned in 1976; this nonprofit organization established the goal of creating a greenbelt along the South Platte's eleven-mile stretch in Denver and along the Cherry Creek and Bear Creek corridors.

Following Denver's lead, the South Suburban Park District, in concert with the Arapahoe Greenway Foundation, established a greenbelt and hike/bike path along the River from Englewood to Chatfield Reservoir. A decade earlier, in 1973, the District had successfully resisted efforts to "channelize" the South Platte as part of the Corps of Engineers flood-control program; by creating South Platte Park, a broad basin of riverside meadows and riparian woodlands, the District offered a natural means of flood control.

This chapter offers three hikes along the South Platte and, hopefully, pays tribute to the foresight of these vital conservation organizations.

Directions:

Gates-Crescent Park is just east of I-25 at 17th Ave. (see map). Take Exit #210 B from I-25 and proceed to the lot, as illustrated.

Access to southern sections of the South Platte is best achieved at Bowles Ave. Take the Santa Fe Drive Exit from C-470 and head north. Drive approximately 3 miles into Downtown Littleton and turn left (west) on Bowles Ave. Parking areas are located on either side of the River, as shown.

Routes:

Gates-Crescent Park to Lower Downtown (2.6 miles roundtrip). From the parking lot, walk northward on the hike/bike path that parallels the South Platte. You will soon pass the **Children's Museum (1)** which opened in 1982. As the path curves to the right, watch for a plaque that directs your attention to **Zang's Brewing Company (2)**, one of 12 structures that comprised the Zang Brewery. Built in 1871, the remnant structure was originally a boarding house (the Red Rabbit) for teamsters who worked at the brewery. Also home to a restaurant and bar since its

The bikeway just south of Fishback Landing.

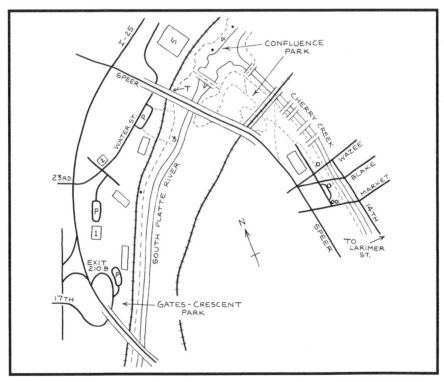

THE PLATTE RIVER GREENWAY NEAR CONFLUENCE PARK

construction, the building is listed on the National Register of Historic Places.

Further along is **Fishback Landing (3)**, the site of Thomas Warren's first chartered ferry service across the South Platte (circa 1859). Beneath the Speer Blvd. viaduct is a **boarding stop (T)** for the **Platte Valley Trolley** which runs between 15th St. and Old Colfax Ave. (2.5 miles roundtrip); for information regarding the Trolley and its schedule call 458-6255.

Confluence Park, at the junction of Cherry Creek and the South Platte River, offers a pleasant reststop along the Greenway and pays homage to the role that this geographic feature played in the development of Denver and, indeed, of the entire Front Range. Major Stephen Long camped here during his explorations in 1820 as did Captain John Fremont and his party in 1842. The Russell brothers discovered gold in Clear Creek, just southeast of the confluence, triggering the gold rush of the late 1850s. On the west bank of the River is **Shoemaker Plaza (4)** where one plaque honors the Platte River Development Committee and another memorializes Thomas Hornsby Ferril's poem *"Two Rivers."* Just west of the Park the **Forney Transportation Museum (5)** occupies the former power plant of the Denver Tramway Power Company (circa 1901).

Cross the South Platte and walk to the southeast above the west bank of Cherry Creek. Several interconnecting paths provide a variety of routes along the waterway. Proceed to Market St. where a plaque commemorates the founding of **Auraria**, in 1858, and another marks the original site of the **Rocky Mountain News** building, established by William N. Byers in April, 1859; the plant was destroyed by the Cherry Creek flood of May 19, 1864.

You may want to head up to Larimer Square for lunch before returning to Gates-Crescent Park via the same route.

Bowles Ave. to Carson Nature Center (4.6 miles roundtrip). From either parking area off Bowles Ave. at the South Platte River, hike southward on the hike/bike path that parallels the stream. Pass the **Riverfront Festival Center (A)**, which opened in 1985, and proceed to **Council Grove (B)** where trees were planted to honor Littleton's Centennial, on July 7, 1990. This grove is but part of an overall goal to plant 10,000 trees along the South Platte Greenway in Arapahoe County.

Follow the River as in winds to the south, passing a **beaver pond (C)**, on your left, and the **Columbine Country Club (D)**, west of the River. Ring-billed gulls, killdeer, kingfishers and a variety of waterfowl are usually present along the stream and bald eagles are occasionally spotted here from November through March. Views of the Front Range foothills and of the Rampart Range, further south, are constant as you hike along the River.

At the northern border of South Platte Park, an **earthen trail (E)** leaves the bikeway and courses along an abandoned channel of the South Platte, crossing through prime riparian habitat. Comprising less than 5% of natural habitat in Colorado, riparian woodlands are perhaps the most threatened ecosystem in our State. Great horned owls, black-billed magpies, northern flickers, red fox, raccoons and fox squirrels are among the fauna that characterize these areas.

Return to the paved bikeway and continue south to the **Carson Nature Center (NC)** which opened in 1991. Named for Theo L. Carson, whose family donated the building to the Park District, the Center serves as a staging area for nature study along the South Platte and will soon house exhibits depicting the flora and fauna of the River Valley. For more information, contact the Center at 730-1022.

After a visit to the Nature Center, return to Bowles Ave. via the same route, completing a roundtrip hike of 4.6 miles.

Bowles Ave. to C-470 (8 miles roundtrip). Park in one of the areas off Bowles Ave. along the South Platte and hike southward to the **Carson Nature Center (NC)**, as described in the preceding narrative.

From the Nature Center, continue

Autumn along the South Platte.

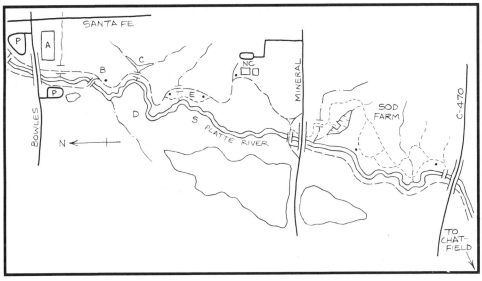

THE GREENWAY SOUTH OF BOWLES AVE.

southward to the bikeway bridge and switch to an earthen trail that continues along the east bank of the River, passing under Mineral Ave. (see map). South of the underpass the trail angles to the east, crosses a sidestream and winds through a floodplain marshland. Muskrats, beaver, mink, bullsnakes, painted turtles and a variety of amphibians typify the fauna of this riverside marsh. Common seasonal residents include red-winged and yellow-headed blackbirds, great blue herons, mallards, Canada geese, pied-billed grebes, black-crowned night herons, yellow warblers, barn swallows and common yellowthroats.

Curving back to the southwest, the trail splits into a variety of potential routes. Stay near the river where cattail marshes, sandbars and rich, riparian woodlands harbor an excellent diversity of plant and animal life. Upon reaching C-470, and if water level permits, cross the old rock dam to the west bank of the River and return to the Nature Center via the paved bikeway. If the River is too high to allow safe crossing, return northward via the earthen trails that course above the east bank.

From the Nature Center, continue northward to Bowles Ave., completing a round-trip hike of 8 miles.

18 LOWER DOWNTOWN/AURARIA/LARIMER ST.

Distance: 2.8 miles
Difficulty: Easy
Walking Time: 3 hrs.
Elevation: 5180-5220 ft.

The discovery of gold near the confluence of Cherry Creek and the South Platte River set in motion a chain of events that, 130 years later, have culminated in the creation of the Mountain West's dominant Metropolitan area. The Russell Party, a band of adventurers from Georgia, made their discovery in 1858 and established the settlement of Auraria along the west bank of Cherry Creek. Word of their find spread quickly to the eastern cities and gold prospectors soon flooded the South Platte valley and nearby canyons.

Among the early arrivals was **General William Larimer**, a banker, military officer and budding politician from Leavenworth, Kansas. Born in western Pennsylvania, in 1809, Larimer founded the Denver City Town Company in November, 1858, and "Denver City," named for James W. Denver, Governor of the Kansas Territory, soon took shape along the east bank of Cherry Creek. Hoping to become Governor of the Colorado Territory or, at least, mayor of Denver, Larimer initially settled for Treasurer of Arapahoe County, which stretched from Kansas to the Rockies, and named Denver City's "Main Street" after himself . . . Larimer Street.

With the establishment of stagecoach service to Denver City, in May, 1859, Larimer's town gained the upper hand over its rival, Auraria, and the two settlements finally merged in April, 1860. By 1862, having lost the battle for Territorial Governor to William Gilpin and having seen Charles Cook voted in as Denver's first mayor, William Larimer returned to his family in Kansas; he died there on May 16, 1875.

The following walk takes you through Lower Downtown (Denver's first business district), across Cherry Creek to Auraria and then back to the Larimer Street Historic District, William Larimer's ultimate claim to fame.

Directions:
The walk begins at 16th and Market Streets. An RTD center is located here and one can catch the shuttle from anywhere along the 16th St. Mall. One of the closer parking lots is in the Tabor Center, between the 1600 blocks of Lawrence and Larimer.

Route:
From 16th and Market, walk northeast along Market St., passing a block of restored, **Victorian Commercial Buildings (1)**. A fire devastated much of this area in 1863 and the current structures were built in the 1880s. A **plaque** at the end of the block **(2)** describes the history of Lower Downtown and the Historic District's designation in 1988.

Turn left on 17th St. The **Hotel Barth (3)**, circa 1882, is now a home for elderly and handicapped residents of the area. The oldest continually-operating hotel in Denver, it was designated a Denver Historic Landmark in 1985. In the next block is the **Oxford Alexis Hotel (4)**; built in 1891, the hotel underwent a complete renovation from 1980-1983 and is listed on the National Register of Historic Places. A **plaque (5)** at 17th and Wynkoop describes the history of the **Union Station** area; the station itself **(6)**, which opened in 1914, offers a fine example of Beaux Arts Classicism architecture. (It replaced the original 1880 depot that burned down.)

Turn right on Wynkoop. This street and the **Edward Wynkoop Building (7)**, erected in 1901, are named for the former commander of Fort Lyon who won fame for his peace-keeping efforts with regional Indian tribes. The **Ice House (8)** dates from 1903 when its original 5-story

Ninth St. Park

Larimer Square

structure arose as the Littleton Creamery; having served as an important cold-storage center for the Mountain West for over 75 years, the building is now home to The Design Center.

Head to the southeast along 18th St. The **Wynkoop Brewing Company (9)** occupies the old J.S. Brown Mercantile Building, circa 1899. This "brewpub," the first in Colorado, opened in October, 1988. Continue along 18th St. to Lawrence St. where the **Denver City Cable Railway Company building (10)** sits on the northeast corner. Built in 1889, this Romanesque Revival structure served as the power plant for Denver's early cable car system.

Proceed to Arapahoe St. and turn westward, walking through **Skyline Park (11)**; crab apple blossoms adorn this urban retreat in mid-April. The **Daniels & Fisher Tower (12)** was inspired by the bell tower at St. Mark's Cathedral, in Venice; constructed in 1909, the 330 foot tower was originally flanked by four-story office buildings. Continue southwestward to 14th St. and turn left. The **Mountain States Telephone & Telegraph building (13)** was built in 1929. This attractive stone and marble structure, with its leaded windows and entryway murals, is home to the **Pioneer Museum**, located on the 14th floor. Cross 14th St. and cut through the **Denver Center for the Performing Arts (14)**, home to Boettcher Concert Hall, the Denver Center Theater Company and the Buell Theater; with the latter's Grand Opening in November, 1991, Denver laid claim to the second largest performing arts center in the U.S.

Descend to Arapahoe St., cross Speer Blvd. (which parallels Cherry Creek), and enter the Auraria Campus, home to three urban colleges. A walkway leads toward **St. Elizabeth Church (15)**, flanked by the **Bonfils Memorial (16)**. The stone, Romanesque Revival church, erected in 1896, was the first consecrated Catholic Church in Colorado. The memorial and rectory, circa 1936, were donated by May Bonfils in honor of her parents.

Proceed westward from the Church to **Ninth St. Park (17)**. The oldest restored residential block in Denver, this fine collection of Victorian homes now serves as the Higher Education Center for the Auraria Campus. Loop along the block where plaques describe the history of each house. A **marker (18)** at the north end of the block provides a synopsis of Auraria's history and pays tribute to organizations that contributed to the neighborhood's renovation.

Walk to the northeast along 9th St. The former **home of Golda Meir (19)** will be on your left; a plaque describes her years in Colorado and the house's role as a center for Jewish intelligentia. Further along is **St. Cajetan's Church (20)**, built in 1926; this Spanish Colonial structure now serves as an education center. To the east, along the mall, is the **Emmanuel-Sherith Israel Chapel (21)**, the oldest surviving church structure in Denver. Erected in 1876, this stone building is listed on the National Register of Historic Places; it is now home to an art gallery.

Continue northward to the **Tivoli (22)**. The site of brewing operations from 1864 to 1969, the buildings of the Tivoli were erected during the late 1800s as part of the "Milwaukee Brewery" which succeeded the Colorado Brewing Company (circa 1876). Taken over by John Good in 1900, the brewery was renamed "Tivoli" after a renowned amusement park in Copenhagen, Denmark. Having merged with the Union Brewery in 1901, the Tivoli-Union Brewing Company finally closed down in April, 1969. The complex of buildings was designated an historic landmark in 1973 and re-opened as a collection of shops, restaurants and theaters in 1985; it may soon become a student center for the Auraria Campus.

Walk along Auraria Parkway, re-crossing Cherry Creek and returning to the downtown area. A **memorial (23)** at the former **site of Denver's City Hall** (1883-1936) includes a bell (circa 1906) that hung in its tower. Proceed eastward along Larimer Street, passing through "**Larimer Square**," one of Denver's most popular

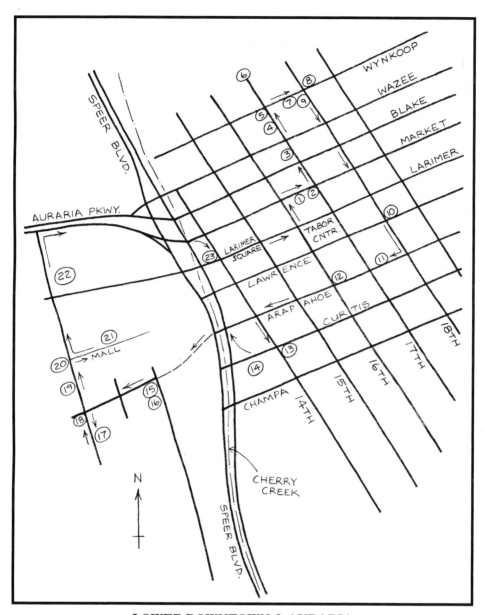

LOWER DOWNTOWN & AURARIA

shopping districts. Having survived the big fire of 1863 and the Cherry Creek flood of 1864, the original frame buildings along Larimer were replaced by the current stone and brick structures between 1870 and 1890.

By the early 20th Century Denver's business district had shifted to the south and "Lower Downtown" began to decay. Revitalization of the area began with the Larimer Square Project, in 1964, and the block between 14th and 15th Sts. became Denver's first Historic District in 1971. Today, Larimer Square offers a fine collection of shops and outdoor cafes, attracting locals and visitors alike.

Continue along Larimer St. to the 16th St. Mall, completing a 2.8 mile tour of Lower Downtown and Auraria.

19   CIVIC CENTER/CAPITOL HILL/QUALITY HILL

Distance: 3.0 miles
Difficulty: Easy
Walking Time: 2.5-3.0 hrs.
Elevation: 5230-5305 ft.

Conceived during the tenure of Mayor Robert Speer, Civic Center Park is bordered by an impressive array of government and cultural buildings. The State Capitol, the City & County Building, the Denver Art Museum and the Denver Public Library all overlook the Park. It is thus not surprising that Civic Center Park has been the site of numerous political rallies, social protests and cultural events over the past seventy years.

Southeast of this urban retreat is the neighborhood of Quality Hill, perhaps the most prestigious residential district in turn-of-the-Century Denver. Stretching between 6th and 11th Avenues, this community sits almost 100 feet above the South Platte River, once affording escape from the valley smog and a spectacular view of the Front Range. No longer an exclusive neighborhood, Quality Hill still harbors many fine, historic homes, including the Governor's Mansion.

A 3-mile walk takes you across Civic Center Park, up through Capitol Hill and out to the Quality Hill district.

Directions:

From Colfax and Broadway in downtown Denver, proceed south on Broadway for two blocks and turn right (west) on 13th Ave. Park in one of several lots along the south side of 13th (see map).

Route:

The walk begins at 13th and Bannock where the **Byers-Evans House (1)** sits on the northeast corner. Built by William N. Byers, founder of the Rocky Mountain News, in 1880, the home was purchased by William Grey Evans, son of the Territorial Governor, in 1890; this fine, Victorian

home is now operated as a museum and is listed on the National Register of Historic Places. The carriage house was recently opened to the public as the **Denver History Museum**. Proceed north to 14th Avenue and then west to Cherokee St. The **U.S. Mint Building (2)**, built in 1904, became the second home of the Denver U.S. Mint; the latter, established by Congress in 1862, had operated at 16th & Market.

Walk east on Colfax and then turn south along the front of the **City and County Building (3)**. Completed in 1932, this 4-story Neo-Classical Revival building, with its Doric columns and concave facade, was designed by a panel of 39 architects. Walk eastward through Civic Center Park. To the south is the **Denver Art Museum (4)** which opened in 1971; founded as the "Artists' Club" in 1893, the Denver Art Museum was formally established in 1922. Halfway across the Park, the **Greek Theater (5)** and its **Colonnade of Civic Benefactors**, built in 1919, looks northward to the **Voorhies Memorial Gateway (6)** which was completed two years later. The **"Broncho Buster (7)"** and **"On the War Trail (8)"** sculptures were both created by A. Phimister Proctor. At 14th and Broadway is the **Denver Public Library (9)**; completed in 1955, the building will soon undergo a major renovation and expansion, tripling its size. The Denver Public Library was established in 1889 and its original home, across 14th Avenue, was razed during the construction of Civic Center Park.

Cross Broadway, entering Lincoln Park. The **Liberty Bell (10)** was donated to the City in 1974 by Stephen Dach in memory of his father who died in a Nazi concentration camp. The **Veterans Memorial (11)** was dedicated on Veterans Day, 1990. Further north is the **Martinez Memorial (12)** which honors Colorado's first recipient of the Congressional Medal of Honor.

Cross Lincoln St. and climb to the **State**

Looking west from the State Capitol Building

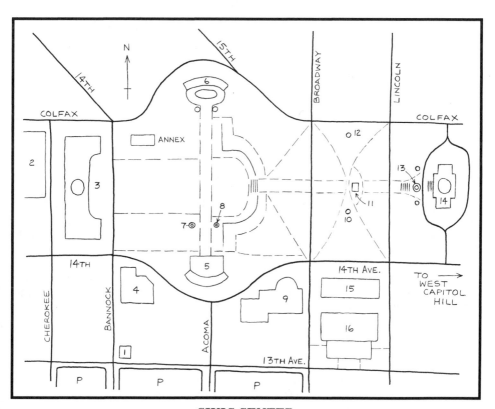

CIVIC CENTER

Capitol Building (14) which is fronted by the Civil War Memorial (13). The land for the Capitol Building was donated by Henry Cordes Brown soon after Denver became the capital of Colorado Territory (December, 1867). However, funding was not approved until 1885, nine years after Statehood was achieved, and ground-breaking ceremonies were delayed until July, 1886. Designed by Elijan E. Myers, who also designed Capitols for Michigan, Texas, Idaho and Utah, the partly-completed building was dedicated on July 4, 1890; gold plating of the dome did not occur until 1908. Be sure to walk through the interior of this magnificent building and, if you're fit enough, climb to the observation gallery for spectacular views of the city and of the majestic Rockies to the west.

South of the Capitol and west of Lincoln St. are the Colorado Judicial Building (15) and the Colorado History Museum (16). The latter opened in 1977 and is the home of the Colorado Historical Society, which was founded in 1879.

Walk eastward along 14th Avenue, passing the State Capitol Annex (17) and the Colorado State Museum Building (18). The latter building, Neo-Classic in style, was built in 1915. At 14th and Grant is the First Baptist Church (19); this Georgian Revival structure dates from 1938. The First Church of Christ Scientist (20), constructed with white lavastone from the Salida, Colorado area, was completed in 1931.

Continue eastward to Pennsylvania St. and turn right (south). The Molly Brown House (21), built in 1889 and designed by William Lang, has a colorful history. Purchased by Molly and James Joseph Brown in 1894, the house later served as the Governor's residence (1902) and as a rooming house (1920s). Changing hands many times, the building was scheduled for demolition when it was rescued by Historic Denver, Inc. in 1970. Inspired by Molly Brown's devotion to historic preservation, the organization restored the home to its turn-of-the-Century condition and now manages it as the Molly Brown House

Museum. For more information, contact Historic Denver Inc. at 534-1858.

Walk southward along Pennsylvania St. which is lined with a motley collection of homes and apartment buildings; most of the older homes date from the 1890s. The Walter Dunning House (22), built in 1889, offers a fine example of Richardson Romanesque architecture. In contrast, the Croke-Patterson-Campbell House (23), circa 1890, manifests the French Chateau Style. The house at 945 Pennsylvania (24), now home to Colorado Outward Bound, was constructed in 1900 for Frank M. Taylor, an internationally renowned mining engineer. At 9th and Pennsylvania is the Clemes-Lipe House (25), circa 1898; originally designed as a Queen-Anne, the home was remodeled in 1915, incorporating the Newport Style of that decade.

Cross over 8th Avenue and walk out to the Grant-Humphreys Mansion (26) which overlooks the Platte Valley and Front Range from Quality Hill. Built in 1902 by James B. Grant, the third Governor of Colorado and founder of Colorado Women's College, this magnificent home was purchased by Albert Humphreys, an oil and mining magnate, in 1917; the mansion is now listed on the National Register of Historic Places. Cut wastward along the driveway to Pearl St. and then turn north to 8th Avenue. The Malo House (27), at 500 E. 8th, exemplifies Spanish Colonial Revival architecture; it was built in 1921. Further west is the Governor's Mansion (28), constructed in 1908 as a residence for Walter S. Cheesman. Purchased by Claude Boettcher in 1926, the Mansion was donated to the State of Colorado in 1960.

Turn north along Logan St. The Hallett House (29) dates from 1892; this Queen-Anne home was built for Judge Moses Hallett, the first Federal Judge in Colorado and the second Dean of the University of Colorado Law School. The houses at 940 Logan (30), circa 1891, and 950 Logan (31), built in 1893, both manifest the Georgian Revival style of architecture. In the next block, at 1034 Logan, is the

The Molly Brown House

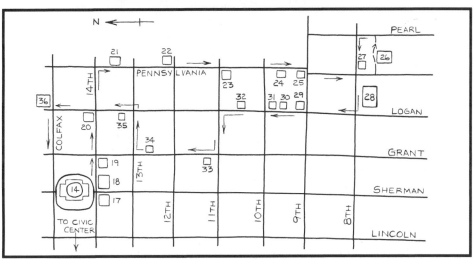

CAPITOL HILL / QUALITY HILL

Daly House (32), built in 1894 for the founder of the Capital Life Insurance Company.

Cross over to Grant St. via 11th Avenue and continue northward. The Queen-Anne house at **1115 Grant (33)** was built for Dennis Sheedy, a banking, cattle and mining magnate, in 1892. The **Creswell House (34)**, at 1244 Grant, dates from 1889. Turn right on 13th and then left (north) on Logan St. The **Denver Women's Press Club**, founded in 1898, moved into the 1910, Eclectic Style building at **1325 Logan St. (35)** in 1924. At Logan and Colfax is the **Cathedral of the Immaculate Conception (36)**, built in 1902. This French Gothic church, with its German stained glass windows, is listed on the National Register of Historic Places.

Turn westward along Colfax Ave., cross Lincoln and Broadway, and cut across Civic Center Park, returning to your car via Bannock or Acoma St.

20 CHEESMAN PARK AREA

Distance: 2.8 miles
Difficulty: Easy
Walking Time: 2-2.5 hrs.
Elevation: 5310-5380 ft.

In 1858, when Auraria and Denver City were still in their infancy, Mt. Prospect Cemetery was informally established on high ground east of the South Platte Valley. Disorganized and poorly maintained, the land was reclaimed by the Federal Government in 1870. Two years later, 160 acres were turned over to Denver to be used as the "City Cemetery." Since the cemetery was primarily controlled by Protestant congregations, Denver's Catholic community purchased 20 acres for their burials and 10 acres, further west, were used for Hebrew interments.

Lack of proper irrigation left the City Cemetery dusty and treeless, an unsightly place to bury the relatives! With the creation of Riverside Cemetery, in 1876, and Fairmont Cemetery, in 1890, the City Cemetery was abandoned and renamed "Congress Park." An undertaker was hired to move some 5000 bodies from the park to the newer, landscaped cemeteries; unfortunately, his efforts were less than honorable and more than 2000 bodies still lie beneath the parkland today.

In 1907, the hilltop refuge was renamed "Cheesman Park," in memory of Walter S. Cheesman, the well-to-do but unpopular chairman of the Denver Union Water Company; his wife's offer to finance construction of the Pavilion sealed the decision to honor Cheesman who had died earlier that year. The Park was the site of an "outdoor university" from 1929 to 1935 and "operas in the park" continued there until 1972.

During the early 1900s, Samuel B. Morgan, a local real estate developer, purchased the southern, un-used portion of what had been the Catholic portion of City Cemetery (known as Mt. Calvary Cemetery). Now encompassing several blocks along the southern edge of the Denver Botanic Gardens, the Morgan Historic District harbors a fine collection of mansion-like homes.

A 2.8 mile walk takes you across Cheesman Park and through the historic neighborhoods that border this hallowed ground.

Directions:

From downtown Denver, drive east on East 6th Ave. Proceed approximately 1.5 miles and turn left (north) on Josephine St. Cross over East 8th Ave. and bear right into a parking lot that services Congress Park. This Park encompasses the Hebrew section of the old City Cemetery.

Route:

Walk to the west along 9th Avenue (see map). Cross York St., entering the Morgan Historic District. Most of the homes in this neighborhood date from 1910-1930. The **Botanic Gardens House (1)**, at 9th and York, dates from 1926; it was donated to the Denver Botanic Gardens by Mrs. Ruth Waring in 1959, facilitating relocation of the Gardens from City Park to the old Catholic portion of City Cemetery (i.e. Mt. Calvary Cemetery).

Wind through the **Morgan Historic District** as illustrated on the map. The **Mason Lewis House (2)**, at 845 Gaylord, dates from 1922. Two fine examples of Georgian Revival architecture are the **Millett House (3)**, at 860 Vine St. (circa 1920) and the **Dines House (4)**, at 900 Race St. (circa 1931). Walk to the west on 8th Ave. and detour along a southern extension of Cheesman Park, lined with stately, early 20th Century homes (see map).

Cut northward along the west edge of **Cheesman Park** and cross over to Humboldt St. via 10th Ave. Turn right (north) for a 2-block walk through the **Humboldt Island Historic District**, the first residential neighborhood in Denver to receive National Historic Register designation

One of the many fine mansions in the Morgan Historic District

A William Lang creation

(1972). The twenty-four homes in this District date from 1895 to 1920. The **Stoiber Reed Humphrey House (5)**, at 1022 Humboldt, exemplifies Renaissance Revival architecture (circa 1907). Further along, the **Thompson Henry House (6)**, built in 1905, depicts the Georgian Revival style. The **Brown MacKenzie McDougal House (7)**, with its Gothic windows and Late Eclectic architecture, dates from 1903.

Turn right on 12th Ave., re-enter Cheesman Park and walk across to the **Cheesman Pavilion (8)**. Dedicated in 1908, this Neo-classical Revival landmark offered a sweeping view of the Front Range, now disrupted by high-rise apartments and the glass towers of downtown Denver.

Exit the north end of the Park via Franklin St. and wind through the oldest neighborhood that borders Cheesman Park; many of the homes in this area data from the 1890s. **Warren United Methodist Church (9)**, built in 1911, is named for Bishop Henry White Warren, the first Methodist Bishop of the Colorado Territory and one of the founders of the Iliff School of Theology (see University of Denver walk). An addition to the Church was completed in 1952 and Warren Village, an apartment complex for low-income, single-parent families, opened south of the Church in 1974. **The McFarlane House (10)**, at 1200 Williams St., dates from 1898; this Neo-Colonial Georgian home, listed on the National Register of Historic Places in 1973, now serves as the Capitol Hill Community Center.

On the northeast corner of 14th and Williams is the **First Divine Science Church (11)**, constructed in 1922 and designed by Jules Jacques Benois Benedict, who also designed Littleton's Town Hall and the St. Thomas Seminary. The homes at **1410 High St. (12; circa 1897)** and **1437 High St. (13; circa 1894)** are both listed on the National Register of Historic Places.

The **Adams-Fitzell House (14)**, at 1359 Race St., dates from 1890; it was the home of George Adams, a local cattle baron. The house at **1320 Race St. (15)**, designed by Harry T.E. Wendell, dates from 1894. The homes at **1415 & 1435 Vine St. (16 & 17)**, both built in 1889-90, were designed by William Lang, one of Denver's more famous architects.

Walk south along Gaylord St., turn left on 11th Ave. and then right on York St. If time permits, plan a visit to the **Denver Botanic Gardens**. Chartered in 1951, the Botanical Gardens Foundation of Denver established its first plant collection in City Park, southwest of the Natural History Museum. When Mrs. Ruth Waring donated her spacious, Normandy house at 9th & York, in 1959, the Gardens were moved to the former site of Mt. Calvary Cemetery. Famed horticulturalist and landscape designer, Saco R. DeBoer, planned the first permanent gardens and Dr. Aubrey Hildreth was named the first director of Denver Botanic Gardens Inc. The Boettcher Conservatory was dedicated in 1965 and an education center was added in 1971.

After your visit to the Gardens, return to the lot off Josephine St., completing a tour of the Cheesman Park area.

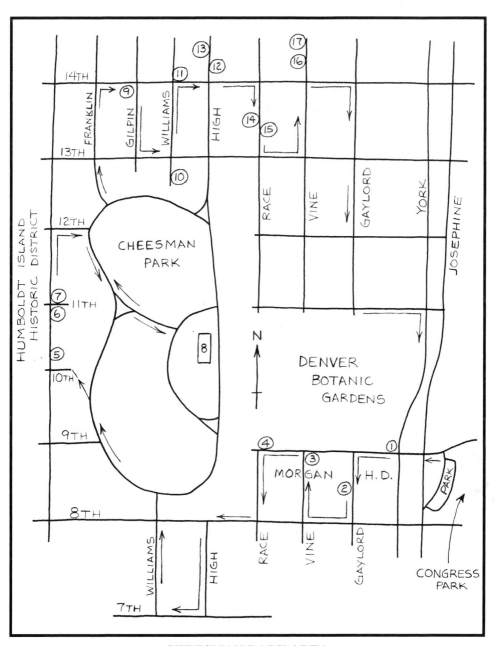

CHEESMAN PARK AREA

21 CURTIS PARK HISTORIC DISTRICT

Distance: 2 miles
Difficulty: Easy
Walking Time: 1.5 hrs.
Elevation: 5210-5220 ft.

Donated to the City in 1868, Curtis Park became Denver's first public park. Over the following two decades a neighborhood of fine, Victorian homes developed in the vicinity of the Park, stretching between 22nd and 33rd Avenues.

A middle-class enclave for much of its history, most of Curtis Park's wealthy residents departed for Capitol Hill during the 1890s and, by the mid 20th Century, the area showed signs of decay. Fortunately, Curtis Park was placed on the National Register of Historic Places in 1975 and a revitalization campaign, spearheaded by Historic Denver, Inc., was spawned in 1978. Forty-three homes were targeted for renovation, with primary emphasis placed on historic preservation.

A 2-mile walk takes you through the heart of this revitalized community.

Directions:

From Downtown Denver, drive northeast for almost 1 mile on Curtis St. and leave your car along Curtis Park.

Route:

From the Park, walk to the southwest along Champa St., entering the Curtis Park Historic District. Most of the homes in the neighborhood date from the 1880s; Italianate and Queen Anne Victorian are the dominant architectural styles. Both **houses at 29th & Champa (1 & 2)** manifest Italianate features.

Continue along Champa to 25th Avenue. The Italianate house at **2649 Champa St. (3)** dates from 1887; across the street, at **2648 Champa (4)**, is a Queen-Anne style home, built in 1890. The brick, multiple-dwelling structure at **2524 Champa (5)** exemplifies Renaissance Revival architecture; completed in 1887, its arched doorway and decorative masonry are typical of the Victorian era.

Turn left on 25th Avenue and then left on Stout St. The **Mallincrodt House (6)**, at 2523 Stout, dates from 1880, while the **homes at 2537 (7) and 2557 (8) Stout**, both Italianate in style, were built in 1886-87. Across 26th Avenue, the **Judge Markham House (9)**, also Italianate, was completed in 1885. The multiple-dwelling structure at **2606-2610 Stout (10)**, circa 1898, manifests Neo-Classical Revival features. In the next block is **Kinneavy Terrace (11)**, a large Victorian building with castle-like turrets and a slate, Mansard roof; it was remodeled into 14 apartments in the early 1980s. The house at **2728 Stout (12)**, Colonial Revival in style, dates from 1905.

Turn left on 28th Avenue, left on Champa, right on 26th Avenue and then right on Curtis St. The 2600 and 2700 blocks of Curtis St. harbor a fine collection of Victorian homes. The Italianate **houses at 2615 (13) and 2621 (14) Curtis** date from 1885 and 1881, respectively. The house at **2626 Curtis (15)**, built in 1890, illustrates the Queen-Anne style of architecture, as does the home at **2712 Curtis (16)**, circa 1897. Two of the finer houses in Curtis Park are at **2735 (17) and 2739 Curtis St. (18)**; the former, built in 1886, exemplifies the Italianate Villa style while the latter, also completed in 1886, is classified as Eclectic. The Queen-Anne home at **28th and Curtis (19)**, with its terrific porch, dates from 1891.

Continue toward the northeast on Curtis St., passing the Park. Just north of the Park are the **Curtis Park Flats (20)**, renovated by the Community Development Block Grant Program of the City and County of Denver. Across 32nd Avenue is **Denver Fire Department House #10 (21)**, dedicated in 1928.

Turn right on 33rd Avenue and then right on Champa St., returning to the Park.

Winter on Champa St.

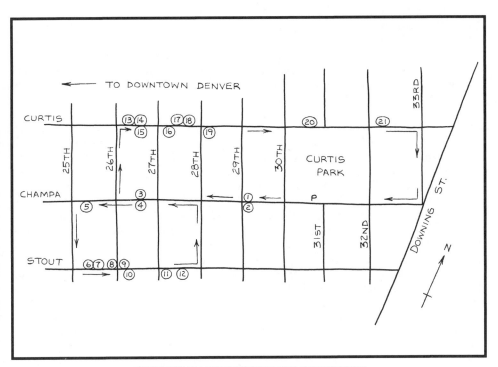

CURTIS PARK HISTORIC DISTRICT

22 CITY PARK/PARK HILL

Distance: 4.4 miles
Difficulty: Easy
Walking Time: 3 hrs.
Elevation: 5250-5335 ft.

The concept of a park system for the city of Denver was first spawned by Mayor Joseph Bates in 1872. William Byers, founder and editor of the Rocky Mountain News, promoted the idea in his editorials and a bill to purchase land for the parks was finally introduced in the Colorado Legislature in 1878. The development of City Park was spearheaded by Mayor Richard Sopris in 1881 and the original design, by Henry Meryweather, was presented to City Council in May, 1882.

The City Ditch, purchased from John Smith's Platte Water Company in 1875, ensured adequate irrigation for most of the Park's 320 acres and tree plantings were begun by local school children in 1885. Denver Tramway cable cars provided transportation to City Park by 1889, greatly increasing public use of the preserve. Sunday concerts began in 1895 and the first Festival of Mountain and Plain was held at the Park that same year. The large lake and its west shore Pavilion were added in 1896 and the Denver Zoo was set in motion when an orphaned black bear cub given to Mayor Thomas McMurray, was housed at the Park.

Mayor Robert Speer, elected in 1904, introduced the concept of European-style boulevards to connect City Park with other sections of town and, perhaps most importantly, established a philanthropic foundation to raise money for the growing Park System.

Residential communities began to appear along the borders of City Park at the turn of the Century. One of these, known as Downington, would soon become the prestigious neighborhood of Park Hill, a community of large, well-spaced homes, manicured lawns and tree-lined boulevards.

A 4.4 mile walk takes you across City Park and winds through the central corridor of Park Hill.

Directions:
From Downtown Denver, proceed east on Colfax Avenue, drive approximately 1.5 miles and turn left (north) on Josephine St. Proceed 8 blocks, turn right on 23rd Ave. and then turn into City Park. Leave your car along one of the Park roads or in one of several small lots near the west end of the Park.

Route:
The **William McLellan Gateway (1)**, now an auto exit, was donated by the former Councilman in 1904; it formerly stood at East 18th St. and was moved to its present site in 1957. Proceed to the **Joseph Addison Thatcher Memorial Fountain (2)**, presented to the City in 1918 and fronted by the magnificent floral gardens of the **Esplanade (3)**. **East High School (4)**, which opened in 1925, will be noted to the south.

The **Martin Luther King Memorial (5)**, designed by Ed Rose, was dedicated in April, 1976. It depicts Reverend King with Emmett Till, a Mississippi youth who was lynched in 1955. Proceed east to the **Pavilion (6)**, circa 1896, which replaced an earlier structure that sat along Duck Lake. The **Bandstand (7)** was added in 1914.

Walk out to the **Robert Burns Statue (8)**, donated by the Scots Caledonian Club in 1904. It honors the famous Scottish poet and is now the centerpiece for a collection of 19th Century artillary. **Duck Lake** was created in 1888 and its island has become a summer home for a large flock of black-crowned night herons. **The Denver Zoo**, now encompassing 76 acres, is renowned for its collection of hoofed mammals. Originally little more than an animal menagerie on the north side of City Park, the Zoo gained momentum in 1918 when Bear

One of the best views in Denver

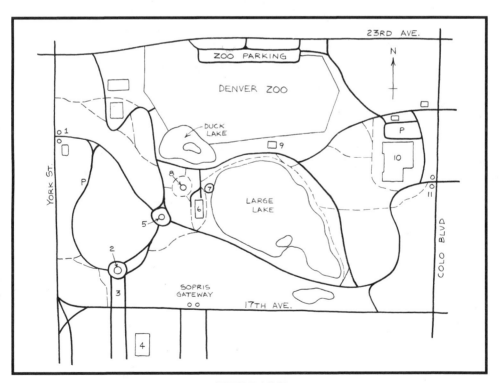

CITY PARK

Mountain was completed. Monkey Island, a WPA project was added in 1936 and the Denver Zoological Foundation was established in 1950. Other historical highlights include construction of the perimeter fence in 1957, addition of the Pachyderm House in 1959, completion of the Animal Hospital in 1969, creation of the Bird World Exhibit in 1975 and the opening of the Northern Shores in June, 1987.

Walk eastward above the north shore of the **Large Lake**, passing the **Pump House (9)**. Built in 1906, this facility was initially used to augment irrigation pressure; it later became a temporary elephant house for the Zoo and now serves as a maintenance building for the Park District. Climb to the west side of the **Denver Museum of Natural History (10)** for a spectacular view of City Park, backed by downtown Denver and the majestic Rockies. The lawns before you were the original site of the Denver Botanic Gardens. The Museum itself sprang from the collection of pioneer naturalist Edwin Carter in 1899. Incorporated in 1900, the Foundation began construction of the original building in 1901 and the Museum officially opened in July, 1908. Inernationally known for its fine collection of wildlife dioramas, which were introduced by Director Alfred Baily in 1936, the Museum underwent extensive renovation and expansion in the early 1980s, including the addition of an Imax Theater.

Circle to the east side of the Museum and cross Colorado Blvd. after passing through the **Joshua Monti Gateway (11)**. Built with Platte Canyon granite in 1916, the gateway was named for a prominant miner who donated the structure to the City. Enter the appealing neighborhood of **Park Hill** and continue eastward along Montview Blvd. The large home at **4101 Montview (12)**, built in 1910, depicts the Italian Renaissance Revival style of architecture. In contrast, **4151 Montview (13)** offers a fine example of the Georgian Style, common throughout Park Hill. Across Ash St., at **4207 Montview (14)**, is an elegant Victorian home dating from 1899.

Proceed eastward to the **Park Hill Library (15)**, built in 1920. Eclectic in style, the Library was funded by a Carnegie grant; a new addition and extensive remodeling were completed in 1964. The **Montview Community Presbyterian Church (16)** organized in 1902. The older section of the Church was built in 1908 using leftover stone from the Central Presbyterian Church in downtown Denver. The Miller Chapel was added in 1918 and the new sanctuary was dedicated in 1958.

Across Montview is the **Masonic Lodge Building (17)**, circa 1924. The **Blessed Sacrament Parish (18)**, established in 1912, was one of the earlier Catholic communities in Denver. The original Church, completed in 1913, now serves as the elementary school; the present Church was built in 1935 and the Junior High Building was added in 1951.

Continue east to Forest St. Parkway. The **Park Hill United Methodist Church (19)** dates from 1924; a new sanctuary was added in 1955. Turn south along Forest Parkway, a pleasant boulevard lined with fine, early 20th Century homes. Proceed 1 block and turn right on 19th Avenue. **Park Hill Elementary School (20)** dates from 1901 when an 8-room schoolhouse was built on the site. Expansion occurred in 1912 and a major renovation was completed in November, 1928, adhering to the Spanish style of the earlier buildings.

Turn right (north) on Elm St. **Machebeuf Catholic High School (21)** is named for Bishop Joseph P. Machebeuf, the first Bishop of Denver, who was transferred from Santa Fe to Denver in 1860 to minister to the gold camps. Cross Montview Blvd. and wind back to City Park as illustrated on the map. Most of the homes in this section of Park Hill date from 1900-1940; bungalows, "Denver Square's," Georgian Revival, Edwardian and Eclectic Styles predominate. **St. Thomas Episcopal Church (22)** was founded in 1908 as a mission parish for St. John in the Wilderness Cathedral; the congregation became a separate parish in 1916 and the Spanish Colonial Church was expanded in 1918.

Montview Community Presbyterian Church

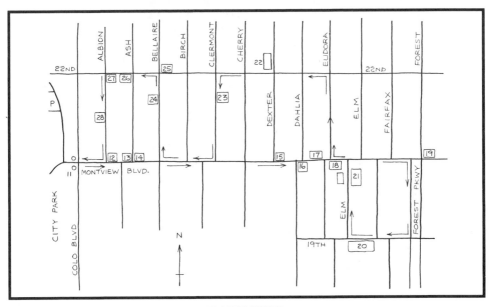

PARK HILL

Reverend Sandra A. Wilson, the rector at St. Thomas, is the first black woman rector in the world-wide Anglican Communion.

The house at **2070 Clermont (23)**, built in 1909, offers a fine example of Georgian Revival architecture. The bungalow at **2073 Bellaire (24)** manifests Romantic Revival features while **2200 Bellaire (25)** is English Tudor in style. The brick home at **2085 Ash (26)** incorporates the Denver Square design and, on the next corner, **2090 Albion (27)**, built in 1910, has Spanish Colonial features. The house at **2037 Albion (28)**, dating from 1905, is Eclectic in style.

Turn right on Montview Blvd., cross Colorado Blvd. and hike westward across City Park to your car.

23 FOUR MILE HISTORIC PARK

Distance: 4 miles roundtrip
Difficulty: Easy
Walking Time: 2-3 hrs.
Elevation: 5300-5360 ft.

During the mid 1800s, the Cherokee Trail served as an important route between Bent's Fort, on the Santa Fe Trail (near present-day La Junta), and the trading posts along the South Platte River in northeastern Colorado. After crossing the Palmer Divide, the Trail followed Cherry Creek northward and westward to its junction with the South Platte. Indeed, the Russell Party had used this route in 1858, when they discovered gold near the confluence of these two streams.

In 1859, a log house was constructed along the Cherokee Trail for Elizabeth and Samuel Brantner. The building site was "four miles" upstream from what would later become Denver's original boundary (established by a Congressional Grant in 1864). The Brantners sold the house to Mary Cawker, a native of Orange County, New York, in September, 1860. She turned the property into a stagecoach station for the Denver & Santa Fe line, adding a tavern and a dance hall.

Devastated by the Cherry Creek flood of May 19, 1864, Mary Cawker sold her property to Levi and Millie Booth who continued the stage station operations that she had started. Business actually picked up in 1865 when the Butterfield Overland Dispatch Company sent stagecoaches across the Smoky Hill Trail, which intersected the Cherokee Trail in present-day Aurora. However, with the arrival of railroad service in 1870, stage lines, and the Cherokee Trail, were soon abandoned.

The Booths purchased additional property around the home and switched their attention to operating a farm and cattle ranch. Irrigation ditches were dug and a brick addition to the house was completed in 1883; the Booths also moved a second frame house (circa 1860s) and attached it to the other structures, creating the present "U-shaped" residence.

In 1934, Four Mile House became the first residential property in Colorado to be registered with the Historic American Building Survey. In December, 1968, it was officially designated a Denver Landmark and, one year later, was listed on the National Register of Historic Places. The Denver Parks and Recreation Department began acquisition of Four Mile House and twelve acres of adjacent land in 1975 and, in 1977, Four Mile Historic Park, Inc., was created to manage the property. The Park was dedicated on May 1, 1978, and the House was opened to the public as a museum three months later.

Four Mile Historic Park is open April through September from 10 AM to 4 PM, Wednesday through Sunday. An admission fee is charged to fund continued maintenance of this historic site. For more information call 399-1859.

Directions:
The Park is located along the east bank of Cherry Creek at S. Forest St. and E. Exposition Ave. Rather than driving directly to the Park, we suggest leaving your car at Cherry Creek Mall, 2 miles downstream. This yields a 4-mile roundtrip walk and will add to your appreciation of the pioneer spirit! The Mall is located at Speer Blvd. & University Blvd., southeast of Downtown Denver.

Route:
Pick up the paved hike/bike path on the south side of Cherry Creek Mall and head

The Four Mile House dates from 1859.

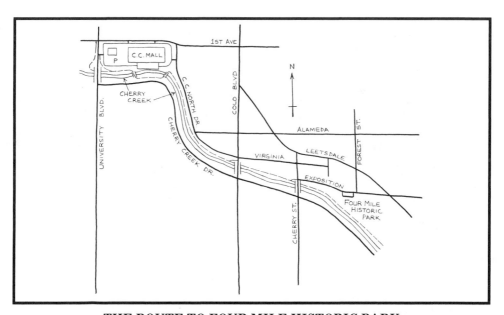

1ST AVE

C.C. MALL

P

N

CHERRY
CREEK

C.C. NORTH DR.

COLO. BLVD.

UNIVERSITY BLVD.

CHERRY CREEK DR.

ALAMEDA

FOREST ST.

VIRGINIA

LEETSDALE

EXPOSITION

CHERRY ST.

FOUR MILE
HISTORIC
PARK

THE ROUTE TO FOUR MILE HISTORIC PARK

east (upstream). The path crosses and then re-crosses the Creek before curving to the southeast through a greenbelt. After passing under Colorado Blvd. and under Cherry St. it ascends to Exposition Ave., just west of the Four Mile Historic Park (see map).

Be sure to plan this walk at a time when the Park is open to the public (times and dates are provided in the preceeding narrative).

24 MONTCLAIR HISTORIC DISTRICT

Distance: 3 miles
Difficulty: Easy
Walking Time: 2 hrs.
Elevation: 5350-5380 ft.

Of all the characters who played a role in Denver's early history, Baron Walter von Richthofen, uncle to the Red Baron of WWII, was surely one of the more eccentric. Born in 1848, the Baron arrived in Denver during the 1870s and began a colorful career that included stints as a real estate broker, a cattle rancher, a beer garden proprietor and a distributor of Rocky Mountain spring water. Bored with family life, the Baron abandoned his wife and children while on vacation in Europe, returned to Denver and joined the Montclair Town & Improvement Company.

Platted in 1885, Montclair was named for its panoramic view of the Front Range. Baron von Richthofen soon acquired much of the town's property and, by 1887, had completed his castle on a high knoll. Unfortunately, his second wife refused to move into the castle until the grounds were landscaped with trees and gardens. This prompted the Baron to have the Montclair ditch constructed, bringing irrigation waters from the Highline Canal.

Montclair was incorporated in 1888 and was eventually annexed by Denver in 1902. A 3 mile walking tour, described below, takes you through the heart of the Baron's domain.

Directions:
From downtown Denver, follow 6th Ave. east for 4 miles. Turn left (north) on Monaco Parkway, drive 6 blocks and turn right on Richthofen Blvd. Proceed 3 blocks and leave your car along Montclair Park.

Route:
Baron von Richthofen donated the Park to the community in 1887 and he constructed what is now the **Montclair Civic**

Building (1) in 1898, using it as a health spa and TB sanitorium. It was converted to an insane asylum in 1902 which soon closed due to public pressure. Denver acquired the Park and building in 1908 and the structure became the city's first community center. A half block southeast of the Park is the **Richthofen Fountain (2)**, circa 1900, in which the ashes of the Baroness were entombed in 1934.

Walk east on 12th St. to the **Baron's Castle (3)**, now obscured by trees. Listed on the National Register of Historic Places, the Castle and its **Gate House (4)** were completed in 1887; both have since been enlarged. Proceed north on Pontiac and then east on 13th. The **Stanley School (5)**, built in 1891, was the site of Colorado's first public kindergarten. Historic Denver, Inc., rescued the school from demolition in 1973 and it is now used as a vocational training center. Backtrack on 13th to **St. Luke Episcopal Church (6)**; the primary structure, completed in 1890, was built as a mission church and was used as a chapel for a boy's school that burned down in 1901.

Jog over to Olive St. and follow it south to 6th Ave. Many of the larger homes in Montclair were built for or by friends of Baron von Richthofen. The **Dennison House (7)**, 1006 Olive, was built in 1890 for the Baron's attorney who became Chief Justice of the Colorado Supreme Court in 1928. The next three homes on the east side of Olive St. **(8)** were three of ten "**TB houses**" built in Montclair between 1900 and 1910; screened porches, since enclosed, encouraged exposure to fresh air.

Heading north along Oneida St. you will pass **Kittredge Park (9)**, the former site of Kittredge Castle (1890-1955). Built by banker and businessman Charles M. Kittredge, the home became a girls' school in 1918. The Mediterranean-style home at **1101 Oneida (10)** was reportedly built by the Baron for his mistress (though he died before its completion in 1906).

The Montclair Civic Building

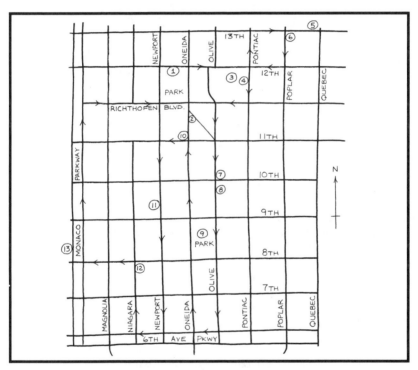

MONTCLAIR HISTORIC DISTRICT

Head south on Newport St. The Queen Anne Victorian house at **919 Newport (11)** was designed by Frank Edbrooke, one of Denver's most famous architects. Returning north along Niagara St. you will pass the former home of Thomas E. Walters, at **790 Niagara (12)**, circa 1893. Walters was an attorney who spearheaded the effort to pave Montclair's streets.

Cut out to Monaco Blvd. via 8th Ave. and head north along this appealing thoroughfare. The Mediterranean-style home at **815 Monaco (13)**, built in 1921, occupies the former site of the Baron's art gallery (C. 1891) and family resort (C. 1901). Proceed north to Richthofen Blvd., turn right and return to Montclair Park... the Baron would be flattered to know you visited!

25 AURORA ENVIRONMENTAL PARK

Distance: 2.2 miles roundtrip
Difficulty: Easy
Walking Time: 1.5 hrs.
Elevation: 5450-5480 ft.

Buckley Field, established in 1942 as an auxillary air field for Lowry Air Force Base, is one of only five primary Air National Guard bases in the country. Its 3500 acres, serviced by two runways, is also home to units from each branch of the military, including the Coast Guard.

During the early 1970s, the U.S. Government turned over 180 acres of the Buckley Field territory to the city of Aurora. Stretching along the upper reaches of Sand Creek, this land harbors prime riparian habitat and the donation stipulated that the area's natural features be protected and that the preserve be used for ecological study.

Today, a paved hike-bike path traverses the length of the Park and earthen trails lead into the rich, streamside woodland. A Challenge Bound Course, administered by the Aurora Public Schools and the city of Aurora, is based at the Park and the preserve is used as an Environmental Day Camp by local scouting groups.

Directions:
From I-225, east of Denver, exit onto 6th Ave. and head east. Drive 4 miles to the Park entrance, on your left. Park in the large graveled lot west of the Coal Creek Rodeo facility.

Route:
Walk to the northwest on the paved path that leaves the western end of the lot. The path winds past the Day Camp area and curves to the right, paralleling the creek and its riparian woodland. Aircraft buffs will enjoy watching commercial airliners as they glide into Stapleton and you may be treated to the spectacular aerial maneuvers of A7D Corsairs and F16 Fighting Falcons, based at Buckley Field.

Bear right at the fork in the trail, staying near the stream channel, and take the next right for a brief excursion through the riparian forest (see map). Cottonwoods, hackberry and willows are the dominant trees and the rich understory attests to the moist soil conditions through much of the year. Numerous songbirds haunt the woodland during the warmer months, feasting on the abundant insects. Magpies, great horned owls and red-tailed hawks nest in the larger trees and raccoons den in the hollowed trunks of old cottonwoods.

Emerging from the woods, continue westward on the hike/bike path and, upon reaching the golf course, turn back along a trail that skirts the archery area (see map). This path leads back to the bikeway; retrace your route to the parking area, completing a 2.2 mile walk.

Riparian woodlands are threatened across the Piedmont.

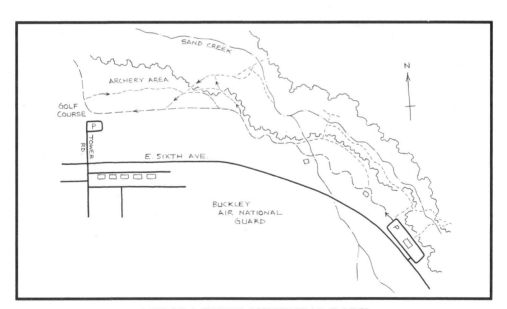

AURORA ENVIRONMENTAL PARK

26 BEAR CREEK LAKE PARK/MORRISON

Bear Creek Loop
  Distance: 3.8 miles
  Difficulty: Easy
  Walking Time: 2.5-3.0 hrs.
  Elevation: 5560-5640 ft.

Morrison Tour
  Distance: 2.4 miles
  Difficulty: Easy
  Walking Time: 2 hrs.
  Elevation: 5750-5800 ft.

Summit Lake sits in a rock-walled cirque on the east face of Mt. Evans, 7500 feet above and 30 miles west of Metro Denver. Melting snows overflow its shallow basin in late spring, giving rise to Bear Creek which trickles eastward across the rocky tundra. Gathering force on steeper terrain and capturing flow from numerous tributaries, the stream rumbles down through a broad, forested valley. In Evergreen (elevation 7072 ft.) it has been dammed to form a scenic mountain lake; below the dam Bear Creek renews itself, cascading through a rugged canyon before pouring onto the Colorado Piedmont at Morrison.

Just east of the foothills Bear Creek and its major tributary, Turkey Creek, have been dammed by the Corps of Engineers, creating Bear Creek Lake. This flood-control Reservoir, completed in 1982, covers 110 acres (up to 718 acres under flood conditions) and is surrounded by Bear Creek Lake Park, characterized by open grasslands, broad plateaus and sweeping vistas.

In this chapter we offer two day hikes at Bear Creek Lake Park and a walking tour of historic Morrison, Colorado.

Directions:
  To reach Bear Creek Lake Park, take the Morrison Road Exit (Colorado 8) from C-470, west of Denver. Drive east for 3.5 miles to the main entrance and proceed to parking areas as illustrated on the map.

Mt. Carbon via Dam
  Distance: 2.2 miles roundtrip
  Difficulty: Easy
  Walking Time: 1.5-2.0 hrs.
  Elevation: 5680-5772 ft.

To reach Morrison, take the same exit but drive west on Colorado 8, pass through the Hogback ridge and park along the south side of the road (see map).

Routes:
  Bear Creek Loop (3.8 miles). From the large parking area (P1) on the north shore of the Reservoir, hike to the west on a jeep road. Nearing the second access lot, switch to a foot path that parallels Bear Creek, heading upstream. One and a half miles from your starting point the trail cuts away from the creek and climbs to a Park road. Turn left on the roadway, cross over Bear Creek and then turn east on a trail that leads back down along the stream.

At the fork, bear right and ascend from the floodplain, soon intersecting the road again. Walk eastward along the road, passing a large prairie dog town and, after 1/3 mile, turn left on a trail that drops down to the floodplain once again. Hike westward along the creek, passing through a rich, riparian woodland. Cross Bear Creek via a footbridge and return to your car above the north bank (see map).

Mt. Carbon via Bear Creek Dam (2.2 miles roundtrip). Mt. Carbon, elevation 5772 feet, is the most striking topographic feature at Bear Creek Lake Park. From the top of this mesa you are treated to sweeping views of the Colorado Piedmont and Front Range foothills, from Metro Denver to the Palmer Divide.

The easiest route to the summit is via a service road that runs atop the dam. Park in the graveled area at the north end of the dam (P2) and hike southward for almost a mile to the edge of Mt. Carbon. The Bear

The Reservoir from Mt. Carbon; Mt. Morrison is in the distance..

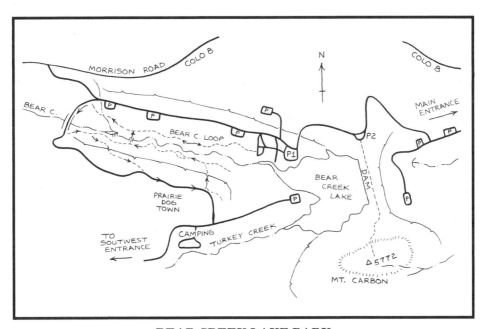

BEAR CREEK LAKE PARK

Creek Valley winds away toward Denver, to the east, and the Reservoir shimmers to the west, 130 feet below your path.

Ascend onto Mt. Carbon via one of several paths that lead up from the south end of the dam. Enjoy a picnic lunch atop this scenic mesa and then return to your car via the same route.

Morrison Tour (2.4 miles). Founded by George Morrison, a stone mason, in 1860, the town of Morrison served as an important gateway to the mountains during the early development of the Front Range cities. Stagecoaches and, later, the Denver, South Park & Pacific Railroad used the town as an entry point to the Rockies and local quarries exported their products through this pioneer village. World famous for its location within a fossil-rich valley of Jurassic shale and sandstone, the town lends its name to the "Morrison Formation," a geologic depository of dinosaur bones.

A walking tour of this historic settlement starts along Colorado 8, just west of the Dakota Hogback (see map). Across from the parking area is the **old Standard Service Station (1)**, circa 1926, now a bakery and gallery. Walk west along Colorado 8 and turn right on Market St. The **small homes (2)** on the east side of this street all date from 1873. On your left is the **Charley Pike House (3)**, built in 1885; he was a local merchant and the nephew of famed explorer Zebulon Pike. Next door is the **Morrison Community Church (4)**, also built in 1885.

Turn left on Mt. Vernon Ave., which hugs the base of the Dakota Hogback, and proceed up to the **Cliff House Lodge (5)**. Now a bed and breakfast establishment, it was constructed by George Morrison in 1873; Morrison died in the house, in 1895, and it was soon thereafter converted to the renowned Cliff House Hotel. Walk south along Stone St. The old **Newland House (6)**, circa 1875, was a boarding house for railroad workers; it now serves as a

museum. The **John Ross Home (7)**, now a restaurant, dates from 1876 when it served as a cafe and stagecoach stop. Across Stone St. is the former **home of Thomas Bergen (8)** who founded Bergen Park, near Evergreen, in 1859.

Turn right (west) along Colorado 8. The **commercial buildings** on your right **(9)** all date from 1876-1880. Just west of Mt. Vernon Creek is the **old Morrison Bank (10)**, circa 1880, now a restaurant. Further along is the old **Gotchalk Bakery (11)**; built on the former site of the Morrison Quarry, the building has been used as a saloon, a bakery and a post office; it now houses a liquor store and a vet clinic.

Cross Colorado 8 and angle to the southwest on South Park Ave., crossing Bear Creek. The old **Stagecoach Building (12)**, built in 1870 by George Morrison, and the adjacent **Livery/Carriage House (13)**, also dating from 1870, are two of the town's more attractive and historic structures. The home at **119 South Park Ave. (14)**, circa 1870, housed a Mexican restaurant from 1945 to 1973.

Continue along South Park Ave. and then turn left on Spring St. The house at **127 Spring St. (15)**, built in 1872 for use by the railroad workers, was moved from the south bank of Bear Creek in 1926. Proceed out to the **old Morrison School House (16)**, now a private home. This attractive, sandstone building was constructed by George Morrison in 1875 and served as an education center until 1955.

Circle back to Spring St., retrace your route along South Park Ave. and turn right (east) on Colorado 8. **Memory Plaza (17)** sits above Bear Creek at the former site of the Morrison newspaper plant (1889-1917). Further along is the **site of Morrison's Railroad Depot (18)**, which served the Denver, South Park & Pacific Railroad from 1873 to 1925.

Continue east along Colorado 8 to your car, completing a 2.4 mile tour of this historic town.

The old Morrison School.

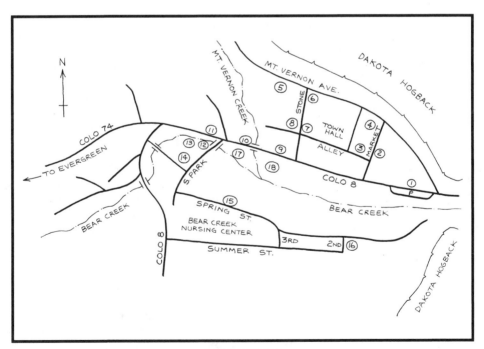

MORRISON

27 WASHINGTON PARK/COUNTRY CLUB HISTORIC DISTRICT

Distance: 5 miles
Difficulty: Easy
Walking Time: 3-4 hrs.
Elevation: 5270-5320 ft.

One of Denver's more enterprising pioneers was John Smith who supervised the construction of an irrigation canal from the South Platte River to the arid lands east of the city. Completed in 1867, the central canal fed numerous side channels, providing precious water for southern and eastern sections of town. Purchased by Denver in 1875 and renamed the "City Ditch," the 27-mile conduit still provides irrigation waters for Washington Park, the Denver Country Club and City Park. Most of the old canal is now piped beneath streets and suburban sprawl but an open section of the ditch still cuts across Washington Park.

Formerly a dairy farm, Washington Park became Denver's 12th public park in 1895. A century later, the 154-acre preserve has become the undisputed mecca for joggers, walkers, rollerbladers and people watchers in the south Denver area. A five-mile walk takes you across northern sections of the Park, down to the Country Club Historic District and back to this urban oasis.

Directions:
From Downtown Denver, follow Speer Blvd. to the southeast. Cross over Broadway and proceed another mile to Downing St. Turn right (south) and drive .7 mile to the Park. Leave your car in one of the lots along the west shore of Smith Lake (see map).

Route:
The **Pump House (1)** was constructed to boost irrigation pressure for the Park. Walk eastward along the southern shore to the lakeside **Pavilion (2)** which was recently refurbished and is rented-out for private receptions. **Smith's Ditch** will be noted just south of the Pavilion, winding in from the southwestern corner of the Park.

Cross the canal, circle to the east side of the **Recreation Center (3)** and walk down to the **old dairy farm buildings (4)**, now headquarters for the South District of Denver's Park and Recreation Department. These attractive structures date from the 1870s and, as mentioned above, were purchased by the City in 1895. The barn has been used as a maintenance facility since that time and once sheltered the horses that were used to mow the Park. The residence, rented out until 1987, now houses the South District offices.

Walk northward along the Park road and stop by the **Eugene Field Cottage (5)**, now headquarters for the Park People. Built in 1875 and situated along Colfax Avenue, this was the home of Eugene Field, managing editor of the Denver Tribune. Saved from demolition by "Unsinkable Molly" Brown in the mid 1920s, the cottage was donated to the City of Denver in 1930 and moved to Washington Park where it served as a library until 1970.

Hike along the east and north shores of **Smith Lake**, passing the "**Colorado Miner**" statue **(6)** by George Carlson, dedicated in April, 1980. Exit the Park and proceed northward along Marion Parkway. The **Park Lane Towers (7)**, visible from much of the Metro area, were built from 1971-73; the **Marion Park Tower (8)** was added in 1976. Further along is **Robert Steele School (9)** which opened in 1913.

Continue northward, passing the west edge of the Denver Country Club along Downing St. Cross Speer Blvd. (and Cherry Creek) and enter the **Country Club Historic District**. The **Denver Country Club** organized in 1901 and, the following year, purchased 240 acres along Cherry Creek; one half of the land was used to

*Smith's Ditch
and the
Washington Park
Pavilion*

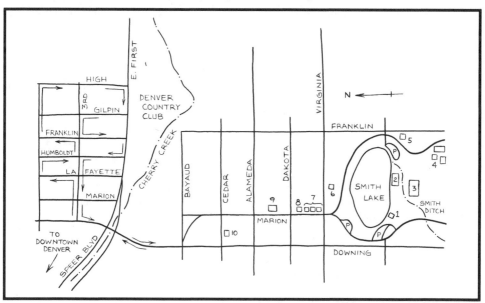

WASHINGTON PARK/COUNTRY CLUB HISTORIC DISTRICT

construct the golf course and the other half was set aside for residential development. Most of the mansion-like homes in the District date from 1905 to 1940 and manifest a wide variety of architectural styles. Some of Denver's most famous architects designed houses in the Country Club neighborhood, including William E. Fisher who created the parkways and gateways that characterized the area. Placed on the National Register of Historic Places in 1979, the Country Club became Denver's largest historic district.

The map in this guide offers a 2-mile tour of the Country Club District, taking you past a diverse collection of architectural styles. Denver Square, Edwardian, Georgian Revival and Spanish Colonial homes dominate the District.

After winding through the Country Club neighborhood, return to Washington Park via Downing St.; cut across to Marion Parkway at Cedar Avenue, passing a fine **Victorian home (10)**, and then continue southward to the Park.

28 UNIVERSITY OF DENVER/UNIVERSITY PARK

Distance: 2.3 miles
Difficulty: Easy
Walking Time: 2 hrs.
Elevation: 5370-5390 ft.

The University of Denver is both the oldest and the largest independent university in the Rocky Mountain region. Founded by Territorial Governor John Evans in 1864, the "Colorado Seminary" was re-organized as the University of Denver in 1880. This chapter offers a walk across this attractive campus and through University Park, the adjacent residential area that was spawned by the college.

Directions:
From Denver, take I-25 south and exit onto University Blvd. Proceed south on University, cross over Evans Ave. and turn left on Warren Ave. Drive 4 blocks to Observatory Park and leave your car at this suburban retreat.

Route:
Walk out to the **Chamberlain Observatory (1)** which was built in 1888, one year after the Park was established. The Observatory was designed by Robert Roeschlaub, the famous architect who also designed the Central City Opera House and University Hall on the University of Denver campus. Flanked by the smaller **Student's Observatory (2)**, the structures were donated to the University by H.B. Chamberlain, a real estate baron and an amateur astronomer.

Take a stroll around the two blocks of Observatory Park; most of the homes along the Park date from 1890 to 1910. The Victorian houses along the 2100 block of Milwaukee St., all built between 1887 and 1898, were known as "**Professors Row (3)**," reflecting their academic residents. Across the Park, at **2127 S. Fillmore (4)**, is the "Honeymoon Cottage," circa 1891, which was often rented to newlywed faculty members. The attractive home at

2201 S. Fillmore (5) was built in 1891 for Dr. Herbert Alonzo Howe, the first Professor of Astronomy at the University of Denver and Director of the Chamberlain Observatory.

Turn west on Warren Ave. and then wind through the neighborhood that stretches from Observatory Park to the University (see map); again, most of the houses date from 1886 to 1910. The house at **2525 E. Evans (6)**, circa 1886, was the first home built in University Park. The bungalow at **2100 S. Columbine (7)**, built in 1905, was used by Colorado Governor Henry A. Buchtel during his two year term.

In our opinion, the 2-block stretch of S. Columbine, from Evans to Iliff, is the most attractive section of University Park. The homes at **2174 (8) and 2233 (9) S. Columbine** offer fine examples of Edwardian architecture, common in this neighborhood. The house at **2255 S. Columbine (10)**, built in 1897, was acquired by the University for use as the Chancellor's residence in 1922.

University Park United Methodist Church (11) was constructed in 1928; a new sanctuary was added in the early 1950s. Cross University Blvd. and enter the University of Denver campus. The entry circle is flanked by three magnificent buildings, the **Iliff School of Theology (12)**, designed by Fuller & Wheeler of Albany, New York, and completed in 1892, **University Hall (13)**, 1890 by Robert Roeschlaub, and the **Mary Reed Building (14)**, perhaps the most recognizable structure on campus.

Walk around the east end of University Hall and proceed to a quadrangle fronting **Margaret Reed Hall (15)**. The **Alma Mater Statue (16)** was dedicated in 1919. Proceed westward, passing the **Buchtel Memorial Tower (17)**, a remnant of the Buchtel Memorial Chapel, circa 1907, that burned down on July 21, 1983. Pass the **Penrose Library (18), Science Hall (19)**

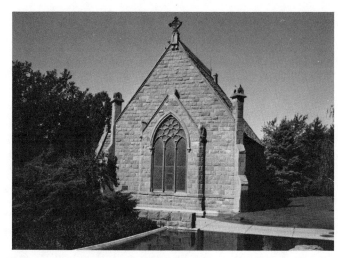

*Evans
Memorial
Chapel*

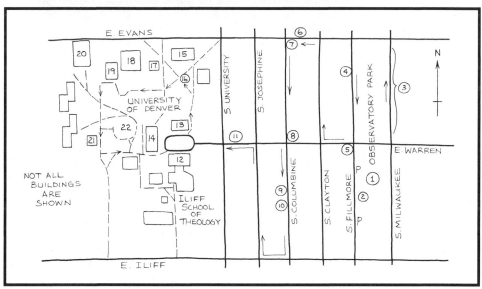

UNIVERSITY OF DENVER / UNIVERSITY PARK

and the **Driscoll University Center (20)** and turn south to the **Evans Memorial Chapel (21)**. Erected in 1878 by Territorial Governor John Evans in memory of his daughter, Josephine, the structure was moved from 13th and Bannock in 1960. The Chapel is a United Methodist Historic Site and was dedicated as a Denver Historic Landmark in 1969.

Circle through the **Harper Humanities Gardens (22)** and then wind through the **Iliff School of Theology** Campus (see map). Founded in 1892 by Bishop Henry White Warren and the family of John Wesley Iliff, a cattle and real estate baron, the School was initially a college within the University of Denver. In 1904, the Iliff School of Theology became a separate institution and now offers Master degrees in various fields of study, including Master of Divinity and Master of Arts in Religion.

Return to Observatory Park via Warren Avenue, completing a 2.3 mile walk.

29 CHERRY CREEK STATE RECREATION AREA

West Side Lot to Nature Trail
  Distance: 2.5 miles roundtrip
  Difficulty: Easy
  Walking Time: 1.5-2.0 hrs.
  Elevation: 5550-5570 ft.

Cherry Creek Loop
  Distance: 3.5 miles
  Difficulty: Easy
  Walking Time: 2-3 hrs.
  Elevation: 5570-5620 ft.

A natural oasis amidst a sea of shake shingles, the area around Cherry Creek Reservoir has been a refuge for wildlife and Front Range residents since the dam was constructed in 1950. The 880 acre lake and the surrounding 3900 acre Recreation Area attract a huge number of visitors throughout the year but most activity occurs on warm weather weekends, on or along the Reservoir. Those who visit the Park during the "off-season" and those who venture away from the lake can still enjoy the solitude that such a vast preserve affords.

Riparian woodlands, perhaps the most threatened habitat in our State, stretch along the course of Cherry Creek where cattail marshes border the wide, sandy channel. Great horned owls nest in this backwater woods and a variety of mammals, including skunks, raccoons and white-tailed deer, retreat to its shelter by day. Ring-necked pheasants, jackrabbits, hawks, prairie dogs and coyotes are among the grassland residents.

Directions:
From Denver, drive south on I-25 and then follow I-225 back to the northeast. Exit onto Parker Road (Colorado 83), turn right (south) and drive 1.2 miles to the Park's east entrance. A nominal day-use fee is charged. Proceed to parking lots south and west of the Reservoir (see map).

Routes:
Numerous foot trails, bikeways and bridal paths provide access to the remote areas of Cherry Creek Recreation Area. We suggest the following day hikes.

West Side Lot to Natural Trail (2.5 miles roundtrip). From the large **lot (P1)** that services the West Side Shelters, walk to the southeast on the paved bikeway that winds above the southwest shore of the Reservoir. Cross through the **Mountain Loop (ML)** and bypass two lanes that lead out to **Sailboard Beach (SB)**. Angling toward the lake the path reaches the **Nature Trail lot** where it forks; bear left and descend into the Reservoir basin, crossing Cottonwood Creek via a footbridge. Scan the adjacent cattail marsh for soras, bitterns and Virginia rails during the warmer months.

The paved path continues to the southeast while the earthen **Nature Trail (NT)** loops eastward into backwater marshlands. Turn onto this loop and wind through the wooded swamp, crossing boggy areas via short boardwalks. Northern harriers are often spotted here and great horned owls nest in the moist woods. Construction of the Nature Trail was funded by the Cherry Creek Women's Club.

Return to the West Side Lot via the same route, completing a roundtrip hike of 2.5 miles.

Cherry Creek Loop (3.5 miles). Park in the **Lot (P2)** just west of the Cherry Creek inlet and walk to the south on a wide, graveled path that parallels the stream. A mile from the trailhead, Cherry Creek curves away to the east while the trail continues southward, crossing upland fields.

As the Creek and trail converge once again, the trail forks; bear left on a bridal path that descends into the floodplain of

*An old
cottonwood
along Cherry Creek.*

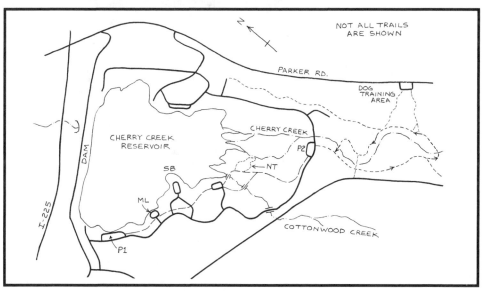

CHERRY CREEK STATE RECREATION AREA

Cherry Creek and soon crosses the stream (high water may negate the full loop; if so, return via the same route). The bridal path leads northward, ascending above the floodplain but paralleling the Creek. Pass cutoff trails to the Dog Training Area and continue above the stream as it curves to the west. Marshes, riparian woodlands and valley meadows make this an excellent area for birdwatching.

Bypass several cutoffs, remaining on the wide path that follows the course of Cherry Creek (see map). The trail eventually narrows and turns westward, crossing the braided channel. Ascend the west bank and turn right, returning to the lot via the graveled path.

85

30 LITTLETON

Distance: 4 miles
Difficulty: Easy
Walking Time: 2.5-3.0 hrs.
Elevation: 5310-5470 ft.

Born in 1829, in Grafton, New Hampshire, Richard S. Little, a civil engineer, surveyed land claims along the South Platte and planned irrigation canals for the Capitol Hydraulic Company. Enamored with the Platte Valley, Little claimed territory along the east bank of the River and, by 1867, had opened the Rough & Ready Flour Mill to process the harvest of local farmers. This proved to be the nidus for "Littleton," which was granted a post office in 1869 and found itself on the Denver & Rio Grande Railroad by 1871. Little filed a plat for his town in June, 1872, and Littleton was finally incorporated in 1890.

A 4-mile walk takes you from the banks of the South Platte, through the city's central business district, up to the Littleton Historic Museum and back to the River again.

Directions:

From C-470, south of Denver, exit onto Santa Fe Drive and proceed north. Drive approximately 3 miles, turn left (west) on Bowles Ave. and park in the unpaved lot north of the road and east of the River (see map); this is the former site of the Rough & Ready Mill, which was demolished in 1959.

Route:

Walk southward along the River and turn east along the south side of the **Riverfront Festival Center (1)** which opened in 1985. Follow Little's Creek, passing under Santa Fe Drive, and turn left on Rapp St. The **Little family home (2)**, built in 1884, is now an office center.

Turn right on W. Alamo. The **white frame buildings (3)** across the street, dating from the 1870s-1880s, are among

the oldest commercial structures in Littleton. Further east is the **Treece House (4)**, built in 1889 and restored in 1977. The stone building at **2505 W. Alamo (5)**, now a gift shop, was built as a residence in 1897. The **Bozarth House (6)**, c. late 1880s, is one of the finer Victorian homes in the city. Cut through the **W. Alamo Center (7)**, a design and art complex that was added to Arapahoe Community College in 1989; the College itself, two blocks south, opened in 1966.

Continue east to **Bega Park (8)** which depicts and honors Littleton's "Sister City" relationship with Bega, New South Wales, Australia. Cross over the railroad and turn right on Bemis St. Walk past a block of early 20th Century homes and cut through **Sterne Park**, one of Littleton's more attractive open spaces. Circle to the east side of the lake and follow the inlet stream up to Lake Ave. (see map).

Proceed east to the **Edwin Bemis Library (9)**. Named for the former editor of the Littleton Independent, the library opened in 1965, having relocated from the Carnegie Building, downtown. Follow Library Lane to S. Gallup St. and jog north to the entrance for the **Littleton Historical Museum**. Opened in 1969, the 14-acre Museum houses a fine collection of structures and artifacts from Littleton's early decades. This living museum is free and open to the public 8 AM-5 PM, M-F, 10 AM-5 PM on Sat., and 1 PM-5 PM on Sunday. Highlights include an 1860s homestead, Littleton's original schoolhouse (c. 1864) and a "turn of the century farm." For more information, call 795-3950.

After winding through the Museum, walk north on S. Gallup St. and then west on Shepperd Ave. to Crocker St. Walk north to the **old Littleton High School (10)**, built in 1920, now the Education Services Center. Continue north to Littleton Blvd. and turn left. The two, fine "**Denver Squares**" just east of Prescott (**11 & 12**)

Littleton's first Schoolhouse.

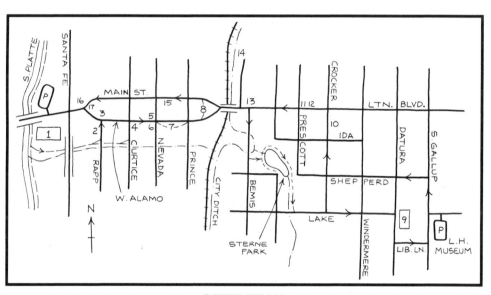

LITTLETON

were built by Harry Nutting, owner of Littleton's Lumber & Fuel Company; the corner house, circa 1907, was his home and he built the other for his daughter.

Named the seat of Arapahoe County in 1904, Littleton witnessed construction of the **County Courthouse (13)** from 1907-1908. Cut behind the Courthouse to the **Depot Art Center (14)**, housed in one of Littleton's old railroad depots, circa 1888. This historic structure and its adjacent 1898 caboose were restored by the Littleton Fine Arts Guild. The Center is open 11 AM-

4 PM, Tuesday-Saturday.

Descend along Main St. into the central business district where Victorian storefronts line the avenue. The old **Town Hall (15)**, built in 1920, became a performing arts center in 1983. At the end of the street is the **old Carnegie Library (16)**, circa 1916, now a popular restaurant, and around the corner is the **Masonic Temple Building (17)**, erected in 1921.

Cross Santa Fe and return to your car, completing a 4 mile tour of Little's town.

31 THE HIGHLINE CANAL

Distance: Hikes from 4.4-11.2 miles
Difficulty: Easy
Walking Time: Walks from 3-6 hrs.
Elevation: 5510-5530 ft.

Originating in Waterton Canyon, the **Highline Canal** was constructed in the early 1880s to bring irrigation waters to the dry farmlands east of Denver. The canal and its pathway now serve as an avenue for exercise and preserve a vital, 80-mile ribbon of riparian habitat through the Metro area.

While any section of the trail will provide a pleasant day hike, its westernmost portion offers easy access and, to date, is somewhat less impacted by urban and suburban development. Nevertheless, private lands border much of the route and respect for the privacy and rights of these landowners is strongly encouraged.

Directions:

From C-470 south of Denver, exit onto Santa Fe Drive (U.S. 85). The map illustrates the location of three parking areas. The first is a small, graveled parking lane on the east side of Santa Fe Dr., .9 mile south of C-470. The second lot is on the south side of County Line Rd., 1.9 miles east of Santa Fe Dr. (.6 mile west of Broadway). The third alternative is to park along Highline Canal Ln. at Writers Vista Park which is on the south side of Mineral Ave., 1 mile east of Santa Fe.

Route:

The following is a description of the **Highline Canal Trail** from Writers Vista Park, on Mineral Ave., to the lot on Santa Fe Dr., a one-way distance of 5.6 miles. Sectional mileage is noted on the map and suggested day hikes are listed below.

From Writers Vista Park the trail parallels the Canal southward. Crossing above and east of McClellan Reservoir,

broad views unfold to the west. Cottonwoods line the canal throughout its length, offering shade in summer and providing choice habitat for fox squirrels, flickers, magpies and numerous songbirds.

The canal angles to the southeast above the inlet of McClellan Reservoir, overlooking backwater marshes where mallards, wood ducks, herons and rails may be spotted in spring and summer. Crossing County Line Road, the trail leads toward the south for .2 mile and intersects a paved bikeway that follows the canal westward. The route winds around feeder streams of the Reservoir and offers spectacular views across the lake to the Front Range. Cormorants fish on the open waters from April to November and seasonal migrations bring loons, grebes, gulls and a variety of diving ducks to McClellan.

Nearing the west end of the reservoir the canal cuts away from County Line Road, angling to the southwest, and crosses under C-470. On the west side of the highway the paved bike path turns westward while the canal and earthen path lead to the south, passing several homesteads. Curving to the west and then back to the south the canal is bordered by open grasslands and pastures. Watch for hawks, kestrels, western kingbirds, red fox and an occasional coyote in this area. The final section of the route loops eastward and then westward again, ending at the small lot on Santa Fe Dr.

The following day hikes are suggested:

Santa Fe Dr. to C-470 - 4.4. miles roundtrip

County Line Rd. to C-470 - 4.8 miles roundtrip

Writers Vista Park to C-470 - 6.8 miles roundtrip

Writers Vista Park to Santa Fe Dr. - 11.2 miles roundtrip

Winter along the Canal.

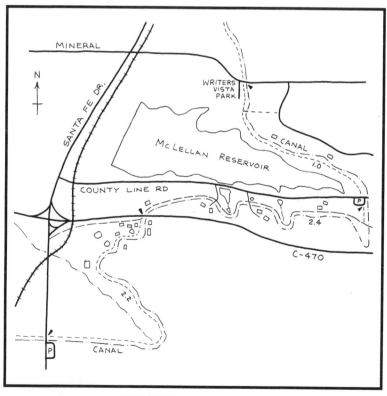

THE HIGHLINE CANAL

32 CHATFIELD STATE RECREATION AREA

South Platte Trail
 Distance: 4 miles roundtrip
 Difficulty: Easy
 Walking Time: 2.5-3.0 hrs.
 Elevation: 5440-5540 ft.

South Platte to Marina
 Distance: 5 miles roundtrip
 Difficulty: Easy
 Walking Time: 3-4 hrs.
 Elevation: 5440-5500 ft.

Combined Loop Hike
 Distance: 11.5 miles
 Difficulty: Moderate
 Walking Time: 6-8 hrs.
 Elevation: 5440-5540

As is common throughout the world, early settlements in Colorado clustered along the primary rivers and streams. Afterall, these vital channels provided water, a source of food and navigational advantages. But river towns are also prone to one of nature's most destructive forces —flooding. This became painfully evident on June 16, 1965, when heavy thunderstorms along the Palmer Divide sent a torrent of water through the South Platte Valley, leveling many homes and businesses.

In response to nature's fury the Corps of Engineers was enlisted to construct a dam at the confluence of Plum Creek and the South Platte River, creating a flood-control reservoir. Chatfield Dam, completed in 1976, now impounds 1450 acres of water surface, offering flood control, varied wildlife habitat and recreation for Front Range residents. The surrounding 4200 acres comprise the Chatfield State Recreation Area, a popular destination for fishermen, hikers, cyclists, horsemen and naturalists.

Directions:

From C-470 southwest of Denver, take the Wadsworth Blvd. Exit (Route 121). Turn south and proceed 1 mile to the Park entrance. A nominal day-use fee is charged.

Routes:

There are varied hiking opportunities at Chatfield. We suggest the following day hikes, all of which originate at the **parking lot (P*)** south of the reservoir and just east of the South Platte inlet (see map).

South Platte Trail (4 miles roundtrip). This **trail (SPT)** follows the river southward from the reservoir, crossing through riparian woodlands and skirting wetlands that dot the valley. Follow the paved path that winds down to the east bank of the South Platte and switch to an earthen trail that meanders upstream, soon climbing above the floodplain and intersecting a horse trail that runs atop the basin.

The **South Platte Trail** descends back to the river bank and, within a half mile, crosses the outflow stream of a pond. Heading due south, the trail crosses through woodlands and meadows that separate the River from a chain of wetlands to the east. After entering a large field the primary trail ends; however, a faint path continues to the south, passing an **old cabin (C)** and climbing from the South Platte floodplain. This latter section, which may be impassable in spring and early summer, intersects the **Highline Canal** just east of the Platte Canyon Reservoir.

Return to your car via the same route, completing a roundtrip hike of 4 miles.

December in the valley.

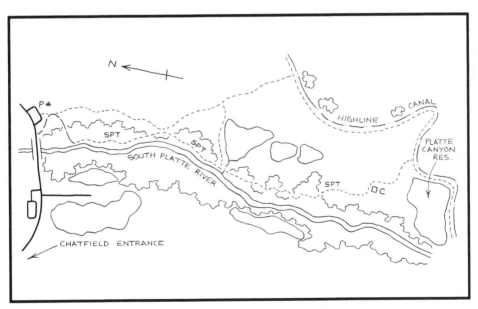

THE SOUTH PLATTE TRAIL

South Platte to Marina (5 miles round-trip). From the parking lot (P*) cross the roadway and follow the paved path that starts above the east bank of the river. It soon veers to the northeast, loops around a drainage and winds above two beaver ponds. The trail then climbs to an **overlook (V)** which affords a view of Chatfield's **heronry (H)**. Drowned cottonwoods support the nests of great blue herons and double-crested cormorants; unfortunately, the trees are beginning to crumble and Park naturalists are encouraging the birds to move to other nest sites, along Plum Creek.

Just past the overlook the trail curves to the southeast and intersects the entry road for the Park Headquarters. Turn left along the road and then veer away to the northwest as the trail begins its loop around the **Headquarters building**. Skirting a deep ravine, the route passes a campground area and continues its excursion above the lake basin. Within a half mile you will begin a gradual descent to the south shore of Chatfield Reservoir; from there a short walk takes you over to the **Marina** where a dock-side lunch is offered during the warmer months.

Return to your car via the same route, completing a roundtrip hike of 5 miles.

Combined Loop Hike (11.5 miles). This long day hike begins and ends at the parking lot (P*) just east of the South Platte inlet. Those who attempt this route should leave early in the day and bring plenty of food and water; most of the route crosses open country, posing the risk of heat exhaustion in the summer and hypothermia in winter.

From the parking lot walk 2.5 miles to the **Marina** as described for the preceding hike. Nearing the Marina, angle to the southeast on a paved path that crosses the Marina access road twice and then intersects a jeep trail (see map). Turn right (south) on this wide path and proceed to the **Nature Area road**. Turn left and walk along the road as it curves to the southeast.

After hiking along the road for .6 mile, switch to another paved trail that climbs above the Plum Creek floodplain and crosses an open grassland. Leveling out along the rim of the basin the trail soon forks; bear right, staying above the floodplain and wind to the southwest. Within a quarter mile you will intersect the **Highline Canal**.

Originating in Waterton Canyon and constructed in the early 1880s, this Canal brought irrigation waters to the dry farmlands east of Denver. Turn right, following the canal's towpath to the northwest. Huge cottonwoods shade the trail, attracting a variety of raptors, songbirds and mammals that hunt and forage on the vast grasslands of the Chatfield preserve. Curving to the west the path yields a broad view to the north, taking in the Recreation Area, Chatfield Reservoir, the Front Range foothills and the distant skyscrapers of downtown Denver.

Cross over Roxborough Park Road and continue along the Canal which curves to the southwest, passes a residential area and then follows a tortuous course to the **Platte Canyon Reservoir**. Switch to a path that leads down to the **South Platte Trail (SPT)** and hike northward above the east bank of the river (see narrative for the South Platte Trail hike).

*Along the
Highline
Canal.*

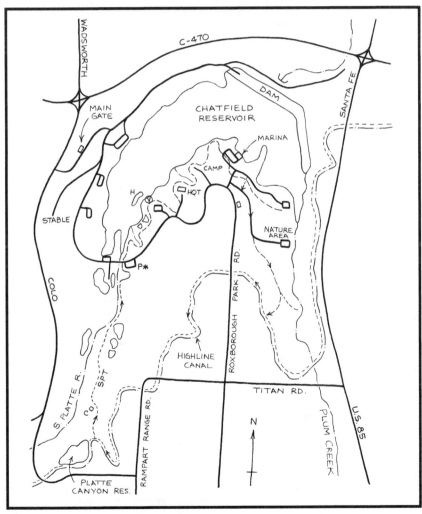

CHATFIELD STATE RECREATION AREA

33 CASTLEWOOD CANYON STATE PARK

Rim Rock/Creek Bottom Loop
  Distance: 3.5 miles
  Difficulty: Moderate
  Walking Time: 2.0-2.5 hrs.
  Elevation: 6160-6580 ft.

Inner Canyon/Lake Gulch Loop
  Distance: 3 miles
  Difficulty: Moderate
  Walking Time: 2.0-2.5 hrs.
  Elevation: 6360-6580 ft.

Cherry Creek rises along the Palmer Divide, fed by the heavy snows and frequent thunderstorms that sweep across that high peninsula of pine. Coursing northward to join the South Platte in downtown Denver, the Creek has carved a scenic gorge through the mesa country of eastern Douglas County.

The rugged gorge is now protected within Castlewood Canyon State Park. Encompassing 873 acres, the Park offers several excellent day hikes through the rock-walled chasm and atop the east rim of the gorge. Of historic interest are the crumbled remains of Castlewood Dam, constructed in 1890 for irrigation of area farms, and the remnants of an old homestead (H) near the west entrance.

Directions:
Follow I-25 south to Castle Rock, Colorado. Take Exit #182, turn left and follow Main St. into the downtown area. Turn left (east) on Fifth St. (Colorado 86), heading toward Franktown. Drive 6.3 miles, ascending across a high ridge and then descending into the Cherry Creek Valley. Turn right (south) on the entry road to Castlewood Canyon (Douglas County 51) and proceed 2.2 miles to the Park's west gate. A nominal day-use fee is charged.

Route: We suggest the following day hikes.
Rim Rock Trail/Creek Bottom Trail Loop (3.5 miles). Park in the small lot just beyond the west entrance gate on the east side of the road. The ruins of the old Lucas Homestead (H) will be noted east of the lot. Walk out to this skeletal structure and follow the trail as it veers to the right and

winds into the Cherry Creek Valley. Upon reaching the valley floor the trail leads southward, crosses a side stream and arrives at a trail intersection.

Turn left and follow the **Rim Rock Trail (RT)** as it crosses Cherry Creek via a footbridge and then climbs the east wall of the gorge using a series of switchbacks. Once atop the mesa the trail leads out to the rim of the chasm, yielding broad views to the west and north. Pike's Peak looms to the southwest while Devil's Head and Windy Peak dominate the western skyline. The Mt. Evans massif rises to the WNW, anchoring the Front Range that stretches northward to the Wyoming border.

Hike southward along the trail as it parallels the east rim of the canyon. Multiple overlooks are spaced along the route, offering spectacular views into the gorge. Two hundred feet above the valley floor, you are walking on Castle Rock Conglomerate, a resistant layer of rock that caps the mesas of the southern Colorado Piedmont. The Conglomerate is a product of outwash from the ancestral South Platte River that once poured eastward across the plains north of Pike's Peak. Altered drainage along the Rampart Range would later divert the River's flow to the north and the mesas have since been carved from the old floodplain by wind and water erosion.

After hiking almost 1.5 miles along the east rim, watch for a trail sign that directs you down to the Dam area via another series of switchbacks. This is rattlesnake country and caution is advised during the warmer months. South of the crumbled Dam the trail intersects the **Inner Canyon Trail (ICT)**. Bear right, cross Cherry

A view from the rim.

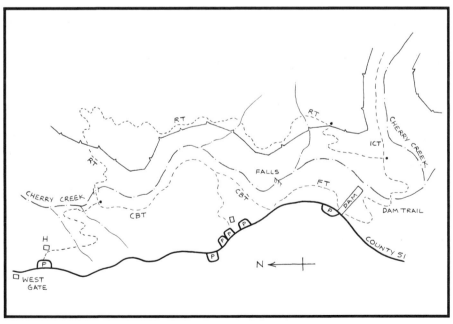

RIM ROCK/CREEK BOTTOM LOOP

Creek via a footbridge and climb onto the west end of the dam. Pick up the **Falls Trail (FT)** which undulates northward along the stream. Bypass several side trails that lead up to picnic areas and continue back to the north end of the gorge via the **Creek Bottom Trail (CBT)**. Ascend back to your car past the old homestead (see map).

Inner Canyon/Lake Gulch Loop (3 miles roundtrip). Park near the old Dam in one of the graveled pulloffs along the County road. Descend the south (upstream) side of the Dam, parallel Cherry Creek for a short distance and cross the stream via a footbridge. Ascend the opposite bank and wind eastward to the intersection with the **Inner Canyon Trail (ICT)**. Turn right onto this path as it curves to the south and then back to the east, entering a narrow, rock-walled canyon.

Bypass the cutoff to the **Lake Gulch Trail (LGT)** and begin a gradual, 1-mile climb through the scenic gorge. Dippers are often spotted in the turbulent waters during the colder months and scrub jays noisily hunt along the dry canyon walls throughout the year. "Slump blocks" of Castle Rock Conglomerate, having broken away from the upper cliffs, rest along the stream. The origin of this bedrock is discussed in the Rim Trail/Creek Bottom Loop narrative.

Nearing the upper reaches of the canyon, the trail crosses the creek and ascends the south wall of the gorge using a series of switchbacks and stairways. The route crosses an open grassland with scattered ponderosa pines and junipers and soon arrives at a parking area. This is the site of a planned east entrance and nature center, to be reached via Colorado 83 south of Franktown.

Pick up the **Lake Gulch Trail (LGT)** and hike westward across the grassland, taking in a magnificent view of the Front Range. The trail soon begins a long descent into the Cherry Creek Valley, edging along the rocky mesa wall. Cattle ranches stretch across the broad basin to the south, threatened with inundation by recent proposals to rebuild the Castlewood Dam. Just another project to divert more water to the golf courses and lawns of Metro Denver, the proposed reservoir would also flood the Inner Canyon. Many of us would rather leave the crumbled dam as it is (it collapsed on August 3, 1933) and protect the scenic canyons for future generations to enjoy.

Cross Cherry Creek, turn left along the **Inner Canyon Trail** and return to your car by backtracking along the **Dam Trail** to the west end of the dam.

The remnants of Castlewood Dam.

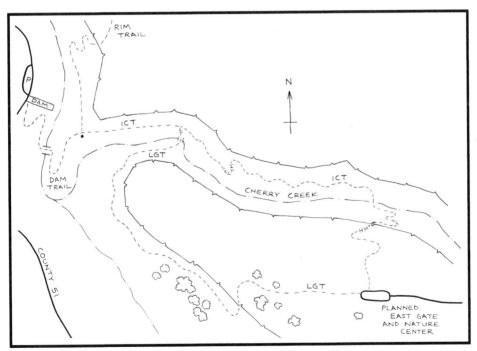

INNER CANYON/LAKE GULCH LOOP

II. THE FOOTHILLS

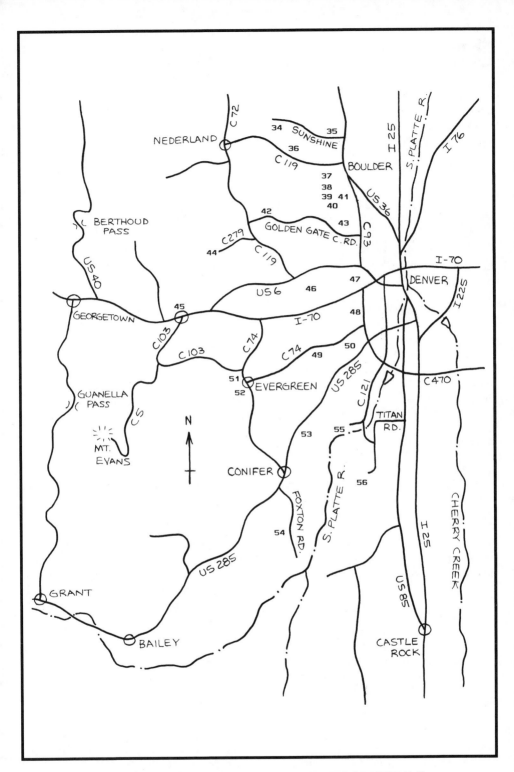

WALK/HIKE AREAS IN THE FOOTHILLS

34 BALD MOUNTAIN SCENIC AREA

Distance: 1 mile
Difficulty: Easy
Walking Time: 1 hr.
Elevation: 6960-7160 ft.

Five miles northwest of downtown Boulder, Bald Mountain Scenic Area is an excellent place for a family picnic and day hike. Rising to an elevation of 7160 feet, the foothill is named for the dirth of trees on its windswept summit. Coarse, shallow soil, steep terrain and drying winds all combine to reduce soil moisture and retard invasion of the surrounding Transition Zone forest. Much of the knob is covered by open meadows and ponderosa parkland. More tolerant of wind and aridity than are trees, grasses such as bluegrama, western wheatgrass and cheatgrass thrive across the sunny slopes of Bald Mountain. Wildflowers are abundant here from spring to early fall.

The first park within the Boulder County Open Space system, the Bald Mountain Scenic Area was dedicated in June, 1973. Its easy, 1-mile trail loop, varied flora and scenic vistas make the Park a popular destination for school groups and families.

Directions:

From Boulder, head west on Mapleton Ave. which leads into Sunshine Canyon and becomes Sunshine Rd. Proceed up the Canyon to the Park which is on the left (south) side of the road, 4.8 miles from the intersection of Broadway and Mapleton Ave.

Route:

From the parking area hike southward along the entry trail (note: the trail loop has been altered since the Open Space brochure was published). Crossing the east flank of Bald Mountain you are treated to a sweeping view of the Boulder Mountain Parks region and of the Colorado Piedmont beyond. The skyscrapers of downtown Denver poke above the horizon to the southeast.

At the trail intersection, bear right onto the **Pines to Peak Trail (PPT)** which makes an excursion around Bald Mountain. The forest thickens on the northern slopes where Douglas fir intermingles with the ponderosa pines. Watch for tassleeared Abert's squirrels in this area.

Circling to the west of the foothill the trail re-enters ponderosa parkland and views extend to the Continental Divide. Arapahoe Glacier, Boulder's primary water source, gleams from the distant southwest. Climbing across the southern shoulder of Bald Mountain, the trail yields a broad view into the valley of Fourmile Creek before turning northward for a short climb to the summit. A shaded park bench awaits your arrival, affording a scenic reststop. The prominant foothills to the southeast are Green, Bear and South Boulder Mountains (north to south), forming the rugged spine of Boulder Mountain Parks.

The return route drops down the west side of Bald Mountain and then curves around the northern flank before rejoining the entry trail (see map).

The open meadows yield sweeping views.

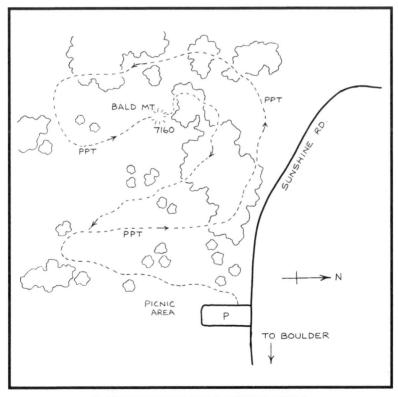

BALD MOUNTAIN SCENIC AREA

35 MOUNT SANITAS

Distance: 3.1 miles
Difficulty: Strenuous; easy along Sanitas Valley
Walking Time: 2.5-3.0 hrs.
Elevation: 5560-6800 ft.

Mt. Sanitas and environs, just west of Boulder, should perhaps be called "The Land of Many Uses." The Seventh Day Adventists established the Colorado Sanitarium at the entrance to Sunshine Canyon in 1895. Primarily a site for treatment of tuberculosis patients, the Sanitarium also provided general medical care to area residents (hence the term "sanitas" which is latin for "health"). Dairy and beef cattle ranches spread across the region during the early 1900s and the University of Colorado managed a sandstone quarry on the east flank of Mt. Sanitas during the 1920s. Acquired by the City of Boulder in the early 1970s, the area is now a popular destination for hikers, birdwatchers and other lovers of nature.

A strenuous, 3.1 mile hike takes you up a rocky ridge to Mt. Sanitas, down its steep eastern wall and back through the peaceful Mt. Sanitas Valley. Unconditioned hikers should confine their wanderings to the valley and perhaps to the lower slopes of the Dakota Hogback (see map); the climb to Mt. Sanitas is strenuous and not recommended for the average weekend trekker.

Directions:
From Boulder, drive west on Mapleton Ave. to the mouth of Sunshine Canyon. Just after entering the foothills, several pulloffs and small parking lots service the Mt. Sanitas area, which stretches northward from the road, and other Open Space trails to the south.

Route:
From the Mt. Sanitas trailhead, pass through the picnic shelter and cross Sunshine Creek via a footbridge. Angle to the left at the trail intersection and begin a steady, 1.3 mile climb to Mt. Sanitas. Log, earthen and rock steps take you to the west side of the ridge where the **Mount Sanitas Trail (MST)** turns northward and parallels the rocky backbone that extends south from the summit. Openings in the rock wall provide glimpses of greater Boulder and the Colorado Piedmont to the east, while Green Mountain (8144 ft.) looms to the south. Views extend up Sunshine Canyon to the west and, as you ascend higher, the Indian Peaks of the Continental Divide appear along the horizon.

Halfway to the summit the trail crosses to the east side of the ridge, offering constant views across the Piedmont, from Denver to the Ft. Collins region. Once atop Mt. Sanitas you are rewarded with spectacular views in all directions. Boulder Mountain Parks' Green Mountain still dominates the view to the south but Jefferson County's Green Mountain (see Hike #13) can also be spotted in the distance. Greater Boulder spreads eastward from the Dakota Hogback; the three large lakes across the eastern edge of the city are Boulder, Valmont and Baseline Reservoirs (north to south). Along the western horizon are the Indian Peaks; the view stretches from S. Arapaho Peak and the Arapaho Glacier to the rounded dome of Mt. Audubon, a swath of peaks averaging over 13,000 feet in elevation.

Mt. Sanitas and its rocky ridge are manifestations of the Fountain and Lyons formations, late Paleozoic sediments that were upturned when the Rockies pushed skyward, 65 million years ago. As you descend along the .6 mile **East Ridge Trail (ERT)**, you travel forward in geologic time,

The Boulder Valley from Mt. Sanitas.

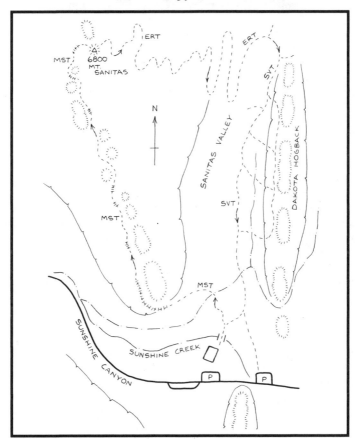

MT. SANITAS AND THE SANITAS VALLEY

eventually reaching the valley floor that is underlain with soft sedimentary rocks from the Mesozoic Era (the Age of Reptiles). Turning southward, the **Sanitas Valley Trail (SVT)** provides a gentle, 1.2 mile descent to the parking area. Hemmed in by the Dakota Hogback to the east and the Sanitas ridge to the west, this scenic valley offers choice habitat for mule deer. These graceful residents are often spotted on the meadows at dawn or dusk.

103

36 BETASSO PRESERVE

Bummer's Rock Trail
  Distance: .5 mile roundtrip
  Difficulty: Easy
  Walking Time: ½ hr.
  Elevation: 6500-6670 ft.

Canyon Loop Trail
  Distance: 2.75 miles
  Difficulty: Moderate
  Walking Time: 2-3 hrs.
  Elevation: 6000-6600 ft.

Stretching across a ridge between Four-mile and Boulder Canyons, the 712 acres of Betasso Preserve offer a pleasant setting for day hikes. Characterized by foothill meadows, ponderosa parklands and mixed, Transition Zone forest, the Preserve was acquired by the Boulder County Open Space Department in 1976.

The Park is named for Steve Betasso, a gold and tungsten miner who purchased the land in 1915 and whose family operated a cattle ranch on the property for over half a century. Now a popular area for group picnics, Betasso Preserve is accessed by a 2.75 mile trail loop. A second trail leads out to Bummer's Rock, an outcropping of Precambrian granodiorite that overlooks Boulder Canyon.

Directions:
From Boulder, head west on Canyon Blvd. and enter the foothills. Drive up Boulder Canyon for 4.2 miles and turn right on Sugarloaf Rd. Proceed .9 mile and turn right on Betasso Road. Drive .5 mile to the Park entrance, on your left; to reach the Bummer's Rock Trailhead, continue on Betasso Road for another .1 mile to a small lot, on your right (see map).

Routes:
Bummer's Rock Trail (.5 mile roundtrip). From the parking lot, hike through open forest on a well-worn trail that leads toward the southeast. The trail soon curves back to the south and then climbs onto a low ridge via a wide switchback to the west. A short walk takes you out to **Bummer's Rock** which commands a fine view of Boulder Canyon. Valmont Reservoir can be seen through the mouth of the Canyon while Arkansas Mountain (7710 ft.) rises to the northwest, backed by Mt. Audubon and the Continental Divide.

Canyon Loop Trail (2.75 miles). Park in one of the lots at the northwest corner (*) of the Preserve's loop road (see map). Hike to the NNW on an old jeep road, crossing above a broad meadow. Angling northward, the trail enters the forest and winds across the upper reaches of the Park's drainage network. Watch for an old cabin (C) that sits along the primary stream.

Emerging from the woods, leave the jeep road and hike to the east through open meadows and ponderosa parkland. Broad views extend southeastward to Green Mountain (8144 ft.) which rises above the Piedmont just southwest of Boulder. Mule deer browse on the meadows at dawn and dusk and Abert's squirrels, tassle-eared residents of the Transition Zone, are often spotted in this area.

Angling to the southeast, the trail descends into Fourmile Canyon and crosses Betasso Preserve's central creek via a foot-bridge. Switchbacks ease your ascent to some degree but the climb onto the south wall of the basin is a bit of a challenge. The grade is steep and loose gravel makes for treacherous footing in some areas. In addition, this section of the trail, shaded by a dense forest of Douglas fir, can be icy during the winter and early spring.

Green Mountain looms to the southeast.

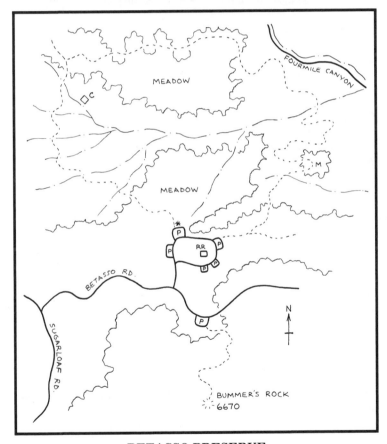

BETASSO PRESERVE

Leveling out atop the ridge the trail angles to the southwest and leads out to the loop road. Just short of the road, a clearing offers a fine view across Boulder Canyon to Green Mountain and out onto the Piedmont where Baseline Reservoir shimmers in the distance. Return to your car by walking westward along the road, thereby completing a loop hike of 2.75 miles.

37 GREGORY CANYON/SADDLE ROCK TRAIL

Distance: 2.6 miles
Difficulty: Strenuous
Walking Time: 3-4 hrs.
Elevation: 5800-7280 ft.

Gregory Canyon is a steep and relatively narrow gorge in the foothills just west of Boulder. As with other canyons along the base of the Front Range, an open ponderosa woodland cloaks the sunny, south-facing wall while a dense forest of pine, Douglas fir and blue spruce covers the shaded, north-facing slopes. The canyon rises 1000 feet over 1 mile, stretching west to east between the sun-scorched dome of Flagstaff Mountain, to the north, and the rocky shoulders of Green Mountain, to the south.

A 2.6 mile loop hike takes you up through **Gregory Canyon**, eastward across the flank of Green Mountain and then down to the trailhead along a winding, rock staircase known as the **Saddle Rock Trail.** Numerous switchbacks, steep terrain and narrow catwalks make the hike seem much longer than the official distance. Plan at least three hours for your excursion and bring plenty of food and water to appease your muscles.

Directions:
From Boulder, head west on Baseline Road to the edge of the foothills. Just as the road turns northward to climb into Boulder Mountain Parks, the access lane to Gregory Canyon angles to the left (south). Proceed to a small, graveled lot at the mouth of the Canyon; elevation here is 5800 feet.

Route:
Hike westward from the parking lot and bear right at the fork, bypassing the **Saddle Rock Trail (SRT).** The **Gregory Canyon Trail (GCT)** parallels the stream for a short distance and then climbs across the dry, northern wall of the canyon. A long

stairway is followed by a brief excursion across rock outcroppings and then a gradual descent to the creek. Cross the stream and begin a long, steady climb via a series of broad switchbacks. Watch and listen for canyon wrens that often perch on boulders along the canyon wall. Rock squirrels may also be seen in this area.

Ascending higher, you are treated to views of Boulder, framed by the rugged walls of Gregory Canyon. Near the top the trail levels out, crosses a jeep road and meanders westward above a wooded meadow. Crossing the creek again the path angles to the south and soon arrives at a rustic lodge (L; elevation 6800 ft.)

Bypass the **Long Canyon Trail (LCT)** and climb to the SSE on the **Ranger Trail (RT).** This path ascends along a creek through a forest of Douglas fir and soon intersects the **H.L. Greenman Trail,** a section of the **Green Mountain Trail (GMT).** Angle to the left at this intersection, curving to the north and then back to the south (see map).

Cross another stream, ascend a short stairway and then bear left onto the **Saddle Rock Trail (SRT).** The Continental Divide stretches along the western horizon as you ascend to the northeast. Approaching Saddle Rock (SR; 7000 ft.) the trail begins its long, winding descent to the mouth of Gregory Canyon. Just east of the Rock the path cuts back to the south and loops above a stream, providing a fine view of the Flatirons on Green Mountain. Halfway down you will intersect the **Amphitheater Trail (AT);** bypass this cutoff and continue along the **Saddle Rock Trail** which maintains its tortuous descent to the floor of Gregory Canyon. Leveling out near the stream, the trail crosses a footbridge, merges with the **Gregory Canyon Trail** and returns to the parking area.

Looking east through Gregory Canyon.

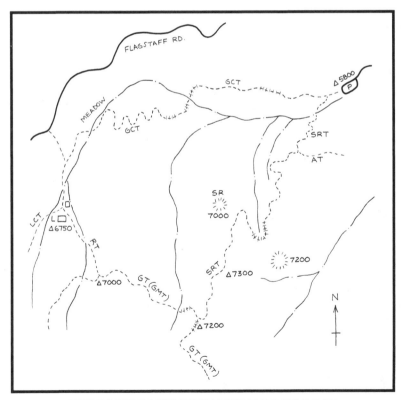

GREGORY CANYON/SADDLE ROCK LOOP

38 GREEN MOUNTAIN/WEST RIDGE TRAIL

To Rock Outcropping
  Distance: 1.5 miles roundtrip
  Difficulty: Easy
  Walking Time: 1.5-2.0 hrs.
  Elevation: 7580-7680 ft.

To Summit of Green Mountain
  Distance: 3 miles roundtrip
  Difficulty: Moderate (last ¼ mile
    strenuous)
  Walking Time: 2.5-3.5 hrs.
  Elevation: 7580-8144 ft.

Rising 2800 feet above the city of Boulder, the summit of Green Mountain (8144 ft.) yields a sweeping view of the Colorado Piedmont, from the Palmer Divide to the Wyoming border and of the Front Range from Mt. Evans to Rocky Mountain National Park. Located within Boulder Mountain Parks, the mountain is accessed by several trail routes, the easiest of which, known as the West Ridge Trail, originates along Flagstaff Road, 4.7 road miles southwest of Boulder.

Directions:
From Boulder, head west on Baseline Road and, at the edge of the foothills, bear right onto Flagstaff Road which winds upward and gradually southwestward. Drive 4.7 miles and watch for a parking lane on the right side of the road, just before the sign "Leaving Boulder Mountain Parks." The trailhead for the **Green Mountain/ West Ridge Trail** is across the road from this parking lane.

Route:
Hike eastward on the wide path that meanders through an open forest of ponderosa pine. An excellent area for birdwatching, the flanks of Green Mountain are home to pygmy nuthatches, hairy woodpeckers, Williamson's sapsuckers, Townsend's solitaires and Steller's jays. Mountain and western bluebirds are common on the meadows during the warmer months while flocks of pine grosbeaks, red crossbills and dark-eyed juncos roam through the forest in winter and early spring.

The trail dips in and out of the Transition Zone forest as it makes its way toward Green Mountain. Three quarters of a mile from the trailhead the path climbs to a **rock outcropping (V)** which yields a fine view of the nearby foothills and of the Indian Peaks along the western horizon. Bear and South Boulder Peaks rise to the SSE, Thorodin Mountain looms to the SSW and James Peak towers above the Continental Divide in the distant southwest. An excellent destination for a picnic lunch, the roundtrip hike to this rocky perch totals 1.5 miles.

Those who continue on toward Green Mountain will soon intersect a jeep road, bear left at this junction and wind through a ponderosa parkland where mule deer often browse on sunny winter days. Within a quarter mile the trail narrows and begins a long, steep climb to the summit of Green Mountain. Continue eastward, crossing the intersection where the **Ranger Trail (RT)** comes in from the north and where the **Green Bear Trail (GBT)** cuts away to the south.

Curving to the southeast the trail now begins its final assault on **Green Mountain**, climbing over the rocky terrain via short, steep switchbacks. Though this last quarter mile is strenuous, the view from the summit rewards your effort. Greater Boulder spreads out beneath the mountain to the northeast and Denver's skyscrapers poke above the Piedmont to the southeast. The mesas of the Larkspur-Castle Rock area create an uneven horizon to the south and the northern Colorado foothills stretch away to the Wyoming border. The view to the west is especially impressive, taking in

The Indian Peaks rise along the western horizon.

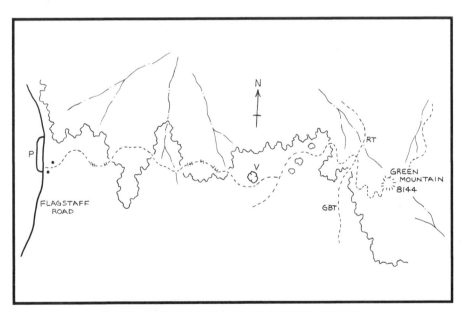

GREEN MOUNTAIN/WEST RIDGE TRAIL

the high peaks of the Front Range, from Mt. Evans to the Mummy Range. Directly west are the jagged summits of the Indian Peaks Wilderness.

Once you convince yourself to leave, return to your car via the same route, completing a roundtrip hike of 3 miles.

39 WALKER RANCH

Meyers Homestead Trail
  Distance: 5 miles roundtrip
  Difficulty: Moderate
  Walking Time: 3 hrs.
  Elevation: 7280-8000 ft.

Eldorado Canyon Trail to South Boulder Creek
  Distance: 2 miles roundtrip
  Difficulty: Moderate
  Walking Time: 2 hrs.
  Elevation: 6440-6920 ft.

Eldorado Canyon Trail to Overlook
  Distance: 4 miles roundtrip
  Difficulty: Strenuous
  Walking Time: 3-3.5 hrs.
  Elevation: 6440-7000 ft.

Listed on the National Register of Historic Places as "historic cultural landscape," the 2566 acres of Walker Ranch were once part of the largest cattle operation along the Front Range. First homesteaded by James and Phoebe Walker, in 1882, the ranch grew to 6000 acres by 1959. Boulder County purchased 2566 acres during the late 1970s and leases another 1132 acres from the Bureau of Land Management.

The vast park, which stretches north from Eldorado Canyon, offers an attractive setting for day hikes. A twelve-mile network of trails provides access to the varied topography of the preserve, from the steep cliffs of Eldorado Canyon to the rolling meadows of Meyers Gulch. Ponderosa parklands, Transition Zone forest, aspen groves and foothill meadows make for a rich mosaic of natural habitat. Mountain lions, black bear, coyotes, mule deer, mountain bluebirds and wild turkeys are among the native fauna. Elk winter on the windswept meadows and dippers work their magic in the turbulent waters of South Boulder Creek.

Directions:

From Boulder, drive west on Baseline Road. At the edge of the foothills bear right onto Flagstaff Road which winds upward and gradually southwestward into Boulder Mountain Parks. Drive 7 miles to a picnic area, on your right, which is the trailhead for the **Meyers Homestead Trail (MHT)**.

To reach the **Eldorado Canyon Trail (ECT)**, continue southward on Flagstaff Road for another .2 mile and turn left on Pika Road. Drive 1 mile, winding downward and eastward, and then turn right on Bison Road. Proceed .2 mile to the **Eldorado Trailhead**, on your right (elevation 6920 ft.).

Routes:

There are several excellent day hikes at Walker Ranch; we suggest the following routes.

Meyers Homestead Trail (MHT; 5 miles roundtrip). From the parking lot off Flagstaff Road, hike westward on a wide path that soon merges with a jeep road coming in from the south. Angle to the northwest at this junction, hiking through an open forest of ponderosa pine. Descending into a valley, the trail crosses a broad meadow where old ranch buildings mark the site of an 1880s homestead. Watch for mountain and western bluebirds that hunt across the grassland from April through October.

The primary route curves to the northeast and then back to the northwest, climbing along Meyers Gulch. As you ascend higher a fine view unfolds back to the southeast where South Boulder Creek has cut its

Arkansas Mountain towers above Boulder Canyon.

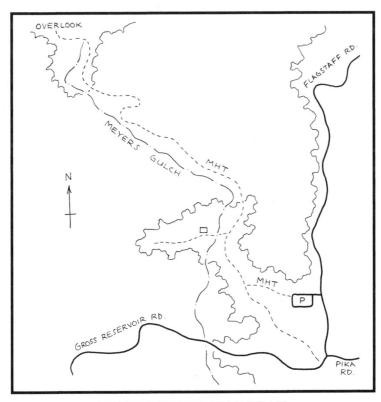

MEYERS HOMESTEAD TRAIL

canyon between Shirttail Peak and Eldorado Mountain. Kinnikinnick, also known as bearberry, flourishes on the sunny slopes of Meyers Gulch and a forest of Douglas fir cloaks the moist, shaded walls of the valley.

Nearing the top of the ridge the trail skirts another meadow and then winds out to an overlook of Boulder Canyon. Arkansas Mountain (7710 ft.) rises to the NNW and the Front Range, from the Arapaho Peaks to the Mummy Range, stretches away in the distance.

After a picnic lunch atop the ridge, return to your car via the same route, completing a roundtrip hike of 5 miles.

Eldorado Canyon Trail (ECT). The **Eldorado Canyon Trail** stretches for 4.5 miles from the Eldorado Trailhead, on Bison Road, to Eldorado Canyon State Park. This chapter covers the northern half of the trail and suggests two possible day hike destinations. The southern half of the trail is covered in the chapter on Eldorado Canyon State Park.

From the **Eldorado Trailhead** the wide, jeep-road trail **(ECT)** descends along Martin Gulch, passing two old ranch buildings on your left. South Boulder Peak (8549 ft.) looms to the east and Eldorado Mountain, topped by a radio tower, rises to the southeast. Bypass the cutoff to the **Columbine Gulch Trail (CGT)** and dip across a stream bed before climbing onto a low ridge.

Over the next quarter mile the trail undulates above Martin Gulch, crossing several sidestreams, and then begins a long descent into the valley of South Boulder Creek. The Denver Rio Grande tracks can now be seen on the northern flank of Eldorado Mountain and the dimpled summit of Scar Top Mountain (8790 Ft.) rises above the canyon to the SSW.

A broad switchback takes you down to the canyon floor where Martin Gulch joins South Boulder Creek and where the **Crescent Meadows Trail (CMT)** intersects the **Eldorado Canyon Trail**. A streamside clearing provides an excellent site for a picnic lunch; returning to your car from this point yields a roundtrip day hike of 2 miles.

Those who continue along the **Eldorado Canyon Trail** will angle to the east and begin a steep climb onto the north wall of the canyon. The trail crosses two sidestreams and ascends to the northeast along the second creek. A series of switchbacks then take you higher onto the ridge where several viewpoints (V) offer spectacular vistas to the south and west. Eldorado Mountain and Scar Top Mountain form the south wall of Eldorado Canyon and Thorodin Mountain (10,540 ft.) looms to the southwest.

As you ascend higher, the Continental Divide appears along the western horizon and your destination, a ridgetop clearing, yields a magnificent view through the mouth of Eldorado Canyon to the southeast. Beyond this natural overlook the trail continues along the north wall of the canyon and descends to Eldorado Canyon State Park (2.5 miles beyond the overlook). Return to your car from this scenic ridgetop, completing a roundtrip hike of 4 miles.

Eldorado Canyon from the overlook.

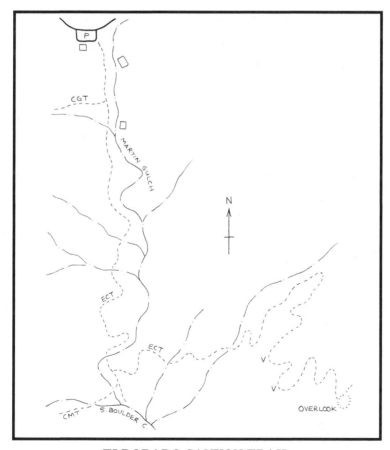

ELDORADO CANYON TRAIL

40 ELDORADO CANYON STATE PARK

Rattlesnake Gulch Trail
  Distance: 3.2 miles roundtrip
  Difficulty: Moderate
  Walking Time: 2-2.5 hrs.
  Elevation: 6040-6840 ft.

Eldorado Canyon Trail
  Distance: 5 miles roundtrip
  Difficulty: Strenuous
  Walking Time: 4-5 hrs.
  Elevation: 6080-7000 ft.

A mecca for local and international rock climbers, Eldorado State Park also offers excellent hiking opportunities. The 845 acre Park, which opened in 1978, stretches along South Boulder Creek and onto the steep rock walls of the canyon. The sheer south face of Shirttail Peak, dropping almost 900 feet to the valley floor, attracts most of the rock climbers while the Park's hiking trails ascend along the rugged cliffs further upstream.

A picnic grounds and **nature center (NC)** sit along the creek, one mile west of the Park entrance. Parking areas are spaced throughout the canyon, as noted on the map.

Directions:

From Denver, drive north on I-25 and exit onto U.S. 36 toward Boulder. Nearing the city, take the Marshall/Eldorado Springs Exit and proceed west on Colorado 170. Cross Colorado 93 and drive another 3 miles to the Park, which begins at the west edge of Eldorado Springs.

From Boulder, follow Colorado 93 south for 4 miles to Colorado 170. Turn right (west) and drive 3 miles to the Park entrance.

Routes:

The following day hikes are suggested.

Rattlesnake Gulch Trail (3.2 miles roundtrip). This is the best and most interesting day hike at Eldorado Canyon State Park. From the trailhead, .6 miles west of the entrance, a wide path heads eastward above the canyon floor (see map). The **Rattlesnake Gulch Trail** then cuts back to the west, climbing onto the north flank of Eldorado Mountain. Curving to

the south path crosses the gulch below an old aqueduct (A) and then turns northward along the west wall of the ravine.

Nearing the center of the canyon the trail switches back to the south for a long, gradual ascent into the upper reaches of Rattlesnake Gulch. One more switchback takes you up to the former **site of the Crags Hotel (H)** which burned down in 1912. Built in 1908, the Hotel was a whistle stop on the Moffat Railroad, offering luxurious accommodations and spectacular views of the canyon. A .5 mile trail (still passable) led down from the tracks and a funicular (gravity-powered incline) provided access from the canyon floor, 800 feet below. Remnants of the foundation, a fireplace and the fountain/fish pond can still be seen today.

Bypass the old trail up to the railroad tracks and wind out to an **overlook (V1)** which offers a view of the Continental Divide, 25 miles to the west. Returning to your car from the overlook yields a roundtrip hike of 3.2 miles.

Eldorado Canyon Trail (5 miles roundtrip). The 4.5 miles **Eldorado Canyon Trail** links the State Park with Walker Ranch, part of the Boulder County Open Space system. A roundtrip hike of 5 miles will take you onto the north wall of Eldorado Canyon and out to a fine **overlook (V2)**, 800 ft. above South Boulder Creek.

Park at the **Nature Center** and pick up the **Eldorado Canyon Trail** just east of the Center building. The trail leads northward, crosses a road and then climbs onto the west flank of Shirttail Peak via a series of switchbacks. Leaving the Park, the route turns westward and undulates across the north wall of the canyon. Views extend

A view to the east from the Rattlesnake Trail.

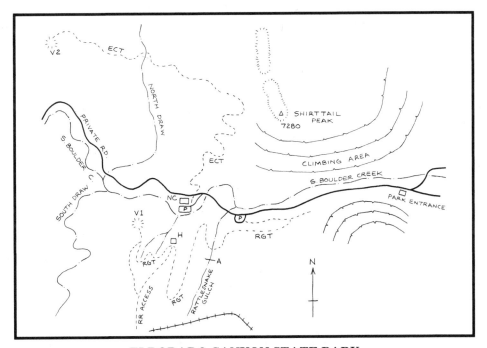

ELDORADO CANYON STATE PARK

south to Eldorado Mountain (8335 feet) and to the Denver & Rio Grande tracks that cross its northern flank. Scar Top Mountain (8790 feet) rises to the SSW and further west is the massive bulk of Thorodin Mountain (10,540 feet).

Two and a half miles from the Visitor Center you will reach a **ridgetop clearing (V2)** which yields a fine view through the canyon to the east and a vista of the Conti-

nental Divide to the west. This is the endpoint of your hike; from here the trail enters the Walker Ranch preserve, descending to the junction of Martin Gulch and South Boulder Creek (see Walker Ranch hikes).

Return to your car from the ridgetop overlook, completing a roundtrip hike of 5 miles.

41 MESA TRAIL/SHADOW CANYON

Distance: 4.5 miles
Difficulty: Moderate
Walking Time: 3-4 hrs.
Elevation: 5600-6640 ft.

The **Mesa Trail** stretches from South Boulder Creek, near the mouth of Eldorado Canyon, to the lower foothills west of Boulder. Combining the southernmost section of this trail with a return route through the lower portion of **Shadow Canyon** yields a pleasant, 4.5 mile day hike. The route winds across foothill grasslands, climbs through open, ponderosa pine forest, hugs the rocky base of the foothills and descends along the moist, thicket-lined valley of Shadow Canyon. Such varied habitat harbors a fascinating diversity of flora and fauna. In addition, remnants of human habitation are found throughout the area, lending an historical perspective to man's impact on the landscape.

Directions:

From Denver, head north on I-70 and Exit onto U.S. 36 toward Boulder. Nearing the Boulder area, take the Marshall/Superior Exit and drive west on Colorado 170. Cross Colorado 93 and drive another 1.6 miles toward Eldorado Canyon State Park. The **Mesa Trail South Trailhead** will be on your right.

Route:

From the parking lot, cross over an irrigation ditch and then cross South Boulder Creek via a fine, wooden bridge. Bypass the cutoff to the **Homestead (HT)** and **Towhee (TT) Trails** where the remnants of the **Doudy-Debacker-Dunn House** will be noted north of the creek. Constructed in 1874, the stone structure that remains was added to an earlier frame house which dated from 1858. The original homestead was the site of a sawmill and gristmill; in later years the property was used as a dairy

farm. Rock walls in the area were built by transient laborers, many of whom had lost their jobs in the gold and silver mines.

Continue northward on the **Mesa Trail (MT)** which ascends gradually from the valley floor and crosses a second irrigation canal. Looping to the west near the mouth of Shadow Canyon, the trail grade increases as it curves around the eastern end of a low ridge and turns westward, climbing through a ponderosa parkland. Watch for mule deer which often rest beneath the pines during the colder months.

Bypass the cutoff to the **Big Bluestem Trail (BBT)** and, 1.5 miles from the trailhead, bear right on the **Mesa Trail** where a spur trail descends into Shadow Canyon (see map). Another .3 mile brings you to a second cutoff to Shadow Canyon; bear right again and you will soon descend into a scenic meadow at the base of the foothills. Devil's Thumb and the famous "flatirons" of the Boulder region adorn the east flank of Bear and South Boulder Peaks.

At the next intersection leave the **Mesa Trail**, climbing back to the south along the edge of the foothills (see map). Passing rock slides and an old burn area, the route turns westward across a sunny cliff and then descends into **Shadow Canyon**. Turn left ("**To Southbound Mesa Trail**"), cross the creek and pass an old cabin. The trail soon leaves the forest and makes a broad swing to the south before curving back into the canyon. Re-cross the stream and, at the next intersection, bear right onto the **Towee Trail (TT)** which descends eastward along the creek. Remain on this trail all the way to the South Trailhead area, bypassing the **Homestead Trail (HT)** along the way.

*Foothill shrublands cloak the lower
section of Shadow Canyon.*

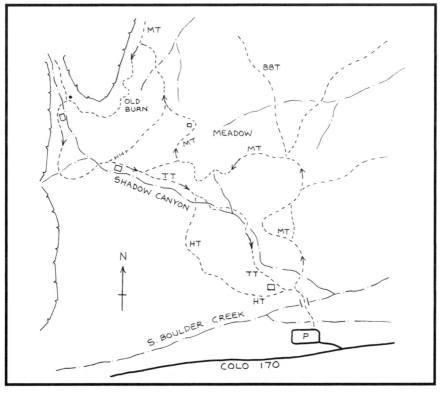

MESA TRAIL/SHADOW CANYON

42 GOLDEN GATE CANYON STATE PARK

Eagle Trail
  Distance: 4.2 miles roundtrip
  Difficulty: Moderate
  Walking Time: 2.5-3.0 hrs.
  Elevation: 7720-8680 ft.

Blue Grouse Trail
  Distance: 3.2 mile loop
  Difficulty: Strenuous
  Walking Time: 3 hrs.
  Elevation: 8320-9320 ft.

Mule Deer-Raccoon-Elk Loop
  Distance: 7.5 miles
  Difficulty: Moderate
  Walking Time: 4.5-5.5 hrs.
  Elevation: 8480-9480 ft.

Horseshoe Trail
  Distance: 3.6 miles roundtrip
  Difficulty: Easy
  Walking Time: 2.5-3.0 hrs.
  Elevation: 8160-9080 ft.

Mule Deer-Coyote-Elk Loop
  Distance: 4.4 miles
  Difficulty: Moderate
  Walking Time: 3.0-3.5 hrs.
  Elevation: 8480-9520 ft.

With a 60-mile network of trails, Golden Gate Canyon State Park offers a superb setting for day hikes. The Park's 10,000 acres sprawl across the flanks of Tremont Mountain (10,388 ft.) and along the valley of Ralston Creek, approximately 13 miles northwest of Golden. Back-country campgrounds are located throughout the Park and the area is a popular destination for cross-country skiers during the winter and early spring.

While the trails are well engineered and blazed with distinctive markers, some of the trail intersection signs are confusing and close attention to the narrative and maps in this guide is recommended.

Directions:

From Colorado 93, one mile north of Golden, turn west on Golden Gate Canyon Road. Wind northwestward for 12.5 miles, crossing Guy Hill and eventually descending into the Ralston Creek Valley. The Park's **Visitor Center (VC)**, located at the intersection of Golden Gate Canyon Road and Crawford Gulch Road, houses Park offices, educational exhibits and a small bookstore. Day use passes and back-country permits can be obtained at the Center.

The **Nott Creek Trailhead (T1)**, which services the **Eagle Trail**, is reached via a short, graveled lane off the north side of Crawford Gulch Road, 3.5 miles northeast of the visitor center. The **Frazer Meadow Trailhead (T2)**, access to the **Horseshoe Trail**, is on the north side of Crawford Gulch Road, .5 mile northeast of the Center. The **Kriley Pond Trailhead (T3)**, an entry point for the **Blue Grouse Trail**, is on the north side of Golden Gate Canyon Road, .9 mile west of the Visitor Center. The **Lower Mountain Base Trailhead (T4)** is a good starting point for both the **Mule Deer-Coyote-Elk Loop** and the **Mule Deer-Raccoon-Elk Loop**; to reach this trailhead follow Golden Gate Canyon Road west from the Visitor center, drive 1.2 miles, turn right on Mountain Base Road and proceed .9 mile to a parking lane, on your left.

Route:

The extensive trail network at Golden Gate Canyon State Park offers a wide variety of potential day hikes; we suggest the following routes.

Eagle Trail (ET; 4.2 miles roundtrip). this 2.1 mile ascent to **City Lights Ridge** leaves the southwest corner of the **Nott Creek parking lot (T1)**, parallels the entry road for a short distance and then angles to the west, climbing across the north wall of the Ralston Creek Valley. A broad switchback takes you to the top of the ridge where the trail leads westward again and soon dips into a saddle where it

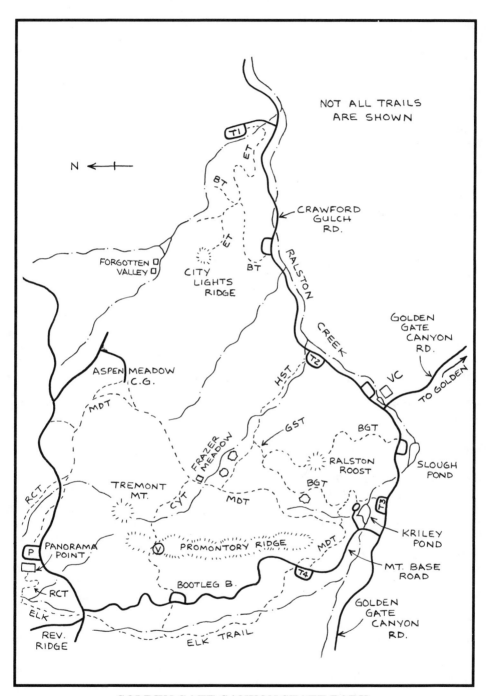

GOLDEN GATE CANYON STATE PARK.

intersects the **Burro Trail (BT)**.

Bear right, walk a short distance and then bear left, staying on the **Eagle Trail**. City Lights Ridge looms straight ahead as you hike toward the northwest. At the next intersection the **Eagle trail** splits to the left and begins a steep, .5 mile climb to the summit. The last .25 mile is very steep and utilizes numerous switchbacks. Once atop the rocky summit you are treated to a panorama of the surrounding foothills. Tremont Mountain rises to the northwest while Thorodin Mountain dominates the view to the north. Forgotten Valley, with its small lake and crumbled ranch buildings, spreads northward from the base of City Lights Ridge.

Looking eastward through the Ralston Creek Valley you can easily spot the craggy silhouette of Ralston Buttes, backed by the Colorado Piedmont. The forested shoulders of Centralia Mountain form the south wall of the valley and, on a clear day, the Continental Divide shimmers on the western horizon.

After a picnic lunch atop the ridge, descend to your car via the same route, completing a roundtrip hike of 4.2 miles.

Horseshoe Trail (HST; 3.6 miles roundtrip). This hike is a gentle, 1.8 mile ascent to Frazer Meadow along the primary drainage from the south side of Tremont Mountain. From the **Frazer Meadow Trailhead (T2)** the **Horseshoe Trail** crosses the stream and winds northwestward through a mixed forest of aspen, pine and spruce. One mile from the trailhead the route intersects the **Ground Squirrel Trail (GST); continue northward on the Horseshoe Trail** for another .25 mile where two rock outcroppings offer sweeping views of the Park and provide excellent settings for a picnic lunch.

The **Horseshoe Trail** continues northward and soon merges with the **Mule Deer Trail (MDT)**. Turn right for a short walk out to **Frazer Meadow** where an old cabin sits along the creek. Tremont Mountain rises to the north and a broad view extends southward through the valley of your ascent.

Blue Grouse Trail (BGT; 3.2 mile loop). This 2.8 mile trail connects the Kriley Pond and Slough Pond areas along Golden Gate Canyon Road via a strenuous ascent and descent of Ralston Roost. Park at Kriley Pond and pick up the **Blue Grouse Trail** above the north shore of the lake. From the **Trailhead (T3)**, the route climbs onto the ridge via a series of well-engineered switchbacks. Bypass the **Ground Squirrel Trail (GST)** along the way, staying on the east wall of the ravine. Nearing the ridgetop the trail passes a rock outcropping which is accessed by two spur trails and offers a fine view across the Ralston Creek Valley.

The primary trail continues northward, levels out and winds through as aspen grove. Bear right at the next two intersections, curving to the southeast through a ridgetop meadow. Re-entering the forest, the trail climbs to the rocky spine of **Ralston Roost** (9320 feet), 1000 feet above the valley floor. The best views are obtained from the northwestern end of the Roost. Mt. Evans looms to the SSW while the double hump of Grays and Torreys Peaks will be noted to the southwest. The chiseled face of James Peak dominates the view to the west and Mt. Neva pokes above the Continental Divide to the northwest. Tremont Mountain, the centerpiece of Golden Gate Canyon Park, rises to the NNW, backed by the shoulders of Thorodin Mountain.

Leaving Ralston Roost the **Blue Grouse Trail** descends toward Slough Pond through open, rocky terrain. Kinnikinnick (bearberry) thrives across the sunny clearings that dot the valley wall. The numerous switchbacks are not as well engineered as those above Kriley Pond and loose gravel makes for treacherous footing in some areas. Nearing the bottom of the slope the path curves through an aspen-lined meadow, snakes along a stream bed and exits onto Golden Gate Canyon Road, across from Slough Pond. Hike westward along the road to Kriley Pond, completing a 3.2 miles loop.

Mule Deer-Coyote-Elk Loop (4.4 miles). This pleasant day hike crosses through an

Tremont Mountain from Frazer Meadow.

excellent variety of terrain and habitat and is highly recommended for the naturalist. From the **Lower Mountain Base Trailhead (T4)**, follow the **Mule Deer Trail (MDT)** as it climbs around the southern end of Promontory Ridge. Curving back to the north, the trail ascends along a ravine above Kriley Pond and then levels out atop the ridge. Bypass a cutoff to the **Ground Squirrel (GST)** and **Blue Grouse (BGT) Trails**, continuing northward toward Frazer Meadow. The **Horseshoe Trail (HST)** cuts in from the southeast and you soon thereafter reach the broad meadow. Cross the creek, pass an old cabin and turn left on the **Coyote Trail (CYT)** which heads toward Bootleg Bottom.

The trail hugs the base of **Tremont Mountain**, leading into the upper reaches of Frazer Meadow and then climbs onto **Promontory Ridge**. A rocky overlook (V) yields a magnificent view of the Front Range, from Mt. Evans to the Indian Peaks of the Continental Divide. From the overlook the **Coyote Trail** drops steeply for a short distance and then moderates, descending along broad switchbacks. Nearing the valley floor the trail runs along a creek, passes an old cabin, crosses the creek and its sidestream and winds through the Bootleg Bottom Picnic Area. It then crosses Mountain Base Road, dips across another stream and intersects the **Elk Trail**.

Turn left (south) on the **Elk Trail** for a pleasant, 1.2 mile stroll back to your car. The route parallels the stream, crossing

through scenic meadows where deer and elk often come to browse. Just past the Ole Barn Knoll Picnic Area the trail crosses the creek and climbs across a low ridge before descending to the trailhead lot.

Mule Deer-Raccoon-Elk Loop (7.5 miles). An alternative hike from the **Lower Mountain Base Trailhead (T4)** is to follow the **Mule Deer Trail (MDT)** all the way to **Panorama Point**. Ascend to **Frazer Meadow** (as outlined in previous hike) and bypass the **Coyote Trail**, remaining on the **Mule Deer Trail** as it continues northward to Aspen Meadow and then curves to the northwest across the northern flank of Tremont Mountain. Approaching **Panorama Point** the route crosses the unpaved road and merges with the **Raccoon Trail (RCT)**.

At the Point a wooden deck yields a spectacular view from Mt. Evans to Long's Peak. Plaques illustrate the scene and identify many of the prominant topographic features. After taking in the view, descend westward along the **Raccoon Trail** using a series of switchbacks. Crossing a stream you immediately intersect the **Elk Trail**.

Turn left on the **Elk Trail** which climbs along the stream, crosses the entry road for Reverend's Ridge Campground and then descends to the south through a valley of streamside meadows and willow bogs. The Lower Mountain Base Trailhead is 2.2 miles from Reverend's Ridge Campground.

43 WHITE RANCH PARK

Wranglers Run Loop
  Distance: 2.7 miles
  Difficulty: Moderate
  Walking Time: 2 hrs.
  Elevation: 7000-7600 ft.

Belcher Hill Loop
  Distance: 3.2 miles
  Difficulty: Moderate
  Walking Time: 2.5-3.0 hrs.
  Elevation: 7200-7880 ft.

Combined Loop Hike
  Distance: 4.7 miles
  Difficulty: Moderate
  Walking Time: 4 hrs.
  Elevation: 7000-7880 ft.

Spectacular vistas, abundant wildlife and a fine network of trails make White Ranch Park an excellent destination for day hikers. Sprawling across Belcher Hill, northwest of Golden, the 3040 acre preserve is the former cattle ranch of the Paul White family. The land was turned over to Jefferson County's Open Space system and is renowned for its diverse population of wildlife. Resident fauna include mule deer, bobcat, mountain lion, black bear and wild turkey. The vast refuge also provides wintering habitat for elk. Wildlife viewing is most productive at dawn or dusk.

Directions:
From Denver, follow U.S. 6 to Golden and, at the mouth of Clear Creek Canyon, proceed north on Colorado 93. Drive just over 1 mile and turn left (west) on Golden Gate Canyon Road. Wind upward and westward for 4 miles and turn right on Crawford Gulch Road. Drive another 4 miles on this well-maintained, dirt-gravel road to the Park entrance, on your right. Proceed about 1.5 miles and park in the first lot, on your left, where you are immediately treated to a sweeping view of the Colorado Piedmont to the east; the Ralston Buttes rise along the edge of the foothills to the northeast. Elevation at this parking lot is 7600 feet.

Route:
We suggest the following day hikes which can be combined into a 4.7 mile loop if desired.

Wranglers Run Loop (2.7 miles). Walk eastward along the road to the second parking lot and pick up the **Rawhide Trail (RHT)** which angles to the northeast and intersects the **Longhorn Trail (LHT).** Turn left, continuing along the **Rawhide Trail** and soon descend into the Wranglers Run Valley through a forest of pine, Douglas fir and blue spruce. Cross the stream and bear left onto the **Wranglers Run Trail (WRT).** This path climbs westward through the scenic valley of Wranglers Run and, .8 mile from the stream crossing, intersects the west arm of the **Rawhide Trail (RHT).** Turn left, re-cross the creek and begin a winding ascent back toward the parking area. After crossing open woodlands and ridgetop meadows the trail intersects the north end of the **Belcher Hill Trail (BHT).** Turn right onto this path for a short but steep climb back to the lot.

North Table Mountain and Metro Denver from White Ranch.

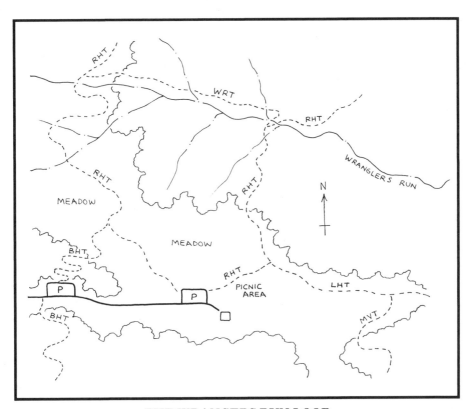

THE WRANGERS RUN LOOP

Belcher Hill Loop (3.2 miles). The **Belcher Hill Trail (BHT)** cuts across the entry road at the first parking lot (see map). Follow this trail southward and endure a short but steep climb to the crest of the Belcher Hill ridge (elevation 7880 ft.). Pick up the **Mustang Trail (MST)** which snakes downward and southward across an open, sun-scorched slope where ponderosa pines cling to the rocky soil. You are immediately treated to a breathtaking view of the Piedmont, foothills and peaks to the south. Devil's Head and Pike's Peak rise far in the distance and the Mt. Evans massif looms to the southwest.

A half-mile descent across this rocky slope brings you to another trail intersection. Turn left onto the **Sawmill Trail (SMT)** which leads eastward across the north wall of the Van Bibber gorge. After hiking .3 mile you will reach a large camping area which affords a magnificent view of downtown Denver and the surrounding Metro area. Signs indicate that black bears may be encountered in this section of the Park.

Continue eastward, loop across a drainage and, emerging from the forest, you will intersect the **Belcher Hill Trail (BHT).** Turn right, walk a short distance and then angle to the left (north) on the **Maverick Trail (MVT).** This 1-mile trail leads through open pine woodlands and across grassy hillsides where mule deer often browse. Views of the Colorado Piedmont unfold along the way.

Upon reaching the **Longhorn Trail (LHT)** turn left and begin a steady climb toward the parking areas. Proceed to the **Rawhide Trail (RHT),** turn left and ascend to the entry road. A short walk to the west will take you back to the first parking lot, completing a 3.2 mile loop.

Combined Loop (4.7 miles). Energetic and conditioned hikers may want to combine the Belcher Hill and Wranglers Run Loops, thereby achieving a hike of 4.7 miles. Park in the first lot and follow the **Belcher Hill Loop** as described above. When you eventually reach the **Rawhide Trail,** turn right and descend into **Wranglers Run.** Complete this loop as described on the preceding page and return to the parking area via the north end of the **Belcher Hill Trail (BHT).**

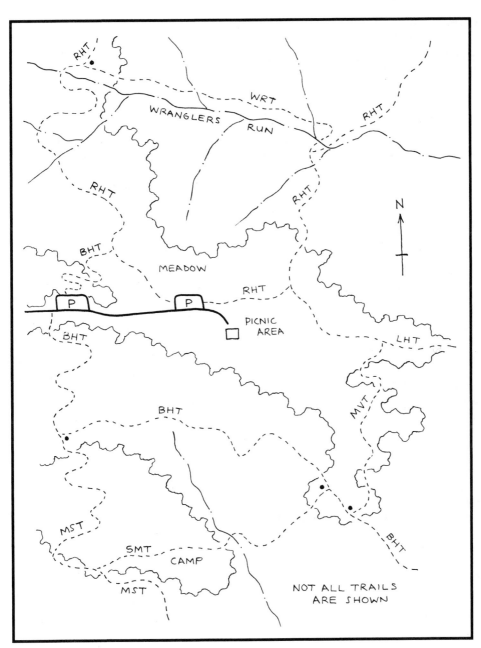

WHITE RANCH PARK

44 CENTRAL CITY

Distance: 1.4 miles
Difficulty: Easy
Walking Time: 1-2 hrs.
Elevation: 8496 ft.

As the Rockies pushed skyward, 65 million years ago, the massive core of Precambrian granite was subjected to unimaginable pressure. Cracks and fissures radiated from the innumerable faults and molten crust spewed upward to fill the crevices. As the mineral-rich lava cooled, it hardened into bands of metamorphic rock which harbored seams of gold, silver and other precious metals.

Such seams are especially rich throughout the "Mineral Belt," a 50-mile wide swath that penetrates the Rockies from the Front Range foothills to the San Juan Mountains of southwest Colorado. Numerous abandoned and some active mines dot the belt throughout its length.

Gold prospectors began to pour into Colorado in 1858-1859, when flecks of the precious metal were found in Clear Creek and other Front Range streams. Among these adventurers was John Gregory who worked his way up the North Fork of Clear Creek and, in the spring of 1859, struck a major seam of gold along the gulch that now bears his name. This bonanza drew thousands of settlers to the area and a collection of mining camps soon lined the gulch. By the mid 1860s Central City had become the dominant town and, with the construction of the Boston-Colorado Smelter, in Black Hawk, economic prosperity was assured for another decade.

The Colorado & Southern Railroad reached the North Clear Creek Valley in 1872 and the Montana Theater offered an oasis of culture for the immigrant miners. Much of the town was destroyed by fire in 1874 but, thanks to the productive mines, it was quickly rebuilt; most of the buildings that line the business district today were erected just after the fire. Central City was less resiliant when the silver boom hit Colorado in the 1880s and much of the town's population moved on to Georgetown, Silver Plume and Leadville.

Central City's second birth occurred in 1932 with restoration of the Opera House. Lillian Gish arrived to star in a production of Camille and the town soon became a popular destination for Denverites and tourists. Seasonal festivals, mine tours and a wave of historical preservation kept the town alive through much of the 20th Century. Then, in October, 1991, limited-stakes gambling opened in Central City and Black Hawk. A new wave of speculators began pouring into Gregory Gulch and, at least for the short term, economic prosperity has returned. On the other hand, free parking has disappeared and casino facades now mask some of the 19th Century architecture. Whether the town will strike a balance between its new venture and its cultural heritage awaits to be seen.

Directions:

From Denver, follow U.S. 6 (6th Ave.) west to Golden. Continue west on U.S. 6, entering Clear Creek Canyon. Drive 11 miles through this rock-walled gorge, passing through 3 tunnels, and turn right (north) on Colorado 119. Snake upward along the North Fork of Clear Creek for 7 miles to Black Hawk and turn left on Colorado 279; proceed 1 mile up Gregory Gulch to Central City. At present, the least expensive parking is in the Public Lot, on the south edge of town (see map).

126

Christmas in the City.

Homes along Eureka St.

Route:

From the parking lot you are treated to a fine view of Central City which sprawls across the upper reaches of Gregory Gulch. Descend along Spring St. The **Narrow Gauge Railroad Depot (1)** will be noted on your right. This scenic and historic line runs between Central City and Black Hawk during the warmer months. Just beyond the railroad yard is the **Central Gold Mine and Museum (2)**, circa 1868, one of the few buildings to survive the fire of 1874.

At the bottom of the hill, bear left onto **Main St.** which is lined with Victorian storefronts, cafes and theaters; casinos are now invading the core business district and it is hoped that the 1870s-1890s architecture will be preserved. The **Golden Rose Inn (3)**, built in 1874, was originally a delicatessan and liquor store. The site of hotel operations since 1917, the Inn is beautifully restored and appointed with antique, Victorian furnishings.

Turn right along Lawrence St., walk two blocks and climb to the **Gilpin County Historical Museum (4)** via a narrow lane (see map). The Museum occupies the old Central City High School and houses a collection of mining artifacts and antiques from the town's glory days. Next door is **St. Paul's Episcopal Church (5)**; both the Church and the old High School were constructed by Cornish stone masons. The Church was built in 1874, replacing a wooden structure (circa 1863) that burned down the previous year.

Walk westward along this narrow street which overlooks the business district. Cut down to Eureka St. between **St. James Church (6)** and the **Gilpin County Courthouse (7)**. Dedicated in 1872, St. James Methodist Church is home to the oldest Protestant congregation in Colorado, organized in July, 1859. Further west on Eureka St. is the **Thomas-Billings House (8)**, built in 1874. Restored by the Colorado Historical Society with the financial assistance of Doug Morton, a Denver publisher, the Victorian home is open to the public.

Backtrack along Eureka St. to the **Central City Opera House (9)**. Constructed in 1878 and designed by Robert Roeschlaub, the Opera House was restored under the direction of the University of Denver, in 1932, setting the stage for the town's cultural resurgence. Next door is the **Teller House (10)**; a renowned hotel from the date of its completion, in 1872, it is now a casino. Across Eureka St. is the **Central City Hall (11)**, circa 1862, the oldest municipal building in Colorado; its second floor is now home to the Gilpin County Art Gallery.

Turn right (south) along an alley that parallels Main St. (see map). **St. Mary of the Assumption Church (12)** was dedicated in 1892. This stone and brick church, with its fine bell tower, replaced an earlier A-frame structure that had occupied the site since 1862. Descend to Nevada St. and then climb back to the parking lot, completing a 1.4 mile tour of this historic town.

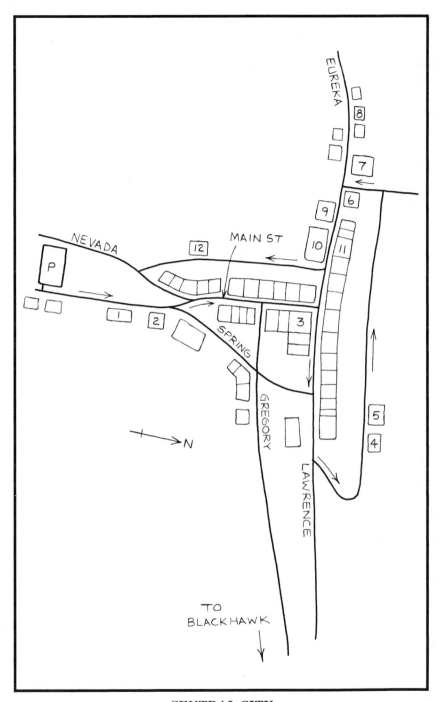

CENTRAL CITY

45 IDAHO SPRINGS

Distance: 2.4 miles
Difficulty: Easy
Walking Time: 2 hrs.
Elevation: 7520-7560 ft.

When George Andrew Jackson, a 24 year old trapper and adventurer from Missouri, wandered into Grass Valley on that fateful day in January, 1859, he made two discoveries that would draw others to the area for many years to come. Hot springs along Soda Creek sent a cloud of steam into the crisp winter air and, beneath the ice of Chicago and Clear Creeks, Jackson discovered nuggets of gold.

Having staked his claim, Jackson returned to the Valley in April, followed by a mini-invasion of prospectors. The town of "Jackson's Diggings," later called Sacramento City and, finally, Idaho Springs (1866), prospered over the next 40 years as the surrounding mountains yielded their mineral wealth. The Idaho Springs Mining District was established in June, 1859, and the townsite itself was officially registered in 1873; Elder Griswold served as the first mayor. Railroad service reached the valley in 1877, spawning further economic growth and bringing visitors to the hot springs resort.

While mining activity declined during the early 1900s, the hot springs continued to draw visitors from across the country. The city is now in the midst of an urban revitalization project and its frontier atmosphere, with Victorian storefronts and beautifully restored homes, offers a pleasant setting for a walk. The 2.4 mile route, described below, takes you back to the late 19th Century, the "Golden Age" of Idaho Springs.

Directions:

From Denver, follow I-70 west, enter the foothills and drive another 20 miles to the Mt. Evans/Idaho Springs Exit (Exit #240).

Turn right into town and then left on Miner St. Park along Miner St., between 10th & 13th Sts.

Route:

Walk east on Miner St., crossing 13th St. Just past the **Carlson Elementary School (1)** is the **Central Hose House (2)**, constructed in 1878. The **Carnegie Building (3)**, housing the Idaho Springs Library, offers a fine example of Colonial Revival architecture; this attractive building was completed in 1904.

On the northeast corner of Miner and 14th is the old **Queen Hotel (4)**, now a Senior Center. Originally a frame structure, the Hotel was rebuilt with brick in 1880. Next door is the **Underhill Museum (5)**, the former home of mining engineer and surveyor James Underhill. Now home to the Historical Society of Idaho Springs, the Museum houses a collection of mining artifacts. Across Miner St. is the **Placer Inn (6)**, established in 1929; the oldest portion of the Inn dates from 1898, when it served as a rooming house and retail center.

On the northeast corner of Miner and 15th is the **Campbell & White Building (7)**, circa 1880, originally a dry goods store. In 1913 a red beacon was placed atop the building, used to notify the town's policeman of an emergency. Across Miner St. is the former home of the **Miner & Merchants Bank (8)**, completed in 1901. The **old Idaho Springs Opera House (9)** is at 1535 Miner St. and, further east, **Citizens' Park (10)** offers a pleasant, mid-town rest-stop. The Park occupies the former site of the Coddington Block, a Victorian commercial building that burned down in 1989.

Looking west along Miner St.

City Hall

The **Buffalo Restaurant (11)** has provided refreshment and recreation since 1906; the building itself dates from 1881. Across Miner St., at "**Across from the Buffalo (12),**" is the former home of the Duck Inn where Buffalo Bill Cody is rumored to have swilled down his last drink; he died four days later, on January 10, 1917. Continue east to the **City Hall Building (13),** fronted by Idaho Springs' **Veterans Memorial**. This attractive, brick building, formerly the Grass Valley Elementary School, circa 1901, was moved to its present site in 1984 and has been completely refurbished.

Circle behind the City Hall to see **Engine #60 (14)** and **Coach #70 (15),** remnants from the era of narrow gauge railroads; educational plaques offer a brief history of their service to Colorado. Walk southward from this display on the trail that parallels Clear Creek and passes under I-70, leading to **Bridal Veil Falls (16)** and the **Charlie Tayler Water Wheel (17)**. Actually the third reconstruction of the original, 1893 wheel, the present replica was built in 1988. With a diameter of 30 feet, it is the largest water wheel in Colorado. Tayler used his original wheel to power a stamp mill along Ute Creek; it was later donated to Idaho Springs by his family and was relocated to the current site in 1946.

Return to Miner St., turn right, cross Clear Creek and then turn right onto Soda Creek Road. A short walk takes you up to the **Indian Springs Resort (18)**. Formerly a meeting site for Arapahoe and Ute Indians, facilities were first constructed here by Dr. E.M. Cummings, who offered "health baths" to local residents in 1863. The central portion of the Hotel dates from 1869 and most present-day facilities were built from 1903 to 1911. The mineral-rich waters, which emerge at a temperature of 125 degrees Fahrenheit, have been credited with healing powers since their first use by native Americans.

Return to Miner St. and turn right. Proceed to the intersection with Colorado Blvd. where the **Idaho Springs Visitor Center**

(19) offers informative brochures on the city and nearby points of interest. The **Steve Canyon Statue** at the Center's entrance was donated to Idaho Springs in honor of Coloradans who served in WWII. Just north of the Visitor Center is the **City Park**, a pleasant streamside greenbelt and an excellent spot for your picnic lunch.

Walk to the west end of the Park and turn right on 23rd St., crossing Clear Creek. Ascend to Virginia St. and turn left, walking above the "Grass Valley" basin. **Zion Lutheran Church (20)**, founded by Swedish immigrant laborers, was built in 1906. Turn left on Illinois St., where a castle-like **stone house (21)** overlooks the city, and descend back to Colorado Blvd. along Placer St.

The **Elks Lodge (22)** dates from 1907 while **Hanson's Lodge (23)**, formerly the Club Hotel, has serviced visitors since 1882. Among them was Doc Holiday who dropped by in the 1880s to indulge in the hot springs. The **United Church** occupies the north side of the 1400 block; the **brick (east) church (24)**, originally the Methodist Church, dates from 1880 while the **frame (west) church (25)**, the former Presbyterian Church, was built in 1871. The congregations unified in 1969 and a large addition to the frame church was completed in 1983. On the northwest corner of Colorado Blvd. and 14th St. is **St. John's Anglican Church (26)**; this Spanish-style structure, originally the Calvary Episcopal Church, dates from 1926. An iron bell, produced in West Troy, New York, in 1873, sits at the Church entrance.

Proceed westward on Colorado Blvd. for another 6 blocks, passing a colorful array of restored Victorian homes; most date from the 1880s and 1890s. Turn left on 8th St., descending to the valley floor and return to your car via Miner St. Along the way you will pass a **football stadium (27)**, home of the Clear Creek Golddiggers . . . figurative descendents of George Andrew Jackson.

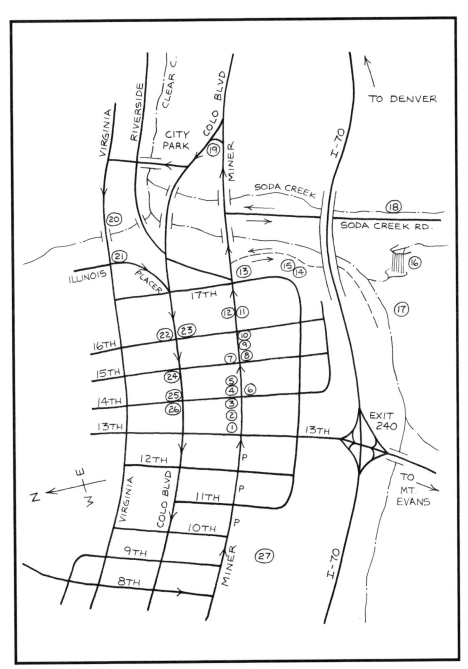

IDAHO SPRINGS

46 BEAVER BROOK TRAIL

West Trailhead to Charm Spring
  Distance: 4 miles roundtrip
  Difficulty: Moderate
  Walking Time: 3-4 hrs.
  Elevation: 6580-7360 ft.

East Trailhead to Meadow Overlook
  Distance: 3 miles roundtrip
  Difficulty: Moderate
  Walking Time: 2.5-3 hrs.
  Elevation: 6920-7200 ft.

Entire Trail:
  Distance: 14 miles roundtrip
  Difficulty: Strenuous
  Walking Time: 10-12 hrs.
  Elevation: 6580-7760 ft.

A joint project of the Colorado Mountain Club and Denver Mountain parks, the **Beaver Brook Trail** has provided a scenic, 7-mile route along the south wall of Clear Creek Canyon for more than half a century. The trail stretches from the shoulders of Lookout Mountain, west of Golden, to the northern terminus of Stapleton Drive, above Bear Gulch. Ironically, only a short segment of the trail runs along Beaver Brook.

Canyon vistas are spectacular along the way but sections of the route, especially near the East Trailhead, are steep and narrow. We thus recommend this trail for sure-footed hikers; children should be watched closely due to the precipitous terrain. Elevations range from 6800 to 7200 along most of the trail, with a high point of 7760 ft. on the north flank of Bald Mountain, just over 2 miles from the West Trailhead.

Directions:
  East Trailhead - From Denver, proceed west on U.S. 6 toward Golden. As the road turns northward along the base of Lookout Mountain, continue to the next traffic light (19th St.) and turn left (west). This street becomes Lookout Mountain Road, winding up to the site of Buffalo Bill's grave. Drive 3.6 miles up this narrow, scenic road and watch for a graveled lot on your right where a sign marks the **Windy Saddle**

Trailhead for the **Beaver Brook Trail.**
  West Trailhead - From Denver, follow I-70 west, enter the foothills and drive another 7 miles to Exit #253. Turn right and take another immediate right onto Stapleton Drive. This road curves back to the northwest and eventually splits into a one-way loop. Proceed to the north end of the loop and park in one of several lots near the picnic area. The **Beaver Brook Trail** starts just to the right of the restroom hut, descending into Bear Gulch.

Route:
  As discussed above, the **Beaver Brook Trail** stretches for 7 miles from Windy Saddle, on the northeast flank of Lookout Mountain, to Bear Gulch, above the junction of Beaver Brook and Clear Creek. The trail itself is blazed with yellow diamonds; in addition, red and white markers are placed every ½ mile, numbered 1 to 14 from east to west. One can thus gauge his or her distance from either trailhead and hikes can be varied accordingly. Adventurous and conditioned hikers can attempt to complete the 14-mile roundtrip distance or, by using two cars, a one-way, 7-mile hike can be achieved.

Most hikers will choose shorter distances, especially considering the rugged terrain. Those preferring cool, shaded side canyons with sparkling streams and abundant wildflowers should start out at the **West**

Canyon vista near the East Trailhead.

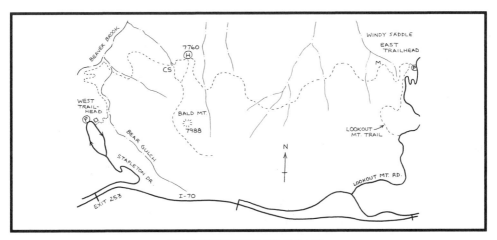

BEAVER BROOK TRAIL

Trailhead. Descending through Bear Gulch the trail curves to the west for a vista of the Beaver Brook canyon before dropping further to the valley floor. After a brief excursion along Beaver Brook the path cuts to the east, crosses Bear Gulch and its tributary and then climbs onto the east wall of the Beaver Brook valley. A steep northward ascent, followed by a less-strenuous climb to the east, brings you to **Charm Spring**, a fine destination for a day hike (4 miles roundtrip from the West Trailhead).

Those who seek broad canyon vistas within a short distance should start at **Windy Saddle (the East Trailhead)**. A 3 mile roundtrip hike will take you westward across rock slides, above forested ravines and out to a **ridgetop meadow (M)** which yields a sweeping view of Clear Creek Canyon.

47 JEFFERSON COUNTY CONFERENCE & NATURE CENTER

Distance: 1.25 miles
Difficulty: Easy
Walking Time: 1 hr.
Elevation: 7440-7560 ft.

If you're more inclined to stroll through woods and meadows than to scale a mountain summit, consider a visit to Jefferson County's Conference and Nature Center. Opened in 1975, the Center is an excellent place to expose children to the study of nature. Educational exhibits introduce visitors to the flora and fauna of the Front Range foothills and a short (1.25 mile), self-guided trail leads you through the nearby forest and across the adjacent meadow.

The Conference Center, housed in Charles Boettcher's 1917 Tudor mansion, is the centerpiece of the estate which was donated to Jefferson County by Charline Breeden in 1968. Now used for business meetings, receptions and art exhibits, the mansion and its 110 acre setting were added to the Jefferson County Open Space System in 1981. The estate is now listed in the National Register of Historic Places.

Directions:

The Conference and Nature Center is atop Lookout Mountain, approximately 15 miles west of Denver. Follow I-70 west, enter the foothills and take Exit #256. Turn right and then turn left onto U.S. 40 West. Drive 1.4 miles and turn right on Lookout Mountain Road. Proceed another 1.4 miles and turn left onto Colorow Road. The Center's entrance drive will be 1.1 mile, on your right.

The **Lookout Mountain Open Space**

Nature Center is open 10 AM to 4 PM, Tuesday, Thursday, Saturday and Sunday, May through October; it is open on Saturdays only from November through April.

Route:

The **Nature Trail** starts just behind (south of) the Nature Center building (NC). Educational plaques are spaced along the route, adding to your enjoyment of the foothills ecology.

Pass a few old farm buildings and bear left at the fork in the trail. Wind down through an open woodland of ponderosa pine, watching for tassle-eared Abert's squirrels along the way. Cross a small stream via a footbridge and, at the next intersection, bear left again.

Leaving the Transition Zone woodland the trail enters a broad meadow where wildflowers abound from late spring through early fall. Bluebirds may be spotted on the meadow and the visitor is treated to a view of Downtown Denver and the Colorado Piedmont to the east. Curving back to the north, the trail crosses through an aspen grove, re-enters the pine woodland and joins the shorter loop (see map).

Proceed straight ahead, crossing another footbridge, and bear left at the next trail intersection. A short walk brings you to gardens behind the historic Boettcher mansion. Continue around the north end of this handsome building and return to the Nature Center, completing your hike.

The Boettcher Mansion.

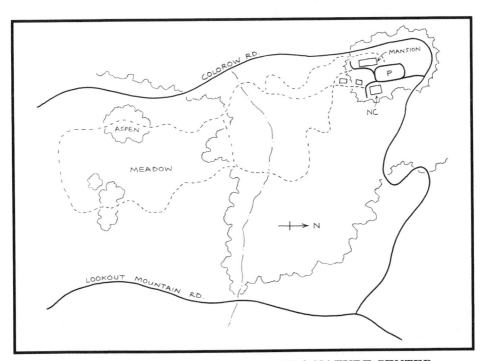

JEFFERSON COUNTY CONFERENCE & NATURE CENTER

48 MATTHEWS/WINTERS PARK-RED ROCKS-HOGBACK PARK

Distance: 5.5 miles
Difficulty: Moderate
Walking Time: 3-4 hrs.
Elevation: 6000-6640 ft.

As the Ancestral Rockies pushed skyward, some 300 million years ago, erosion was already spreading aprons of silt and sand along the base of the range. Over the millenia that followed, these layers of rock dust compacted into the sandstones and siltstones of the Fountain Formation, the "Redrocks" that we find along the edge of the foothills today. Dating from the Pennsylvanian Period of the late Paleozoic Era, the Fountain Formation rocks were covered by younger deposits of shale and sandstone from the Mesozoic Era, the Age of Reptiles. Late in the Mesozoic, during the Cretaceous Period (65-135 million years ago), shallow seas invaded Colorado; sand from these ancient seas compacted into Dakota Sandstone which, itself, was overlain by Pierre Shale during the late Cretaceous Period.

The Modern Rockies began to rise about 70 million years ago. A core of Pre-Cambrian granite pushed upward through the Paleozoic and Mesozoic sediments, forcing these younger rocks to tilt upward along the eastern flank of the mountains. "Differential erosion," whereby softer rocks erode faster than harder ones, has left behind ridges of sandstone and valleys of shale.

A 5.5 mile hike takes you across this fascinating landscape and yields sweeping views of the Front Range foothills and Colorado Piedmont. The hike begins at the Mt. Vernon Historic Townsite, within Matthews/Winters Park (part of the Jefferson County Open Space system). The Townsite is the former location of Mt. Vernon, founded by Dr. Joseph Casto in 1859. Dr. Casto, a preacher, land barron and gold rush pioneer, arrived from Ohio and soon established the town as capitol of the Jefferson Territory. When the Territory of Colorado was created in 1861, regional economic and political power was centered at Denver City, on the South Platte River, and Mt. Vernon, along with many other pioneer towns, faded into oblivion.

Directions:
From Denver, follow I-70 west to the foothills. Cross through the Dakota Hogback and exit onto Colorado 26 (Exit #259). Turn left (south) and proceed .3 mile to the Matthews/Winters Park entrance, on your right.

138

Redrocks Park and Mt. Morrison from the Dakota Ridge Trail.

*(L. to R.) Mt. Morrison, Redrocks, the Hogback and
Green Mountain as seen from Mt. Falcon.*

Route:

From the parking lot, walk back along the entry road, cross Colorado 26 and ascend the Hogback via the **Dakota Ridge Trail (DRT)**. Bypass a cutoff on your right, pass a gate and ascend further before cutting back to the south (watch for the trail sign). The trail climbs steadily across the west flank of the hogback, yielding broad views of Mt. Vernon Canyon, Red Rocks Park, Mt. Morrison and the Front Range foothills.

Reaching the crest of the Hogback you are walking atop Dakota Sandstone, deposited during the reign of Tyrannosaurus rex. Green Mountain looms to the east and, beyond its mass, Metro Denver sprawls across the Piedmont. Far to the south are the varied mesas of the Castle Rock region and the concrete corridor of C-470 snakes away along the base of the foothills. Mule deer are abundant on the slopes of the Hogback but rest in sheltered ravines by day and are best seen at dawn or dusk. Junipers and ponderosa pines cling to the dry, rocky soil of the ridge, providing food and shelter for scrub jays, magpies, towhees and chickadees. Golden eagles and red-tailed hawks soar along the ridge throughout the year.

The trail undulates atop the hogback, soon crossing an open meadow (M) that sits in a saddle of the ridge. Views of Red Rocks Park become more spectacular as you approach Colorado 26 which loops eastward to cross the Hogback. Wind down to the road and then climb back onto the Dakota Ridge south of the roadcut (see map). Upon reaching the crest of the Hogback the trail angles back to the north and begins a long descent of the western flank via a series of switchbacks.

Cross the road, turn right, walk a short distance and turn left onto an entry road for Red Rocks Park. Follow the road for about .1 mile and watch for **Red Rocks Trail (RRT)** on your right (see map). Angle onto this path which cuts across an open scrub grassland, dotted with yuccas and framed by scattered groves of juniper and pine. The massive sandstone slabs of the Fountain Formation rise to the west, leaning toward the slopes of Mt. Morrison (elevation 7881 ft.).

The trail crosses a dirt road and then parallels it, climbing gently toward the north. Crossing a paved roadway the **Red Rocks Trail** begins to climb more steeply, winding past outcroppings of sandstone and turning westward along a thicket-lined stream. Birding can be excellent in this area and rock squirrels are often spotted on the sandstone monoliths.

Bypass the cutoff for the **Mt. Morrison Slide Trail (MST)** and cross back to the east wall of the valley, descending gradually toward the north. The trail turns westward to cross the upper reaches of Cherry Gulch where dense thickets cluster in the shaded ravine. North of the Gulch the sun-parched hillsides are cloaked by yuccas, prickly pear cactus and an extensive scrub grassland. Entering the Mt. Vernon Historic Townsite the Red Rocks Trail intersects the **Village Walk Loop (VWL)**. Bear left onto the loop and take a short walk out to an old cemetery (C) where graves date back to the 1860s. Complete the west arm of the Village Loop and return to the parking area (see map). Your undulating route has totalled 5.5 miles.

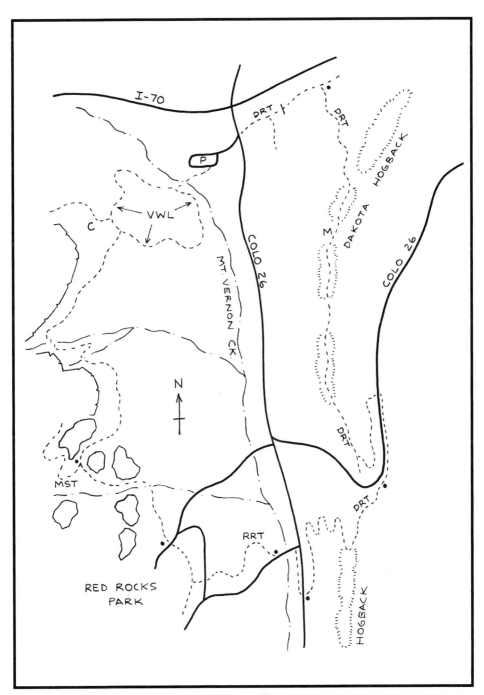

MATTHEWS/WINTERS PARK - REDROCKS - HOGBACK PARK

49 LAIR O' THE BEAR PARK

Distance: 2.7 miles
Difficulty: Easy
Walking Time: 2 hrs.
Elevation: 6520-6800 ft.

A relatively new addition to Jefferson County's superb Open Space system, Lair O' The Bear Park offers a pleasant day hike through the scenic gorge of Bear Creek. Located 4.5 miles west of Morrison, the Park's 300 acres stretch along the stream and onto the south wall of the rugged canyon. A 2.7 mile route takes you through riparian woodlands, across streamside meadows and into a fragrant forest of pine and fir. Wildflowers are abundant along the trail from late spring through summer.

Directions:

From C-470 west of Denver, take the Morrison Exit. Turn west on Colorado 8, proceed through town and continue straight ahead on Colorado 74 toward Evergreen. Wind upward and westward for 4.5 miles to the Park entrance, on your left. Elevation at the parking lot is 6538 feet.

Route:

From the parking lot, follow the trail that leads southward to Bear Creek. Turn right on the **Creekside Trail (CST)** and wind westward through riparian woodland. Bear left at the next intersection and, at the **Dipper Bridge (DB)** continue straight ahead along the **Creekside Loop (CSL)** for a .5 mile excursion across the floodplain of Bear Creek. Kingfishers patrol the waterway while yellow warblers, rufous-sided towhees and black-headed grosbeaks brighten the woodland during the warmer months. Wildflowers are spectacular here in June and July.

Complete the **Creekside Loop** and bear right, crossing the **Dipper Bridge**. This span and the **Ouzel Bridge (OB)**, at the east end of the Park, are named for a fascinating bird that feeds on insects and larvae by plunging into turbulent mountain streams. A bit smaller than a robin, the blue-gray dipper is best found at the Park during the colder months when higher streams have frozen over.

Once across the bridge, bear right on the **Bruin Bluff Trail (BBT)**. Climbing westward above the creek, the trail soon angles to the south and leads upward into the rich, Transition Zone forest that cloaks the north-facing wall of Bear Creek Canyon. Ponderosa pine and Douglas fir are the dominant trees while mountain mahogany, scrub oak, yuccas and prickly pear cactus adorn the sunny meadows. The showy, yellow flowers of the prickly pear are best seen in late June or early July.

Crossing a sidestream the **Bruin Bluff Trail** angles back to the north, climbs higher and then zigzags to the east, dipping through a second ravine. Curving to the northeast the route passes a rocky overlook (V) and then begins a long, gradual descent to the Bear Creek floodplain. At the bottom of the slope the **Caster Cutoff (CC)** merges from the west; turn right, continuing eastward along the **Bruin Bluff Trail**, and cross a streamside meadow where a vast stand of thistle attracts American and lesser goldfinches in late summer.

Cross the **Ouzel Bridge (OB)** and return to the parking area via the **Creekside Trail (CST)**. A fishing deck (F) offers a shady retreat for anglers and a pleasant reststop for hikers.

The Bruin Bluff Trail.

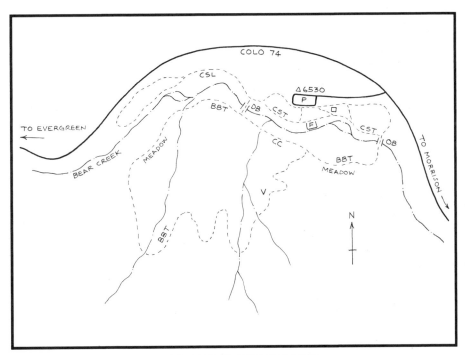

LAIR O' THE BEAR PARK

50 MOUNT FALCON PARK

Combined Loop Hike
  Distance: 5 miles
  Difficulty: Moderate
  Walking Time: 3-4 hrs.
  Elevation: 7400-7760 ft.

To White House Site
  Distance: 3 miles roundtrip
  Difficulty: Easy
  Walking Time: 2.0-2.5 hrs.
  Elevation: 7480-7760 ft.

For a family hike of modest difficulty close to Denver, you cannot beat the scenic trails of Mount Falcon Park. Part of Jefferson County's Open Space System, the 1415 acre Park sprawls across a rolling plateau in the foothills, just west of Metro Denver. Elevations range from 7400 to 7851 feet and steep climbs are limited to routes that venture onto the rugged walls of the plateau. Flanked by Bear Creek Canyon to the north and Turkey Creek Canyon to the south, the Park offers spectacular views of the Front Range, from the Piedmont to Mount Evans. Foothills stairstep to the Continental Divide north of the Park and vistas across the Piedmont extend from Greater Boulder to Larkspur.

Most of the plateau is covered by Transition Zone forest. Open woodlands of ponderosa pine thrive across the sunny, dry slopes while a mix of pine, spruce and Douglas fir cloaks the shaded, north-facing hillsides. A broad meadow covers the central portion of the plateau and steep, rocky cliffs descend into the adjacent canyons. Resident fauna include mule deer, bobcats, coyotes, Abert's squirrels, golden-mantled ground squirrels, mountain and western bluebirds, Steller's jays and wild turkeys.

In addition to the natural beauty, Mt. Falcon offers a fascinating tale of human history. **John Brisben Walker**, a businessman, land baron and one-time owner of Cosmopolitan Magazine, built a stone mansion above Bear Creek Canyon in the early 1900s. From that hideaway he planned the construction of a "Western White House" for U.S. Presidents on a ridge at the northeastern edge of Mt. Falcon. Unfortunately, the mansion burned down in 1918 and later business failures prompted Walker to abandon his White House dream. Remnants of the **mansion (M)** and a foundation for the **White House (W)** can still be seen at the Park today.

Directions:
Take U.S. 285 southwest from Denver, enter Turkey Creek Canyon and proceed another 2.3 miles to Parmalee Gulch Road. Turn right and wind northward for 2.8 miles. Turn right on a dirt road and follow the signs to Mount Falcon Park; the 2-mile entry zig-zags through a residential area and then crosses a broad meadow before reaching the Park.

Routes:
The following day hikes are suggested.
  Combined Loop Hike (5 miles). From the parking lot hike eastward on the entry trail and then turn south along **Parmalee Trail (PT)**. This 1.7 mile path snakes down through open, ponderosa pine forest and then turns eastward across the dry, rocky wall of Turkey Creek Canyon. Deer and blue grouse often forage on these sunny slopes and this is a good area to watch for hawks, falcons and golden eagles.

The **Parmalee Trail** eventually turns northward and climbs back onto the plateau. Bear right onto the **Meadow Trail (MT)**, walk a short distance and then angle to the right on the **Old Ute Trail (UT)**. This .5 mile loop circles a forested knob, yielding views in all directions. Bypass the cutoff to **Devil's Elbow Trail (DET)** and circle back to the **Meadow Trail**. Turn right and hike northward across the eastern end of the meadow, crossing Strain Gulch. The **Meadow Trail** soon intersects the **Castle Trail (CT)** and just north of this

Crossing the meadow.

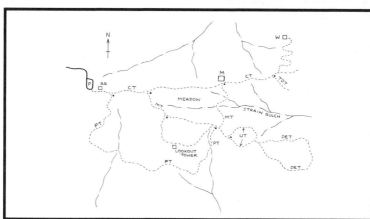

MOUNT FALCON PARK

junction is the site of the **Walker Mansion ruins (M).** Ascend to this historic yet tragic monument which yields a sweeping view of the Bear Creek Valley.

Hike eastward on the **Castle Trail** atop a narrow ridge. Bypass the **Two-Dog Trail (TDT)** and turn northward, climbing higher via a series of switchbacks. The abandoned foundation of **Walker's White House (W)** sits atop a rocky crest that juts out above the Bear Creek Valley. The views are spectacular, more than justifying Walker's Dream. Metro Denver sprawls across the Piedmont to the east and Red Rocks Park nestles below Mt. Morrison (7881 ft.) to the north of the Canyon. To the west, the Bear Creek Valley descends from Mt. Evans, flanked by a succession of lowering and ever-drier ridges.

A 1.5 mile hike along the **Castle Trail (CT)** takes you back to the parking lot, completing a route that has totalled 5 miles.

Hike to White House Site (3 miles roundtrip). One of the easier and perhaps the most popular day hike at Mt. Falcon Park is a roundtrip excursion on the **Castle Trail (CT)** with stops at the **Walker Mansion ruins (M)** and at the site of the abandoned **White House (W).** From the parking lot, walk eastward along the entry trail, bypass the **Parmalee Trail (PT)** and continue eastward on the **Castle trail (CT).** After skirting a small meadow the path ascends to the western edge of Mount Falcon's central grassland where bluebirds often hunt from the scattered pines. Bypass the **Meadow Trail (MT)** and descend gradually along the northern edge of the grassland. Near the eastern end of the meadow you will reach the **mansion ruins (M)** and another .8 mile will take you out to the **White House site (W).** Please refer to the Combined Loop Hike for details of this route. Return to your car via the same trail, completing a roundtrip hike of 3.0 miles.

145

51 ELK MEADOW PARK/BERGEN PEAK

Meadow Loop
  Distance: 4 miles
  Difficulty: Easy
  Walking Time: 2.5-3.0 hrs.
  Elevation: 7600-8200 ft.

Bergen Peak Trail
  Distance: 9.2 miles roundtrip
  Difficulty: Strenuous
  Walking Time: 4-5 hrs.
  Elevation: 7750-9708 ft.

Bergen Peak, elevation 9708 feet, is the eastern end of a high ridge that extends toward Denver from the Mt. Evans massif. This ridge divides the Bear Creek Valley, to its south, from the broad basin of Clear Creek.

The southern and eastern flanks of Bergen Peak are protected by adjacent holdings of Jefferson County Open Space, Denver Mountain Parks and the Colorado Division of Wildlife. The open meadows along the base of the mountain offer prime winter habitat for elk (hence the name Elk Meadow Park for Jefferson County's preserve) and a hike to the summit of Bergen Peak takes you through several distinctive Rocky Mountain life zones.

The lower meadows, dotted with groves of ponderosa pine, are home to western and mountain bluebirds, pocket gophers, coyotes, badgers and Richardson's ground squirrels. Transition Zone forest, characterized by Douglas fir, blue spruce and ponderosa pine, cloaks middle elevations of the mountain. There you will find Steller's jays, pygmy nuthatches, hairy woodpeckers, black-headed grosbeaks, golden-mantled ground squirrels and numerous chipmunks. Wildflowers abound on the sunny clearings from June through August. Above 8000 feet the Transitional forest gives way to the Subalpine Zone, typified by lodgepole pine and quaking aspen. Red squirrels chatter from their arboreal lofts while gray jays, ravens and yellow-rumped warblers hunt across the wooded slopes.

A superb network of trails provides access to these varied mountain habitats. Parking lots are located along Colorado 74,

east of the meadow, and on Stagecoach Blvd., at the southern edge of the Park (see map).

Directions:
Follow I-70 west from Denver. Enter the foothills and drive approximately 8 miles to the El Rancho Exit (Exit #252). Follow Colorado 74 toward Evergreen; the Elk Meadow lot will be 3.9 miles, on your right. To reach the Stagecoach Blvd. lot, continue southward on Colorado 74 for another 1.75 miles, turn right on Stagecoach Blvd. and proceed 1.1 mile to the parking area, on your right.

Route:
We recommend the following two hikes.
Meadow Loop - This easy, 4 mile route combines sections of the **Meadow View Trail (MVT)**, **Elkridge Trail (ERT)**, **Sleepy S Trail (SST)** and the **Painter's Pause Trail (PPT)**. From the lot along Colorado 74, hike northward and then westward on the **Meadow View Trail**, entering an open woodland of ponderosa pine. Angling back to the south, the trail skirts a broad meadow at the base of Bergen Peak, undulating across the eastern flank of the mountain and dipping in and out of Transition Zone forest. Clearings yield broad views to the east, extending out to the Colorado Piedmont. Crossing numerous drainages, the Meadow View Trail eventually intersects the **Elkridge Trail**.

Bear left (east) onto this trail which runs atop a finger of high ground and then descends to the meadow via several switchbacks. Turn left on the **Sleepy S Trail**, hike eastward above Bergen Creek and then

Looking south across the meadow.

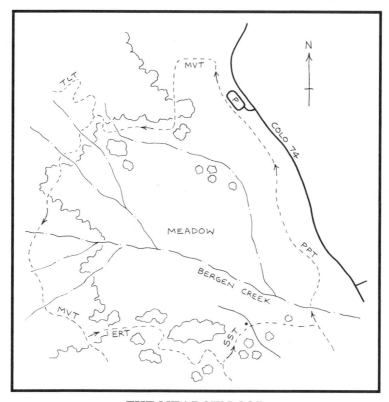

THE MEADOW LOOP

return to the parking lot via **Painter's Pause Trail** which parallels Colorado 74.

Bergen Peak Trail - A strenuous, 4.6 mile ascent of Bergen Peak from Stagecoach Blvd. (9.2 miles roundtrip) offers a physical challenge but rewards the hiker with superb mountain vistas. The initial portion of the hike uses the southernmost section of the **Meadow View Trail (MVT)** which leads northeastward from the lot, climbing onto a low ridge. Bypass the cutoff to the **Sleepy S Trail**, angling back to the northwest and entering the Transition Zone forest. Another .6 mile brings you to the intersection with the **Bergen Peak Trail (BPT)**. Turn left and begin an assault on the mountain via a series of well-engineered switchbacks. Crossing into Denver Mountain Park territory the forest begins to open up and you will soon arrive at the first of many viewpoints (V) above the Bear Creek Valley. Climbing higher the trail crosses through a "lodgepole pine desert" where thick stands of this subalpine tree suppress growth of an understory and discourage habitation by all but a few species of birdlife.

Nearing the edge of the Bear Creek Valley once again, the trail winds westward through open forest and several rocky overlooks provide a broad view from the eastern Colorado Piedmont to the rounded summit of Mt. Rosalie. Pikes Peak looms to the south, 60 miles distant.

Climbing higher and angling to the northwest, the trail crosses through Bergen Peak Wildlife Area, passes beneath the rocky summit of Bergen Peak and intersects the **Too Long Trail (TLT)**. Stay on the **Bergen Peak Trail**, cutting back to the southwest and climbing through a mixed forest of lodgepole pine and quaking aspen via another series of switchbacks. Nearing the summit the trail winds to the north side of the mountain, yielding spectacular views across the Clear Creek basin. Santa Fe Mountain (10,537 feet) looms to the northwest and the Continental Divide stretches away in the distance. Lookout Mountain, with its numerous radio towers, will be noted to the northeast, backed by the Colorado Piedmont. Sections of I-70 appear in the foreground, winding through the Front Range foothills.

Curving southward the trail leads out to the rocky summit of Bergen Peak, a perfect site for a picnic lunch. The view is magnificent. Metro Denver spreads out to the east, just beyond the vanguard of foothills. The craggy silhouette of Devil's Head will be spotted in the distant southeast while Pikes Peak rises above the southern horizon. The Mount Evans massif dominates the western view; further away and to the right of the Mt. Evans group are the twin fourteeners, Grays and Torreys Peaks. The city of Evergreen, and its sparkling reservoir, 2700 feet below your rocky perch, stretch across the valley to the southeast.

After rest and nourishment atop the mountain, return to your car via the same route, completing a roundtrip hike of 9.2 miles. Plan to start out early in the day and depart the exposed summit by noon, thereby avoiding the frequent afternoon thunderstorms.

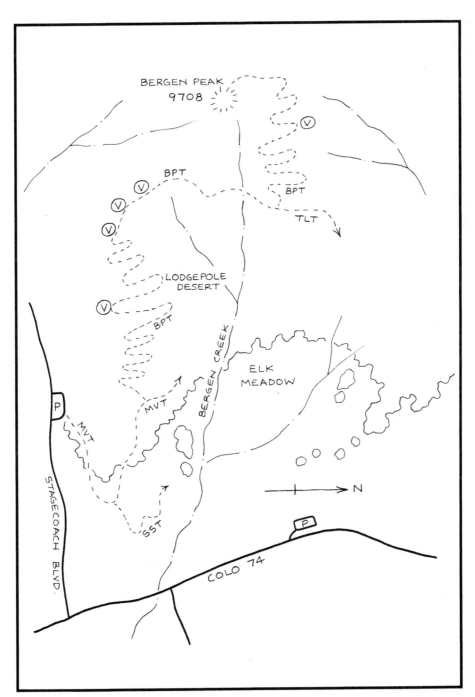

BERGEN PEAK TRAIL

52 ALDERFER/THREE SISTERS PARK

Distance: 2.3 miles
Difficulty: Moderate
Walking Time: 2 hours
Elevation: 7400-7800 feet

Rock spires adorn many of the foothills throughout the Evergreen-Conifer region. Four of these outcroppings, just southwest of Evergreen, form the centerpiece of Jefferson County's Alderfer/Three Sisters Park. Composed primarily of Precambrian, Silver Plume Quartz, "The Brother and Three Sisters" are reached by a fine network of trails and offer spectacular views of the Bear Creek basin.

Land for the Park, which stretches north from Buffalo Park Rd., was donated to Jefferson County by the E. J. Alderfer and Spencer Wyant families. Located within the Transition Zone, the preserve is characterized by an open forest of ponderosa pine. Wild turkeys, blue grouse, Steller's jays, porcupines, Abert's squirrels and mule deer are among the resident fauna. Wildflowers abound on the sunny meadows from May through late summer.

Directions:
From Denver, follow U.S. 285 toward the southwest. Enter the foothills and proceed 14 miles to Conifer. Turn right and wind northward on County Route 73, toward Evergreen. Drive 8 miles and turn left (west) on Buffalo Park Rd. Proceed 1.3 miles to the parking lot, on your right.

Route:
A 3.9 mile trail network provides access to the Park. We suggest the following 2.3 mile route which takes you to the Brother Lookout and across the ridge of the Three Sisters.
From the parking lot, hike northward on the **Sisters Trail (ST)**. Bypass the first cutoff to the **Ponderosa Trail (PT)** and proceed to the second trail intersection. Now turn left on the **Ponderosa Trail** and begin a gradual climb across the sun-scorched south wall of The Brother. Just over ¼ mile from the last intersection you will reach the cutoff to the **Brother Lookout**. Proceed up to the rocky summit for a sweeping panorama of the Bear Creek basin. The city of Evergreen fills the foreground to the east, backed by the wall of Bear Mountain (8629 feet). In the distant southeast are the triple summits of Doublehead Mountain, Mt. Legault and Berrian Mountain. The massive, tree-covered dome to the SSW is Evergreen Mountain (8536 feet) while Mt. Evans and its cohort of peaks looms 16 miles to the west. The dark silhouettes of Hicks Mountain and Squaw Mountain rise in the northwest, just to the left of Bergen Peak (9708 feet) which overlooks the Evergreen area. The Three Sisters will be spotted through the trees to the north of The Brother.

Descend back to the **Ponderosa Trail**, turn right for a short distance and then angle right again, onto the **Sisters Trail (ST)**. The trail gradually ascends along the west flank of the Three Sisters ridge and then crosses between two of the rocky triplets. From the east side of the ridge you are treated to a view of Evergreen Lake, almost 800 feet below. Numerous switchbacks take you down to the base of the ridge where you will reach another trail intersection. Cut back to the left on the **Hidden Fawn Trail (HFT)** for a pleasant, .8 mile loop back to the parking area.

The Three Sisters as seen from The Brother.

ALDERFER/THREE SISTERS PARK

53 MEYER RANCH PARK

Distance: 4.3 miles
Difficulty: Moderate
Walking Time: 2.5-3.0 hrs.
Elevation: 7875-8727 ft.

Thanks to the generosity of Norman and Ethel Meyer, another scenic park was added to Jefferson County's superb Open Space system. Meyer Ranch Park encompasses 397 acres across the southern wall of the South Turkey Creek Valley, approximately 16 miles southwest of Denver. Characterized by a broad meadow along the valley floor, higher sections of the Park are cloaked by transitional and subalpine forest. Large ponderosa pines dot the drier, sunny slopes near the meadow while a thicker forest of lodgepole pine and aspen covers the higher, shaded ridge that extends westward from Mt. Legault (9074 feet).

Late spring and summer bring a colorful display of wildflowers to the meadows of Meyer Ranch. Indian paintbrush, columbine, larkspur and wood lily are among the more common species. Resident wildlife include mule deer, chipmunks, red squirrels, mountain bluebirds and wintering herds of elk.

Directions:
Follow U.S. 285 southwest from Metro Denver. Enter the foothills and proceed another 11 miles. The parking area will be on the left (south) side of the highway.

Route:
Access to the preserve is via four interconnected trail loops. Mileages and elevations are noted on the map. We suggest the following hike which yields a total route of 4.3 miles.

From the parking area, cross South Turkey Creek and hike across the meadow on the **Owl's Perch Trail (OPT)**. After passing the restroom hut (RR) the trail divides into a loop and cuts through the Park's picnic grounds. Take either branch, winding southward through this open woodland of ponderosa pine. At the trail intersection, turn right onto the **Lodgepole Pine Loop (LPL)** and hike westward above the South Turkey Creek Valley. Views extend across the valley to the rocky bulk of Berrian Mountain (9147 ft.) and westward to the dark, flat-topped form of Black Mountain (10,756 ft.)

Gaining elevation and angling back to the east, the trail leaves the open pine woodland and enters the dense, subalpine forest of lodgepole pine and quaking aspen. At the trail intersection turn right onto the **Sunny Aspen Trail (SAT)** and climb southward. Occasional clearings offer views of Doublehead Mountain (8938 feet) to the NNE and across to the imposing mass of Berrian Mountain.

Reaching a small meadow at 8325 feet, turn onto the **Old Ski Run Trail (OSR)** for a final assault on the ridge. A steady climb brings you to a fine overlook (V) of the South Turkey Creek Valley and of the foothills and mountains beyond. Mt. Evans looms to the WNW while the double-hump silhouette of Chief and Squaw Mountains again dominate the view northward across the valley.

Another .25 mile brings you to the upper loop of the **Old Ski Trail**. Bear left onto the loop and then take the short spur trail to a rocky outcropping (A) for your picnic lunch. Alternatively, find a second side trail further along the loop (B) which leads into a small meadow beneath the rocky summit of Mt. Legault. If you choose the latter site be sure to respect the private property line and stay within Meyer Ranch Park. After your lunch break, return to the parking area via the **Old Ski Run Trail** and the eastern arms of the **Sunny Aspen** and **Lodgepole Pine Trails.** Your round-trip hike will total 4.3 miles.

The Meyer Homestead below Berrian Mountain.

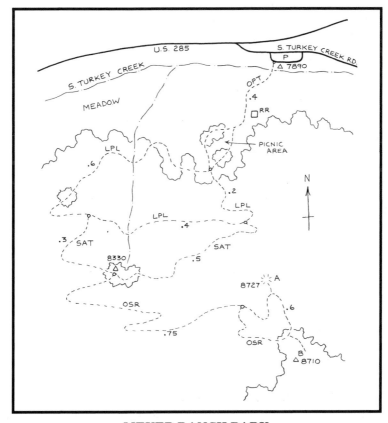

MEYER RANCH PARK

54 REYNOLDS PARK

Eagle's View Overlook
  Distance: 3.4 miles
  Difficulty: Moderate
  Walking Time: 2.5-3.0 hrs.
  Elevation: 7280-8100 ft.

The 1260 acres of Reynolds Park stretch across the valley of Kennedy Gulch, 5 miles south of Conifer. Now part of the Jefferson County Open Space system, this scenic area was the home of Idylease, a well-known dude ranch from 1913-1942. Named for John A. Reynolds, whose family donated the land to Jefferson County, the Park hosts an excellent diversity of flora and fauna. Black bear, mule deer and wild turkey are among the native residents. Well-engineered trails lead into the varied habitats of the preserve and offer scenic routes for the day hiker.

Directions:
  Follow U.S. 285 southwest from Denver. Enter the foothills and proceed 14.3 miles, passing through Aspen Park and Conifer. Turn left onto Foxton Road (County Route 97) and descend along Kennedy Gulch for 4.8 miles to the Reynolds Park access lot, on your right.

Route:
  Though there are several potential day hikes at Reynolds Park, we suggest the following 1.8 mile climb to **Eagle's View Overlook** with a return route along Oxen Draw (3.4 miles roundtrip).

From the parking area follow the entry trail as it passes a picnic area, crosses Kennedy Gulch creek and curves to the right. Just past the restroom hut the path intersects the **Elkhorn Interpretive Trail (EIT)**. Bear right onto this loop, winding along a meadow and through an open, ponderosa pine woodland. Wildflowers are abundant here in late spring and summer. A broad switchback leads onto a low shoulder of the valley wall and the route soon intersects the **Raven's Roost Trail (RRT)**.

Switch to this trail which climbs steadily through a forest of ponderosa pine and Douglas fir. Views of the Kennedy Gulch valley unfold at several of the switchbacks, providing an excellent excuse to stop and rest. Nearing the upper reaches of Oxen Draw, the **Raven's Roost Trail** levels out and curves along a sun-scorched, rocky slope before descending to the creek bed. Cross the stream and switch to the **Eagle's View Trail (EVT)**.

This .7 mile trail climbs to the top of the ridge, fording several small streams and crossing through a wooded meadow. Watch for brightly-colored western tanagers along the trail during the warmer months. At the crest of the ridge the trail emerges from the forest, curves to the west and leads across an open meadow. Strolling along at 8100 feet, you are treated to a magnificent view of foothills, mountains and deep, forested valleys. The craggy silhouette of Devil's Head stands out to the southeast. To the SSE is the majestic form of Pike's Peak, flanked by Long Scraggy Peak to the left and the Cathedral Spires to the right. Green Mountain (10,421 feet) to the SSW and Windy Peak (11,970 feet) to the southwest anchor the Kenosha and Platte River Mountains whose snowy summits peek above forested ridges to the west.

After a picnic lunch on the meadow, descend the **Eagle's View Trail** and switch to the **Oxen Draw Trail (ODT)**, descending .6 mile through a moist woodland of aspen, Douglas fir and blue spruce. The trail crosses the stream no less than twelve times before intersecting the **Elkhorn Interpretive Trail**. Bear right and follow the southern end of this loop, crossing a wooded meadow and soon returning to the parking lot.

154

Magnificent views reward your climb to the Overlook.

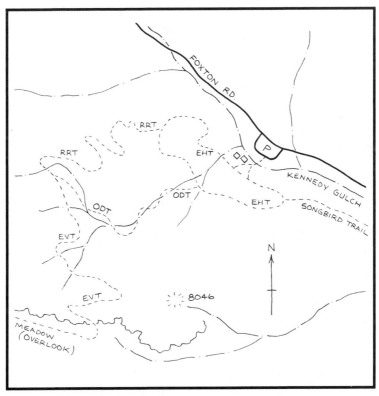

ROUTE TO EAGLE'S VIEW OVERLOOK

55 WATERTON CANYON

Distance: Variable; 2-12 miles roundtrip
Difficulty: Easy
Walking Time: Variable; plan at least 2 hrs.
Elevation: 5480-6000 ft.

The south branch of the South Platte River heads in the high alpine meadows that overlook the vast, intermountain grassland of South Park. Its many tributaries course into the broad valley, joining the main channel as it flows southeastward to the Pike's Peak region. Exiting Elevenmile Reservoir, the River angles back to the northeast and rumbles through the foothills.

The north branch of the South Platte rises along the Continental Divide near Guanella and Kenosha Passes. Flowing eastward, the north fork hugs the base of the Platte River Mountains and eventually joins the south branch eleven miles NNE of Deckers, Colorado. It is at this junction, in a land of scenic canyons and legendary trout fishing, that the Denver Water Board has proposed the creation of the Two Forks Reservoir. Fortunately, to date, the E.P.A. has not supported this devastating project.

Three and a half miles below the junction is the Strontia Springs Dam, completed in the early 1980s, which created yet another reservoir along the South Platte. Below the dam the River renews itself and snakes for another six miles through the spectacular gorge of Waterton Canyon before exiting the foothills and coursing northward across the Colorado Piedmont.

A visit to Waterton Canyon affords an easy hike through magnificent scenery. Native bighorn sheep offer a special treat for the naturalist and are best seen on the sunny, south-facing walls of the Canyon. Other resident mammals include rock squirrels, chipmunks, mule deer and an occasional mountain lion. The birdlife is especially varied; golden eagles, Steller's and scrub jays, canyon wrens and rufous-sided towhees are found here throughout the year. During the warmer months look for rock wrens, white-throated swifts, violet-green swallows, lesser goldfinches and lazuli buntings. Dippers are often spotted along the turbulent waters during the winter and early spring.

Directions:
From C-470 in southwest Metro Denver, exit at Wadsworth Blvd. (Route 121). Turn south and drive approximately 4.5 miles. As the road curves westward into Martin Marietta, turn left toward Waterton, proceed .2 mile and turn right into Waterton Canyon parking area. Be advised that the area is often congested on warm weather weekends; plan a weekday visit if possible. Also, in an effort to protect the resident deer and bighorn sheep, dogs are not permitted in the Canyon.

Route:
From the parking area cross through a gate and follow a service road westward to the mouth of the Canyon. The first half mile of your journey takes you across the flat floodplain of the South Platte River, characterized by a few ponds, scattered thickets and groves of cottonwood trees. Entering the canyon the roadbed parallels the river, winding toward the southwest and gradually ascending to the Strontia Springs Dam, six miles upstream.

The length of your hike can be varied depending upon time constraints and your level of fitness. Rather than completing the 12-mile roundtrip hike to the Dam, many visitors stop at the Marston Diversion site, approximately three miles upstream. Regardless of the distance that you choose,

November snow blankets the Canyon.

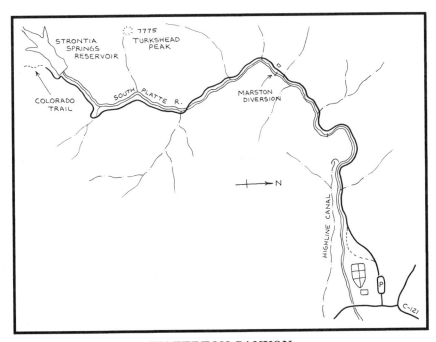

STRONTIA
SPRINGS
RESERVOIR

7775
TURKSHEAD
PEAK

SOUTH PLATTE R.

MARSTON
DIVERSION

COLORADO
TRAIL

N

HIGHLINE CANAL

P

C-121

WATERTON CANYON

your effort will be rewarded with spectacular canyon scenery, varied flora and a plethora of wildlife.

The hike through Waterton Canyon corresponds with the eastern end of the **Colorado Trail** which stretches from Metro Denver to Durango. For more information on that Trail, contact the **Colorado Trail Foundation** at the address listed in Appendix II.

56 ROXBOROUGH STATE PARK

Fountain Valley Trail
  Distance: 2.25 miles
  Difficulty: Easy
  Walking Time: 1.0-1.5 hrs.
  Elevation: 6000-6200 ft.

South Rim Trail
  Distance: 3 miles
  Difficulty: Moderate
  Walking Time: 2 hrs.
  Elevation: 6080-6480 ft.

Carpenter Peak Trail
  Distance: 5.5 miles roundtrip
  Difficulty: Strenuous
  Walking Time: 3.5-4.0 hrs.
  Elevation: 6200-7175 ft.

Designated a National Natural Landmark, Roxborough State Park harbors some of the most spectacular scenery in Colorado. Complementing its natural beauty, the Park also offers a dramatic display of Front Range geology.

Looking north from the South Rim Overlook, the visitor can readily appreciate the distinct rock strata that characterize the region. At the west edge of the Park, an uplift of Precambrian granite has created a chain of foothills, culminating in Carpenter Peak (7175 feet above sea level). Along the base of the foothills a ribbon of red sandstone fins lean toward the higher summits. Known as the Fountain Formation, this bedrock dates back to the Pennsylvanian Period (300 million years ago) and is the product of erosional debris from the Ancestral Rockies.

Running down the center of the Park and separated from the Fountain Formation by a narrow valley is a band of yellow-gray sandstone known as the Lyons Formation. Deposited as sand dunes and riverbanks during the Permian Period (225 million years ago), the Lyons sandstone was forming as the earth's land masses were merging into the mega-continent of Pangea. Forming the eastern border of the Park is a broken ridge known as the Dakota Hogback. Dating from the Cretaceous Period (135 million years ago), the resistant Dakota sandstone harbors fossils from the age of dinosaurs.

Prior to the Laramide Orogeny (the rise of the modern Rocky Mountains, 70 million years ago), the above rock strata were aligned horizontally, with younger deposits overlying older sediments (see figure next page). As the Rockies pushed skyward, the sedimentary layers were tilted upward toward the west. Subsequent erosion has created the present day landscape; the more resistant sandstone layers tower above the intervening valleys which are underlain with less resistant shale. Walking east to west through the Park, the visitor thus travels back in time, crossing through 500 million years of geologic history.

In addition to Roxborough's physical beauty and striking geologic features, the Park harbors a diverse population of plants and animals. Scrub oak blankets dry, sunny areas of the lower ridges while a Transition Zone forest of pine, Douglas fir and blue spruce cloaks the shaded slopes of the foothills. Resident fauna include mule deer, coyotes, bobcat, rock squirrels, chipmunks and an occasional mountain lion. The mule deer, very tolerant of nearby hikers, are best found along the hogback or on the meadows east of the Lyons Formation. Scrub jays, rock wrens, towhees and golden eagles characterize the Park's avian population.

158

Sandstone fins of the Fountain Formation.

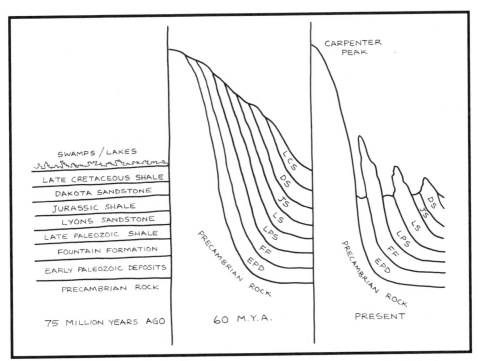

THE GEOLOGIC EVOLUTION OF ROXBOROUGH PARK

159

Directions:

From C-470 south of Denver, exit onto Santa Fe Drive and head south. Proceed 4.2 miles and turn right (west) on Titan Rd. Drive about 4 miles and continue on this road as it curves to the south and becomes Rampart Range Rd. Another 2.2 miles brings you to a stopsign adjacent to the Roxborough Fire Department. Turn left and then take an immediate right onto the entry road of Roxborough State Park. A nominal day use fee is charged; be advised that the Park closes at 8 PM in the summer and before dark during the winter months.

Routes:

Roxborough State Park is accessed by four trail loops which range in difficulty from easy to strenuous. All originate from the **Visitor Center (VC)** or from nearby parking lots. The Center houses natural history exhibits, a small bookstore/gift shop and a theater.

The following day hikes are recommended.

Fountain Valley Trail (2.25 mile loop).

The **Fountain Valley Trail (FVT)** leads northward from the visitor center. After hiking a short distance turn left and walk out to the Fountain Valley overlook (V1) which affords spectacular views to the north and south.

Return to the primary trail and turn left. The Fountain Valley Trail soon splits to form an elongated loop. Bear right and begin a gradual descent across open meadows between the Lyons Formation (LF) and the Dakota Hogback (DH). Mule deer often browse on the meadows and are best seen at dawn or dusk. At the north end of the loop is Persse Place (PP), a stone cabin constructed in 1906. The structure is a remnant from a resort that occupied the valley in the early 1900s.

The trail curves back to the south, gently climbing between the Lyons Formation and the Fountain Formation (FF). Complete the loop and return to the visitor center via the entry trail.

South Rim Trail (3 mile loop).

This hike begins at the parking lot just west of the Hogback (see map). Cross the creek via a footbridge and walk southward along the edge of the valley. Bypass the **Willow Trail (WT)** which splits off to the west and you will begin to climb along the west flank of the Dakota Hogback. Gradually ascending, the route yields sweeping views to the north and west. A broad switchback takes you onto the crest of the Hogback and out to the South Rim Overlook (V2) which offers a magnificent panorama of Roxborough Park and the surrounding countryside.

The **South Rim Trail** soon curves back to the north and winds into the valley between the Lyons and Fountain formations. Passing near the sandstone monoliths, watch for rock squirrels that den in the crevices and often sun themselves on the rock ledges. Leading across the valley floor, the trail crosses the primary stream channel. Bypass the cutoff to **Carpenter Peak (CPT)** and, at the next intersection, turn right onto the **Willow Trail** and return to the parking lot.

Carpenter Peak Trail (CPT).

This is a strenuous, 2.75 mile climb from the Visitor Center (elevation 6200 feet) to the summit of Carpenter Peak (elevation 7175 feet). Take the **Willow Trail (WT)** from the Visitor Center, bear right onto the **South Rim Trail** and then angle west onto the **Carpenter Peak Trail**. The trail crosses a dirt road, loops across a stream channel and then begins a steep assault on the ridge. A series of switchbacks leads upward into a sheltered ravine where Douglas fir thrives on the shaded, north-facing slope. The trail crosses the stream bed and leads northward across the dry, rocky wall of the foothill. Angling to the west, it climbs along another forested stream bed, loops across the creek and leads onto the crest of the ridge. Turning westward again, the trail negotiates a third drainage before a final climb takes you to the summit of Carpenter Peak.

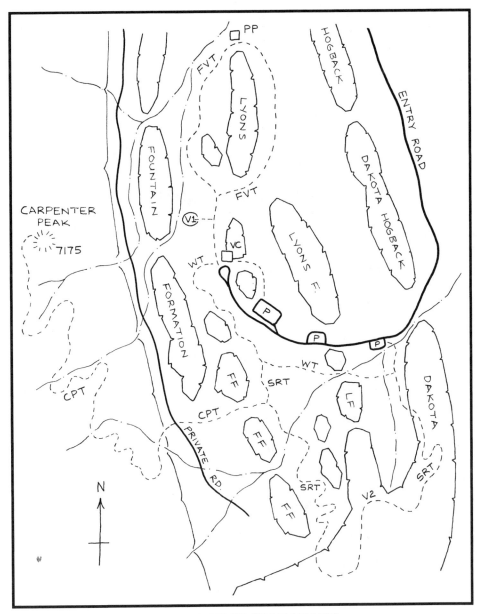

ROXBOROUGH STATE PARK

From this rocky prominance you are treated to superb views in all directions. The rounded summit of Bennett Mountain (8045 ft.) rises to the southwest while the craggy silhouette of Windy Peak dominates the western view. Turkshead Peak (7775 ft.) towers over Waterton Canyon to the WNW and Metro Denver sprawls across the Piedmont to the northeast. The varied rock formations of Roxborough Park stretch below you to the east and Wildcat Mountain (6640 ft.) pokes up from the flatlands to the southeast.

Return to the Visitor Center via the same route, completing a roundtrip hike of 5.5 miles.

III. THE HIGH COUNTRY

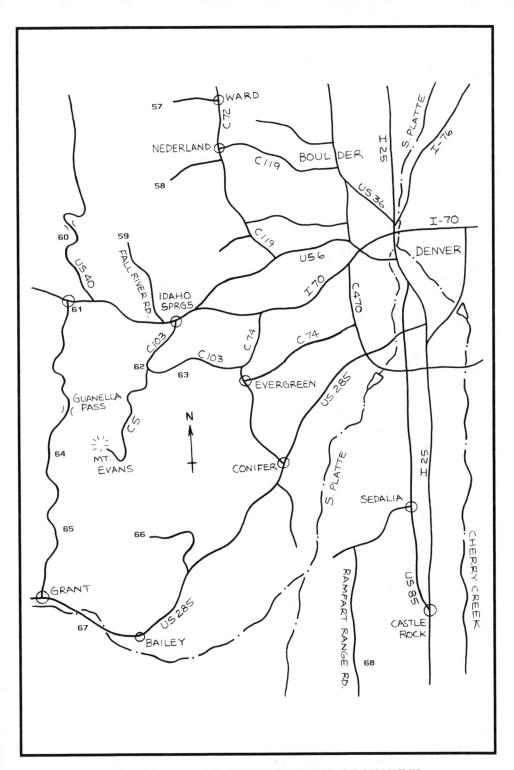

HIKING AREAS IN THE HIGH COUNTRY

57 INDIAN PEAKS WILDERNESS

Hike to Lake Isabelle
  Distance: 4.5 miles roundtrip
  Difficulty: Moderate
  Walking Time: 3-4 hrs.
  Elevation: 10,500-10,868 ft.

Hike to Blue Lake
  Distance: 4 miles roundtrip
  Difficulty: Moderate
  Walking Time: 3-4 hrs.
  Elevation: 10,480-11,320 ft.

The Indian Peaks Wilderness, twenty miles west of Boulder, is a paradise for campers, fishermen and day hikers. Characterized by rugged peaks, pristine alpine lakes, glacial valleys and a rich, mountain forest, the area draws hords of Coloradans and tourists during the warmer months. Human congestion has become a real problem and back-country permits are now required for overnight camping from June 1 through September 15 (call 303-444-6001).

Of the many access points to the Indian Peaks Wilderness, Brainard Lake, near Ward, Colorado, is surely the most popular. A paved entry road and relatively easy hikes to scenic alpine lakes explain the area's appeal. Since this guide is designed primarily for families, weekend trekkers, naturalists and visitors, we would be remiss not to include this area. However, in light of its popularity, we suggest a weekday visit after the summer crowds have dispersed. Mid-late September is an excellent time to visit the Wilderness.

Directions:
From Boulder, head west on Canyon Blvd. which leads into Boulder Canyon. Colorado 119 continues up the canyon and winds westward for 14.8 miles to Netherland. Turn right (north) on Colorado 72 toward Ward, Colorado, and drive 11.5 miles to the Forest Access Road, just north of town on the west side of the highway. Follow the paved road for almost 5 miles to Brainard Lake. Circle to the west side of the Lake and turn right (west) onto the road that leads to the Mitchell Lake and Long Lake Trailheads; bear right for the hike to Blue Lake (which originates at the Mitchell Lake Trailhead) or left for the hike to Lake Isabelle (which begins at the Long Lake Trailhead).

Route:
There are many potential day hikes that can be achieved from the Brainard Lake area; we suggest the following day hikes. Both hikes are of modest length and moderate difficulty and the trails are easily followed.

Lake Isabelle (4.5 miles roundtrip). The trail to Long Lake, Lake Isabelle, Isabelle Glacier and Pawnee Pass leaves the south side of the Long Lake Trailhead lot, curves to the east and then turns westward. Within .25 mile you will reach the Wilderness boundary and the eastern shore of Long Lake. Bypass the cutoff to the south, bearing right and hiking to the west on the **Pawnee Pass Trail (PPT)**. This trail meanders above the north shore of Long Lake (elevation 10,521 ft.), remaining almost level until it reaches the west end of the lake. There it begins to climb at a very modest grade and soon skirts a large meadow which affords a broad view of the Niwot Ridge to the south.

Approaching the west end of the lower valley the trail crosses a side stream and then climbs steeply to the basin of **Lake Isabelle**. Sitting at an elevation of 10,868 feet, the Lake is surrounded by alpine meadows and scattered parcels of forest. The pinnacle of Navajo Peak (13,409 ft.) rises at the north end of the Niwot Ridge and Apache Peak (13,441 ft.) forms the central high point of your mountain vista.

Lake Isabelle

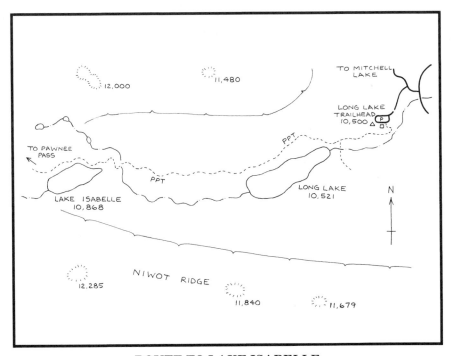

ROUTE TO LAKE ISABELLE

Shoshoni Peak (12,967 ft.) leans in above the northwest end of the valley, its sheer south face dropping 800 feet. The Isabelle Glacier, nestled between Apache and Shoshoni Peaks, is not easily seen from the Lake basin.

After a picnic lunch along the lake, return to the trailhead via the same route, completing a roundtrip hike of 4.5 miles.

Blue Lake (4 miles roundtrip). The trail to Blue Lake passes Mitchell Lake along the way and is labeled the **"Mitchell Lake Trail"** at the access lot. This wide path, blazed with blue diamonds, leaves the southwest corner of the lot and winds to the west through a fragrant, subalpine forest. A quarter mile from the trailhead the route crosses a side stream and, soon thereafter, negotiates the primary creek via a wooden footbridge.

Making a swing to the south the trail reaches the Wilderness boundary beyond which the blue markers disappear. The route curves back to the north and soon emerges from the forest above the south shore of Mitchell Lake (10,700 ft.). Mt. Audubon (13,223 ft.) looms to the northwest as the trail turns westward and parallels the shoreline.

Crossing the inlet stream via a log bridge, the path climbs steeply through open, rocky terrain, yielding a magnificent view back across Mitchell Lake. It then levels out, skirts an alpine marshland and winds to the west across a swath of high ground. Curving southward the trail overlooks a pair of high country lakes before making a final climb to the basin of Blue Lake. The last section of the hike is an exercise in patience; rock cairns guide you across the tundra landscape, meltwater puddles impede your progress and the route negotiates a series of rock ledges, each promising a view of the lake.

Nevertheless, the reward is worth the effort. **Blue Lake**, elevation 11,320 feet, sits above timberline in a world of snow, rock, sun and ice. Mt. Toll rises beyond the Lake, its pyramidal form topping out at 12,979 ft. The broad shoulders of Mt. Audubon still loom to the north and the eastern ridge of Pawnee Peak separates the Blue Lake basin from the valley of Lake Isabelle, 1.5 miles to the south.

Return to the Mitchell Lake Trailhead via the same route, completing a roundtrip hike of 4 miles.

Mt. Toll rises above Blue Lake.

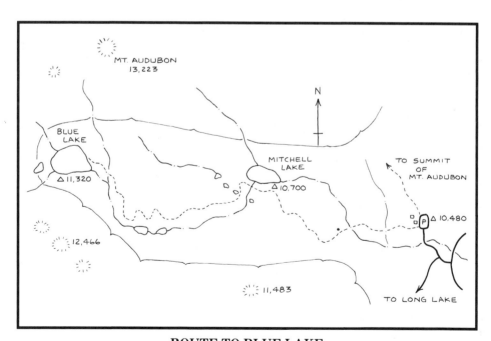

ROUTE TO BLUE LAKE

58 EAST PORTAL/CRATER LAKES

To Valley Meadow
  Distance: 2.4 miles roundtrip
  Difficulty: Easy
  Walking Time: 1.5-2.0 hrs.
  Elevation: 9200-9600 ft.

To Crater Lakes
  Distance: 6 miles roundtrip
  Difficulty: Strenuous
  Walking Time: 4 hrs.
  Elevation: 9200-10,600 ft.

To gain acceptance as important centers of commerce, it was imperative that western cities be located on one or more of the major railroads that pushed into the Rocky Mountain region during the latter half of the 19th Century. Dismayed by Union Pacific's decision to bypass Denver and run their transcontinental route through southern Wyoming, local civic leaders went to work to ensure vital rail service for the Queen City. Among these determined men was **David Moffat** who, despite many critics, had been calling for a rail tunnel through the Continental Divide since his arrival in Denver in 1860.

Born in New York in 1839, Moffat was a banker, businessman and entrepreneur who developed a local reputation as a bit of a dreamer. Nevertheless, he had powerful political allies and, by 1870, managed to engineer the interconnection of the Union Pacific and Kansas Pacific Railroads in Denver, creating an alternative route to the West Coast from the big eastern cities. By 1904 Moffat had a rail line built over Rollins Pass, three miles northwest of East Portal. Ironically, he died, perhaps by suicide, in 1911, sixteen years before his ultimate dream was realized. Constructed from 1923 to 1927, the 6.2 mile **Moffat Tunnel** placed Denver on a prime transcontinental railroad.

A visit to **East Portal**, the eastern terminus of the Tunnel, can be combined with an invigorating hike along South Boulder Creek. At present, the side trails in this area are poorly marked and close attention to the map and narrative in this guide is advised. The climb to **Crater Lakes**, which sit in a rock-walled basin at 10,600 feet, is recommended for fit and experienced hikers.

Directions:
  From Colorado 93 between Golden and Boulder, turn west on Colorado 72 and ascend through Coal Creek Canyon to Wondervu. Descend westward, crossing South Boulder Creek at Pinecliffe and continue to the intersection with Colorado 119 (this is 18.4 miles west of Colorado 93). Turn left (south) on Colorado 119 and proceed 1.8 miles to Rollinsville. Turn right (west) on the dirt road that leads toward Tolland and East Portal and drive 8 miles to the Moffat Tunnel entrance. Park in the large lot north of the tracks; stay east of the restricted work area.

Route:
  The following day hikes are suggested. The hike to the **Valley Meadow** is a pleasant stroll along South Boulder Creek on a wide, even path; it is recommended for all visitors to East Portal. On the other hand, the climb to **Crater Lakes** is strenuous and should be attempted only by those who are conditioned to hiking at altitude.

Valley Meadow Hike (2.4 miles roundtrip). Cross the railroad tracks, cross a bridge over a drainage channel and, if necessary, climb over a metal gate (see map). Continue southwestward, pass through a second fence and hike along South Boulder Creek on a wide gentle path. Pass several private cabins and wind through a series of small, sunny meadows over the first half mile.

The trail crosses the braided channel of Arapaho Creek and then skirts another meadow before entering the cool, mature

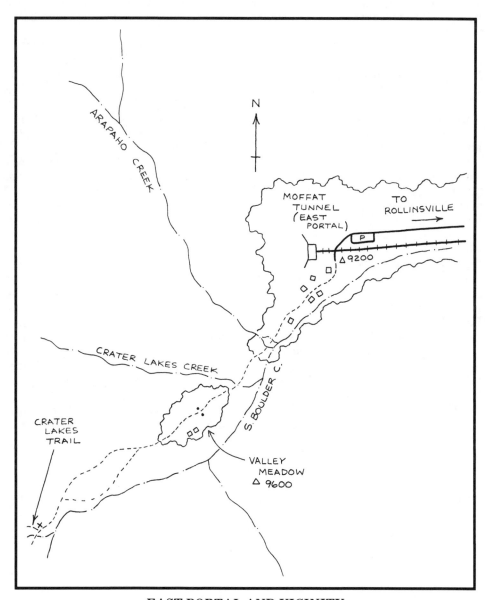

EAST PORTAL AND VICINITY

forest of spruce and pine. After a gentle climb through the woods the trail crosses the outlet creek for the Crater Lakes and, within 100 yards, enters a large meadow where the crumbled remains of two cabins sit near the stream. Affording a fine view to the northeast, this is an excellent destination for a family picnic. Returning to East Portal from this area yields a round-trip hike of 2.4 miles.

Crater Lakes (6 miles roundtrip). Those who are energetic and fit enough to attempt a hike to these secluded lakes should continue southwestward from the **Valley Meadow**, re-entering the forest. The primary trail soon forks; bear right and climb along a rocky channel at a moderate grade. Within a half mile the trail levels out and, a short distance later, snakes just above South Boulder Creek. As the trail and creek diverge once again you will enter a clearing and reach a small side stream. Look to your right where a rock pile (x) marks the entrance to the **Crater Lakes Trail (CLT).**

Turn onto this narrow path which climbs very steeply onto the west wall of the valley, using a natural stairway of rocks, roots and fallen logs. After a quarter mile the trail levels a bit and angles to the southwest. Walk a hundred yards or so and watch closely for a point (*) where the trail cuts back to the right and begins another very steep climb to the west. Two short spur trails lead out to rock overlooks (V) of the South Boulder Creek Valley; James Peak (13,294 ft.) pokes above the ridge to the south.

The main trail continues upward to the west, levels off and then makes a third steep ascent. Moderating once again, the path curves to the northwest, passes a small meadow (M) and then climbs gently along a rock ledge. A final steep section is followed by a descent to the basin of the Crater Lakes.

Leaving the forest the trail enters a wet meadow and forks; stay on the south side of the stream and walk out to the east shore of the first Lake. Though smaller than its twin, this is the more scenic of the Lakes, backed by rocky cliffs of the Continental Divide.

Before returning to East Portal, take the other trail fork which crosses the creek and leads out between the larger two of the Crater Lakes (see map). The Lake to your north is the largest of the five lakes and reminds one of the loon and moose country of northern Minnesota or Maine. It is also interesting to know that the Moffat Tunnel passes directly beneath this tranquil alpine lake.

Return to East Portal via the same route, completing a roundtrip hike of six miles.

The southern Lake is especially scenic.

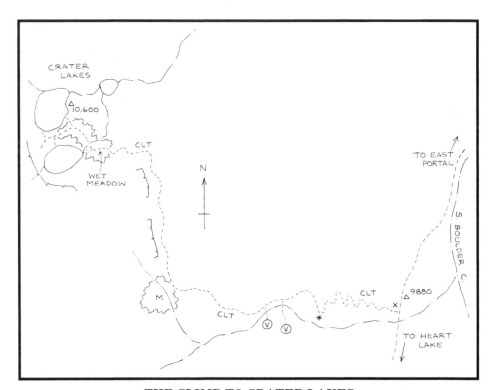

THE CLIMB TO CRATER LAKES

59 ST. MARY'S GLACIER

Distance: 1.5 miles roundtrip
Difficulty: Moderate
Walking Time: 1.5-2.0 hrs.
Elevation: 10,400-11,000 ft.

St. Mary's Glacier, northwest of Idaho Springs, is a popular destination for flatlanders during the summer months. The ten-acre snowfield, a remnant from the Pleistocene Epoch, sits at 11,000 ft., beneath the south flank of Kingston Peak. The "Glacier" and its scenic meltwater lake offer a cool retreat from the hot, dusty Piedmont and a short, rocky trail makes the haven readily accessible to families and weekend trekkers. Though many visitors bring skis, sleds and snowboards to the Glacier, its icy face drops 400 feet over ¼ mile and caution is strongly advised.

Directions:
Follow I-70 west from Denver. Enter the foothills and drive another 22 miles to Exit #238 (Fall River Rd.). From the ramp, proceed straight ahead for .2 mile and then turn right onto Fall River Rd. Wind toward the northwest for 8.6 miles to a large parking area, on your left.

Route:
From the parking lot, walk further up the road and then angle left onto a wide, rocky path that climbs toward St. Mary's Glacier. The trail winds upward through an open forest of lodgepole pine and is intersected by several other routes coming in from either side (see map).

A half-mile ascent brings you to the east shore of St. Mary's Lake which sits at 10,690 feet, beneath towering walls of rock. Hike northward along the lakeshore and then cut across to the glacier via one of several paths (see map). From your perch at the edge of the snowfield you are treated to a magnificent view to the south. A hundred feet below is St. Mary's Lake and 17 miles distant is Mt. Evans, often shrouded in clouds. Just east of the lake is Fox Mountain (10,921 ft.), a pinnacle of rock reminiscent of Devil's Tower in Wyoming.

A cool breeze usually sweeps across the snowfield and you'll be glad to have a sweater here even on a mild summer day. Pikas bark from nearby boulder fields and raucous ravens soar across the surrounding cliffs. Gray jays, chipmunks and golden-mantled ground squirrels often turn up to scavenge remnants from your picnic lunch.

After your refreshing visit to this scenic alpine basin, descend to your car via the same route, completing a roundtrip hike of 1.5 miles.

The Glacier sits above its scenic meltwater lake.

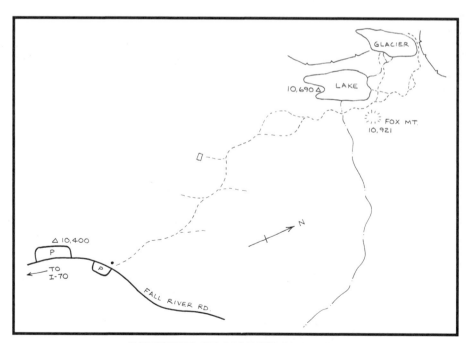

ROUTE TO ST. MARY'S GLACIER

60 THE CONTINENTAL DIVIDE/BERTHOUD PASS

Distance: 4 miles roundtrip
Difficulty: Strenuous
Walking Time: 3-4 hrs.
Elevation: 11,315-12,424 ft.

The Continental Divide, a geographic, hydrologic and romantic feature of the American West, is the line of high ground that stretches north to south through North America, separating the Pacific-bound streams from those that flow toward the Atlantic Ocean. In Colorado, the Continental Divide zigzags through the north-central and southwestern portions of our State, passing within twenty-five miles of Boulder. The **Continental Divide Trail** follows the Divide from New Mexico into Canada and is easily accessed from several high passes in Colorado.

The day hike discussed below originates at Berthoud Pass on U.S. 40, forty miles WNW of Denver, and leads upward along the Divide to a peak with breathtaking views in all directions. Were it not for the elevation, the hike would be classified as moderate in difficulty. However, the rarefied air at 12,000 feet makes for strenuous exercise at even modest grades and we thus recommend this hike for conditioned walkers who are also adapted to the altitude.

Cold winds and intense sunlight are features of the alpine tundra throughout the year. Sunglasses, sunscreen and warm, layered clothing are strongly advised. Thunderstorms develop rapidly along the Divide, especially from May through July, and it is wise to plan your hike for the morning hours. The dry, sunny month of September is an ideal time to venture into the "Land above the trees."

Directions:

Follow I-70 west from Denver. Enter the foothills and drive 28 miles to the Empire-Granby-U.S. 40 West Exit (Exit #232). Proceed slowly through Empire and then follow U.S. 40 to the summit of **Berthoud Pass** (about 15 miles from I-70). Park in the large lot on the east side of the pass.

Route:

Cross U.S. 40 and head up the **old jeep road** at the southwest corner of Berthoud Pass (see map). Follow this wide path as it climbs through open, subalpine forest, winding toward the northwest. Reaching timberline near a ski lift, you are treated to your first views of surrounding peaks. Engelmann Peak (13,362 ft.) is the massive mountain to the south, notched by a large glacial cirque. In the distant southeast is the jagged crest of Mt. Evans and its four-teener companion, Mt. Bierstadt. To the east is Colorado Mines Peak (12,493 ft.), topped by an FAA radar facility. Parry Peak (13,391 ft.) is the prominent cone to the ENE.

Climb westward along the chair lift and, at the fork, take either route, circling behind the summit lift station. The jeep road then angles to the southwest and descends into a basin; bear right at this junction, picking up the **Continental Divide Trail** which is blazed by an elevated marker (see map). The route climbs onto a higher plateau, following the course of the Divide; streams to your left flow toward the Atlantic via the Platte River system while those on your right flow westward via the massive watershed of the Colorado River.

A short descent brings you to the base of a steep slope that you must now climb via a lung-busting series of switchbacks. Once atop the ridge (12,280 ft.) your views broaden significantly. Rest your legs for a few minutes and then continue along the **Continental Divide Trail**, climbing to Peak 12,391 and then curving to the southwest to reach **Pebler Peak (12,424 ft.)**. This summit, which yields a spectacular panorama, is an excellent destination for a day hike.

Engelmann Peak still dominates the

Vasquez Peak

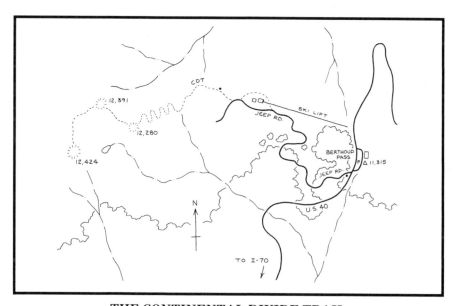

THE CONTINENTAL DIVIDE TRAIL

view to the south, with Bard Peak (13,641 ft.) now poking above its western shoulder. Mt. Evans and Mt. Bierstadt are again noted to the southeast, with the triple formation of Squaw, Papoose and Chief Mountains further east. The Continental Divide, across Berthoud Pass, stretches away to the north; the sheer west face of the Arapaho Peaks will be spotted to the northeast with the flat-topped cone of Long's Peak (14,255 ft.) further north. The other summits of Rocky Mountain National Park are to the northwest of Long's Peak and the rugged Never Summer Range pushes skyward on the northern horizon. The less-imposing Park Range stretches westward from the Upper Colorado Valley, forming a backdrop for the rolling farmlands of Middle Park. Directly west of your lookout is Vasquez Peak (12,947 ft.) and Byers Peak pokes above lower mountains to the northwest.

Return to Berthoud Pass via the same route, completing a roundtrip hike of 4 miles.

61 GEORGETOWN

Distance: 1.6 miles
Difficulty: Easy
Walking Time: 1.5-2.0 hrs.
Elevation: 8480-8560 ft.

The gold rush of the late 1850s enticed many young men to leave their homes and jobs in the eastern States to seek fortune in the rugged canyons of the Rocky Mountains. Among these hopeful pioneers were George and David Griffith who left their farm in Kentucky and reached the Clear Creek Valley in the summer of 1859. Discovering gold at the junction of Clear Creek and its South Fork, the brothers founded the Griffith Mining District and "George's Town" grew up along the banks of the two streams. A second settlement, Elizabethtown, arose during the silver rush of 1864; named for the sister of George and David Griffith, this village merged with George's Town in 1868, marking the birth of Georgetown.

Gold was never found in large quantities along this stretch of Clear Creek and the twin settlements of Georgetown and Silver Plume owed their economic vitality to the silver boom of the late 19th Century. With the arrival of the Central Colorado Railroad from Denver, in 1877, Georgetown reached the zenith of its short-lived prosperity. Sixteen years later, the Sherman Silver Purchase Act was repealed by the U.S. Congress, placing our country on the gold standard and triggering a free fall in the price of silver. The glory days of Georgetown and Silver Plume had come to an abrupt end; by 1939, even the railroad link between Idaho Springs and Georgetown had been abandoned.

Fortunately, an interest in historic preservation, coupled with a boom in tourism, revitalized the Clear Creek Valley during the mid 20th Century. The Georgetown-Silver Plume National Historic District was established in 1966 and, over the past two decades, Georgetown has witnessed a gradual restoration of its business and residential areas.

A 1.6 mile walking tour, described below, takes you through this historic mining town. Beautifully restored Victorian homes, refurbished storefronts and nicely landscaped parks, all framed by the steep rock walls of the Clear Creek Valley, make for an appealing stroll.

Directions:

From Denver, drive was on I-70, enter the foothills and proceed another 32 miles to the Georgetown Exit (Exit #228). Turn left, crossing under I-70, and then turn right on the main thoroughfare into town (Argentine St.). Just beyond the overhead "Historic Georgetown" sign, turn left into a parking lot that stretches along the road and services the Old Georgetown Depot.

Route:

From the parking lot, cross Clear Creek via a footbridge and proceed to the old **Georgetown Depot (1)**. Constructed to service the Central Colorado Railroad upon its arrival in 1877, the Depot now houses the Alpine Inn, a visitor center and a gift shop. Tickets to the **Georgetown Loop Railroad**, a reconstructed, narrow-gauge line between Georgetown and Silver Plume, can be obtained at the Depot. The Railroad, which was dedicated in August, 1984, and which is operated by the Colorado Historical Society, generally runs from mid May through mid October, depending on the fickle mountain weather.

From the Depot, walk south along Rose St. Georgetown's **City Park**, graced by a **gazebo (2)**, is one block ahead. Across

The Blackman-Seifried House.

Victorian storefronts line 6th St.

Rose St. from the park are several nicely restored **Victorian cottages (3)**. Continue to the south on Rose St., crossing the South Fork of Clear Creek. The **John Adams Church House (4)**, dating from 1877, offers a fine example of Gothic Revival Architecture, common throughout Georgetown. In contrast, the **Blackman-Seifried House (5)**, constructed in 1881-82, exemplifies the Italianate Style. It was the home of Henry Seifried, president of the first Bank of Georgetown. On the northwest corner of Rose and 9th Sts. is the **Bowman-White House (6)**, built in 1892; it combines elements of the Gothic-Revival and Italianate Styles. Finally, the beautifully restored **Robeson House (7)**, erected in 1901, illustrates the Queen Anne Style of architecture.

Further along Rose St. is the old **Dewey Hotel (8)**, circa 1874, which is now the Georgetown Mercantile Company. Turn right on 6th St., the central corridor of Georgetown's Historic Business District. The **Fish Block (9)** occupies the northwest corner of Rose and 9th Sts. and is the former home of the Bank of Clear Creek County. Next door is the **Masonic Hall (10)**, an Italianate structure completed in 1891. Across 9th St., a **stone memorial and plaque (11)**, dedicated in 1935, pay tribute to the Georgetown Mining District. West of the monument is the **John Tomay Memorial Library (12)**, constructed in 1924, and the **Georgetown Community Center (13)**, circa 1867. The latter building, which served as the Clear Creek County Courthouse from 1868-1976, was moved from its original site at 5th and Argentine Sts. in 1976.

Turn left (south) on Argentine St. where the **old Georgetown Jail (14)**, dating from the 1860s, contrasts with the modern buildings of the Clear Creek County Courthouse. At the corner of 4th and Argentine are two brick homes, the **Cornish House (15)**, built in 1893, and the **Clark House (16)**, circa 1875. The **Hamill House (17)**, the former home of mining baron and banker William A. Hamill, dates from 1867. Hamill bought the house in 1874, enlarging

the structure and landscaping the lot over the following decade. The property was acquired by the Georgetown Society in 1971 and tours of the House are now open to the public. The **Stowell House (18)**, across Argentine St., dates from 1869.

Walk east on Third St to Taos St. and turn left. Several **attractive homes (19)** line the block to your right, all dating from the late 19th Century. Turn up 4th St. for a fine view (V) across the city and through the Clear Creek Valley.

The **Grace Episcopal Church (20)** dates from 1869. One half block to the west, on 5th St., is the **Alpine Hose House #2 (21)**, built in 1874. William Hamill donated the bell which still hangs within the tower.

Descend to the business district along Taos St. and turn right on 6th St. The **Hotel de Paris (22)**, now a museum, was constructed in sections, from 1875 to 1890, by Louis DuPuy; it was one of the finer dining and lodging establishments during the glory days of the silver boom. Across 6th St. is the **Star Hook and Ladder Company (23)**, erected in 1886; the structure now houses the police station and town hall. At the east end of 6th St. is the **power station (24)**; originally built by United Light and Power in 1900, the structure has been owned by Public Service of Colorado since 1924.

Angle to the northeast, cross South Clear Creek and then bear left onto Main St. The **Butler House (25)**, circa 1871, has a beautifully landscaped lot fronting the banks of the creek. Walk west on 8th St. and then turn right (north) on Taos St. The **Presbyterian Church (26)** was constructed from 1872-74 and has serviced the community ever since. Across Taos St. is the **old Public School (27)**, an attractive brick structure dating from 1874.

Cross South Clear Creek once again and continue northward on Taos St. **Our Lady of Lourdes Church (28)**, constructed in 1918, is the third church built by Georgetown's Catholic parish; the congregation outgrew the first, 1872 structure and the second church burned down in 1917. Further along Taos St. and just east of City

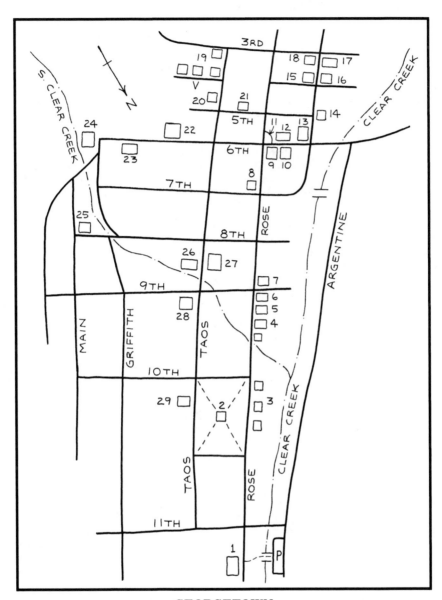

GEORGETOWN

Park is the **Old Missouri Firehouse (29)**, the home of Georgetown's first volunteer fire department (Georgetown Fire Company #1). Organized in 1870, the company enlarged the Old Missouri House in 1881.

Cut across **City Park** and return to the **Georgetown Depot**, completing a 1.6 mile walking tour of this historic and attractive community.

62 CHICAGO LAKES TRAIL

To Idaho Springs Reservoir
Distance: 3.4 miles roundtrip
Difficulty: Moderate
Walking Time: 3 hrs.
Elevation: 10,400-10,617 ft.

To Chicago Lakes
Distance: 8 miles roundtrip
Difficulty: Strenuous
Walking Time: 6-7 hrs.
Elevation: 10,400-11,760 ft.

On the north side of Mt. Evans the terrain plummets into the Chicago Basin, a scenic, rock-walled valley reminiscent of Yosemite National Park. Hemmed in by towering peaks, the upper basin sits above timberline where two alpine lakes entice campers and fishermen throughout the warmer months. The Chicago Lakes, 11,430 and 11,760 feet above sea level, are reached via a four mile trail that originates at Echo Lake, a popular Denver Mountain Park thirteen miles southwest of Idaho Springs. Those hoping to complete the 8-mile roundtrip hike in one day should plan to leave early in the day and bring plenty of water and nourishment. A more reasonable destination for most day hikers is the Idaho Springs Reservoir, 3.4 miles roundtrip from Echo Lake.

Directions:
From Denver, follow I-70 west. Enter the foothills and drive another 20 miles to the Mt. Evans exit (Exit #240) in Idaho Springs. Turn left (south) and follow Colorado 103 for 13 miles, winding up the Chicago Creek valley to Echo Lake. Adequate parking stretches along the road east of the Lake.

Route:
Hike around the north rim of Echo Lake and, halfway down its western shore, bear right onto a wide path that leads into the adjacent forest. Walk approximately 30 yards and watch for a sign that directs you to the right; this faint spur trail leads out to the edge of the Chicago Creek Valley where it intersects the primary route, blazed with tree notches.

The **Chicago Lakes Trail** angles to the south and begins an excursion along the rim of the valley. Views of the Continental Divide unfold to the northwest and Bard Peak (13,641 ft.) dominates a cluster of mountains to the west. Further along you are treated to your first view of the upper Chicago Basin, framed by the forested walls of the lower valley.

About ½ mile from the trailhead the route begins a long descent to the valley floor via a series of switchbacks. Crossing Chicago Creek, the trail intersects a jeep road. Turn left onto this wide path and begin a gradual climb through the valley. Another .5 mile brings you to the **Idaho Springs Reservoir**, elevation 10,617 ft. Lined with boulders, full of trout and offering a spectacular view of the upper basin and surrounding peaks, the Reservoir is a fine spot for a picnic lunch. This destination, 3.4 miles roundtrip from Echo Lake, is recommended for families and most weekend hikers.

More adventurous and well-conditioned trekkers, and those planning an overnight stay in the upper basin, should continue southward along the jeep road as it parallels the west shore of the Reservoir. Curving to the southwest the route narrows to a foot-trail and begins the final 2.3 mile climb to the **Chicago Lakes**. The final half-mile is above timberline and the Lakes sit beneath towering walls of granite. To the east are Rogers Peak (13,391 ft.) and Mt. Warren (13,307 ft.), to the south is Mt. Evans (14,264 ft.) and to the west are Mt. Spaulding (13,842 ft.) and Gray Wolf

The Idaho Springs Reservoir.

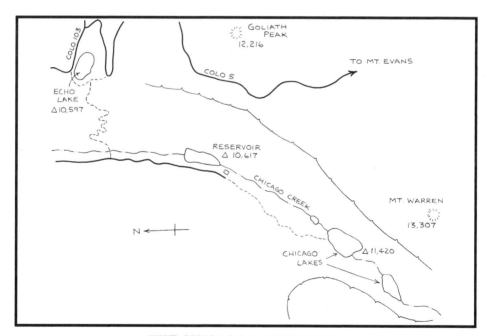

THE CHICAGO LAKES TRAIL

Mountain (13,602 ft.). Ravens soar across the cliffs and sure-footed mountain goats are often spotted on the steep walls of the basin.

After plenty of rest and nourishment in this spectacular gorge, descend through the valley, cross Chicago Creek and climb back to Echo Lake, completing a roundtrip hike of 8 miles.

63 CHIEF MOUNTAIN

Distance: 3.2 miles roundtrip
Difficulty: Strenuous
Walking Time: 2.5-3.0 hrs.
Elevation: 10,680-11,709 ft.

If regional hikes were ranked by scenic reward per mile, then the 1.6 mile ascent of Chief Mountain would surely be near the top of the list. Rising to 11,709 feet, Chief Mountain is the high point along an alpine ridge that extends northeastward from the Mt. Evans massif. To the south of the ridge the terrain plunges into the scenic basin of Bear Creek while, to the north, the broad drainage of Clear Creek sculpts the landscape. Jutting above timberline, the summit of Chief Mountain yields one of the grandest panoramas along the Front Range.

Directions:
Follow I-70 west from Denver. Enter the foothills and drive 8 miles to the El Rancho Exit (Exit #252). Turn left and follow Colorado 74 toward Evergreen. Proceed 2.5 miles and bear right onto Colorado 103 which leads up to Echo Lake and Mt. Evans. Wind upward and westward for 12.5 miles to a pull-off lot on the right side of the road. The trail to Chief Mountain begins across the road, blazed with marker #290.

Route:
The **Chief Mountain Trail** ascends from the road, makes a broad switchback to the west and, within .5 mile, crosses an old jeep road. A trail marker at this junction indicates a distance of 1.2 miles to the summit of Chief Mountain.

Cross the jeep road and climb southward onto the saddle between Papoose Mountain (11,174 ft.) to the east and Chief Mountain to the west. Crossing open woodland atop the saddle the trail angles to the west, enters the subalpine forest and swings onto the north flank of Chief Mountain. Nearing timberline the trail crosses through an open, stunted forest of spruce, limber pine and subalpine fir. Spectacular views soon unfold to the north and west, dominated by the jagged spine of the Continental Divide. Long's Peak, 40 miles to the north, towers above Rocky Mountain National Park.

Crossing the open, rocky tundra the trail climbs to the summit of Chief Mountain via a series of switchbacks. A bit of boulder-hopping is required to scale the last few meters but the panorama from the wind-swept pinnacle is well worth the effort. Metro Denver and the Colorado Piedmont stretch across the eatern horizon. Pike's Peak looms to the south and the Kenosha and Platte River Mountains form a high wall to the SSW. Mt. Evans dominates the view to the WSW, with Mt. Bierstadt (14,060 ft.) rising just behind. Grays and Torreys Peaks, both fourteeners, form a distinctive double-hump to the west and the Continental Divide leads northward to the Wyoming border. Portions of I-70 and the city of Idaho Springs, 4200 feet below, will be spotted within the Clear Creek basin.

Mountain goats occasionally wander out to Chief Mountain from the higher terrain of Mt. Evans and pikas, hamster-like residents of the rocky tundra, are common about the summit. After enjoying a picnic lunch and taking in the sights, return to Squaw Pass Road (Colorado 103) via the same route, completing a round trip hike of 3.2 miles.

Mt. Evans from Chief Mountain.

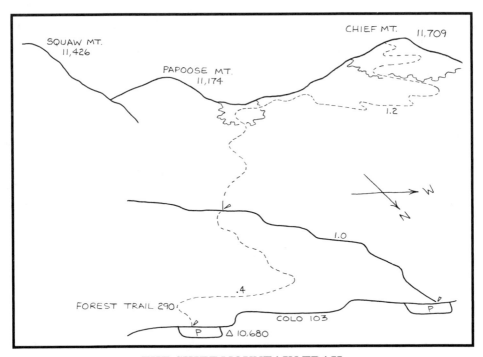

THE CHIEF MOUNTAIN TRAIL

64 ABYSS LAKE TRAIL

To First Meadow (M1)
  Distance: 3 miles roundtrip
  Difficulty: Moderate
  Walking Time: 2-3 hrs.
  Elevation: 9620-10,040 ft.

To Large Meadow (M2)
  Distance: 4.5 miles roundtrip
  Difficulty: Moderate
  Walking Time: 3-3.5 hrs.
  Elevation: 9620-10,200 ft.

To Timberline
  Distance: 11 miles roundtrip
  Difficulty: Strenuous
  Walking Time: 6-7.5 hrs.
  Elevation: 9620-11,500 ft.

Of all the trails that lead into the Mt. Evans Wilderness, the **Abyss Lake Trail** is surely the most popular. Horseback riders, fishermen, campers and hikers create a virtual parade along the route on warm weather weekends; a late-season, weekday visit is recommended if possible.

The appeal of this trail is easy to understand. Stretching for 8 miles from the Guanella Pass Road to the secluded, rock-walled gorge of Abyss Lake, the well-worn path climbs at a modest grade along most of its route. Alpine meadows are spaced along the valley of Scott Gomer Creek, offering scenic reststops or attractive destinations for a picnic lunch.

The entire 16-mile roundtrip hike to Abyss Lake is a bit long for a one day trip; we thus suggest shorter destinations, described below.

Directions:
From Denver, follow U.S. 285 to the southwest. Enter the foothills and drive another 40 miles to Grant. Turn right (north) on the Guanella Pass Road and proceed 5 miles to the **Abyss Lake Trailhead,** on your right.

Route:
From the parking lot the **Abyss Lake Trail** enters the subalpine forest and curves to the north. Just over ½ mile from the trailhead the path crosses Francis Creek and angles to the northeast. Another mile brings you to a **small meadow (M1)** along Scott Gomer Creek; returning to your car from here yields a roundtrip hike of 3 miles.

If possible, continue along **Abyss Lake Trail** to a **large meadow (M2)** that sits at 10,200 feet. This destination yields a spectacular view of Mt. Evans through the valley to the NNE, flanked by Mt. Bierstadt (14,060 feet) to the west and Epaulet Mountain (13,523 feet) to the south. The rocky shoulders of Geneva Mountain rise above the valley to your north and the massive dome of Kataka Mountain (12,441 feet) looms to the east. Returning to the trailhead from this scenic meadow yields a roundtrip hike of 4.5 miles.

Those who continue on will cross Scott Gomer Creek, skirt the east edge of the meadow and continue toward the northeast through a dense forest of aspen. Crossing the creek a second time the route climbs along a rocky path and, curving northward, intersects the **Rosalie Trail (RT)** 4 miles from the trailhead. This trail stretches 12.5 miles from the Deer Creek Trailhead to Guanella Pass (see Tanglewood Trail hike).

Cross the **Rosalie Trail** and continue toward the northeast on the **Abyss Lake Trail,** soon passing two ponds. Another .7 mile takes you across Scott Gomer Creek and along the west bank of Lake Fork

*Mt. Bierstadt and Mt. Evans
viewed through the Scott Gomer Valley.*

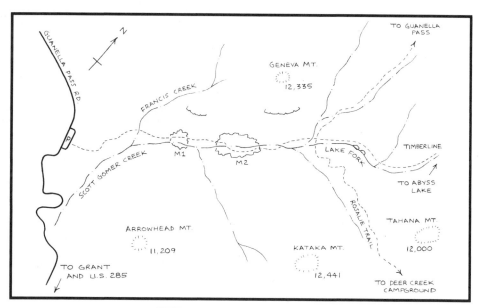

THE ABYSS LAKE TRAIL

Creek (see map). **Timberline,** which averages 11,500 feet in our region, will be less than ½ mile ahead.

The sheer rock wall of Mt. Evans and Epaulet Mountain rises to the northeast and the steep south face of Mt. Bierstadt looms to the north. Across the Scott Gomer basin to the southwest is Geneva Mountain (12,335 feet) while Tahana, Kataka and Arrowhead Mountains form the east wall of the valley.

Returning to Guanella Pass Road after your timberline picnic yields a roundtrip hike of 11 miles.

65 THREE-MILE TRAIL

To Lower Meadow (M1)
  Distance: 2.2 miles roundtrip
  Difficulty: Easy
  Walking Time: 2 hrs.
  Elevation: 8980-9280 ft.

To Upper Valley (M2)
  Distance: 6 miles roundtrip
  Difficulty: Moderate
  Walking Time: 4-5 hrs.
  Elevation: 8980-10,700 ft.

Three-mile Creek drains the remote southwestern corner of the Mt. Evans Wilderness, emptying into Geneva Creek three miles north of Grant, Colorado. The trail along this scenic stream climbs at a very moderate grade, making the hike ideal for families and weekend trekkers. Aspen are abundant along the valley and sheer rock cliffs add to the grandeur of the alpine scenery.

Directions:

Follow U.S. 285 southwest from Denver. Enter the foothills and drive another 40 miles to Grant. Turn right (north) on the Guanella Pass Road and proceed 2.9 miles to the Three-mile Trail access lot, on your right.

Route:

The **Three-mile Trail** climbs 3000 feet over 4.5 miles, leading from the Geneva Creek Valley to the northern flank of Mt. Logan. Several destination points along the way offer a variety of potential day hikes, from easy to moderate in difficulty.

The trail exits the northeast corner of the small parking lot and leads northward above the Geneva Creek basin. Passing several private residences the trail crosses Three-mile Creek via a log bridge and turns northeastward, paralleling the stream. An old irrigation ditch and its rusting inlet valve (1) will soon appear on the north bank of the creek.

Continue northeastward, re-cross the stream and enter a narrow section of the valley, hemmed in by rock cliffs. The path climbs over an outcropping (2) and descends back toward the stream. As the canyon opens up you will cross the creek a third time and soon arrive at a **large meadow (M1)**, elevation 9280 feet. Just over one mile from the trailhead, this meadow is an easy destination for families and offers a sunny picnic site with a magnificent view to the northeast. Returning to your car from this point yields a day hike of 2.2 miles.

Those who continue on will re-enter the forest, pass a small pond (3) and, after crossing the creek two more times, will reach a second small meadow; this is approximately 1.5 miles from the trailhead. Just beyond this meadow is the ruins of a log cabin (4) which sits along the north bank of the stream.

Continuing past the cabin the trail crosses Three-mile Creek for a sixth time and begins to climb at a somewhat steeper grade. Entering another narrow section of the valley the trail crosses the stream four more times and then angles to the right (east) below an impressive wall of rock cliffs and pinnacles (5).

Another mile, and eight more stream crossings, brings you to a **broad alpine meadow (M2)** where the primary stream forms from southeastern and northeastern tributaries. Three miles from the trailhead, this meadow is an excellent destination for a day hike. The bare summit of Mt. Logan (12,870 ft.) looms to the southeast and the rocky crest of Mt. Kataka (12,441 ft.) rises to the north. Looking back down the Three-mile valley, rock cliffs adorn the sun-scorched, south facing wall while a dense, subalpine forest cloaks the shaded slopes of Spearhead Mountain (11,244 ft.), south of the valley. Directly west is

*Aspen and.
spruce frame
a view of
Mt. Logan.*

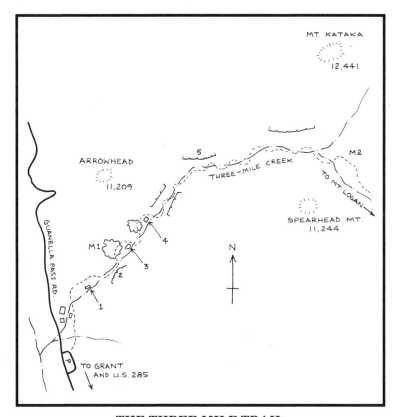

MT. KATAKA

12,441

ARROWHEAD

11,209

5

THREE-MILE CREEK

M2

TO MT LOGAN

GUANELLA PASS RD.

SPEARHEAD MT.
11,244

M1

4

3

2

N

1

P

TO GRANT
AND U.S. 285

THE THREE-MILE TRAIL

Mt. Arrowhead (11,209 ft.) which separates the Three-mile valley from the basin of Scott Gomer Creek (see Abyss Lake Trail).

Returning to the trailhead from this high, alpine meadow yields a roundtrip hike of 6 miles.

187

66 TANGLEWOOD TRAIL

To Timberline:
  Distance: 7 miles roundtrip
  Difficulty: Strenuous
  Walking Time: 4-5 hrs.
  Elevation: 9380-11,600 ft.

To Pegmatite Points
  Distance: 8 miles roundtrip
  Difficulty: Strenuous
  Walking Time: 5-6 hrs.
  Elevation: 9380-11,960 ft.

Your first treat on this excursion is a drive through the magnificent valley of Deer Creek. Quilted with horse pastures and hay fields, the broad valley stretches eastward from the high domes of Mt. Logan and Mt. Rosalie. Aspens glow across the valley walls in late September, contrasting with the deep green of the subalpine conifers.

Heading on a southern ridge of the Mt. Evans massif, Deer Creek rumbles to the southeast, merging with Tanglewood Creek beneath the southern flank of Bandit Peak (12,444 ft.). Just below this junction is the trailhead for the Rosalie and Tanglewood Trails which provides access to southern portions of the Mt. Evans Wilderness.

The **Rosalie Trail** leads upstream along Deer Creek and continues northward to Guanella Pass, a one-way distance of 12.5 miles. **Tanglewood Trail,** the subject of this chapter, cuts to the north, ascending 2600 feet over four miles to the pass between the Deer Creek and Bear Creek Valleys. The first three miles are of moderate difficulty but the last mile, above 10,800 feet, is steep and strenuous. Nevertheless, those who are conditioned enough to take the hike should make every effort to reach timberline, 3.5 miles from the trailhead. From the windswept tundra, over 2000 feet above the valley floor, you are rewarded with a spectacular view of mountains, foothills and canyons to the south.

Directions:

Follow U.S. 285 southwest from Denver. Enter the foothills and drive almost 25 miles to Deer Creek. Turn right and then right again onto Park County Route 43.

Follow this scenic road as it curves back to the west and runs through the valley of Deer Creek. Six and a half miles from U.S. 285 bear left at the fork and proceed another 1.3 miles to the Deer Creek Campground. Bear right along a graveled road for another mile to the Trailhead parking lot.

Route:

A common entry path leaves the southwest corner of the lot, heading west. Bear right onto the **Tanglewood Trail,** hiking above Deer Creek. The trail crosses the stream via a footbridge and then angles to the north along Tanglewood Creek, crossing its channel three times within the first mile. One and a half miles from the trailhead you will enter the Mt. Evans Wilderness and, within another half mile, you will cross a sidestream of Tanglewood Creek.

As the grade steepens you are treated to your first views of the Platte River and Kenosha Mountains to the south and the high ridge of the Pegmatite Points, your ultimate destinatin, looms straight ahead. Another mile brings you to a final crossing of Tanglewood Creek which comes in from the west, heading between Bandit Peak and Mt. Rosalie. The trail now begins to steepen significantly, climbing through the upper reaches of the subalpine forest with only limited use of switchbacks.

Reaching timberline the path curves out to the east, offering a broad view to the south. Devil's Head rises above the Rampart Range to the southeast and Pike's Peak, almost 60 miles away, pokes above the crest of Buffalo Peak. Just to the west of Buffalo Peak is Windy Peak (11,970 ft.) and the high ridges of the Tarryall,

Near timberline along the Tanglewood Trail.

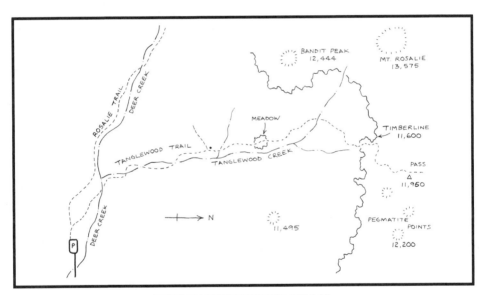

THE TANGLEWOOD TRAIL

Kenosha and Platte River Mountains stretch along the horizon to the SSW. The smooth dome of Mt. Logan blocks out the view to the southwest and Bandit Peak, a shoulder of Mt. Rosalie, rises to the west. Returning to the trailhead from timberline yields a roundtrip hike of 7 miles.

Those who have the energy to continue up to the pass, just under 12,000 feet above sea level, will be rewarded with additional views to the north. From this high ridge the terrain slopes into the valley of Bear Creek, backed by the double-hump of Chief and Squaw Mountains. Mt. Rosalie (13,575 ft.) looms to the west and Long's Peak will be spotted to the north, 47 miles away. The Pegmatite Points stretch away to the east, huge piles of rock atop this windswept arm of the Mt. Evans massif.

Return to the Deer Creek Trailhead via the same route, completing a roundtrip hike of 8 miles.

67 BEN TYLER TRAIL

To Lower Meadow:
   Distance: 2.5 miles roundtrip
   Difficulty: Moderate
   Walking Time: 2-2.5 hrs.
   Elevation: 8260-8800 ft.

To Crest of Platte River Range
   Distance: 14 miles roundtrip
   Difficulty: Strenuous
   Walking Time: 10-12 hrs.
   Elevation: 8260-11,650 ft.

To Upper Valley Meadow:
   Distance: 11 miles roundtrip
   Difficulty: Strenuous
   Walking Time: 6-7 hrs.
   Elevation: 8260-10,900 ft.

Ben Tyler Gulch incises the northern flank of the Platte River Mountains, approximately 2 miles west of Shawnee, Colorado. A 5.5 mile hike (11 miles roundtrip) takes you through this scenic valley, climbing from the North Fork of the South Platte to high alpine meadows, 3000 feet above the River. The valley is characterized by rugged cliffs and extensive stands of aspen, the latter producing a spectacular blanket of gold in late September.

Though seldom steep, the **Ben Tyler Trail** climbs steadily through most of its length and the hike to the Upper Valley, or to the Crest of the Platte River Range, is recommended for fit and experienced hikers. Others should set their sites on the Lower Meadow which yields magnificent views of Ben Tyler Gulch and of the North Fork Valley to the east.

Directions:

Follow U.S. 285 southwest from Denver, enter the foothills and proceed 35.8 miles to the Ben Tyler Trailhead, on the left (south) side of the highway. This parking area is 2 miles beyond the Pike National Forest boundary, at Shawnee.

Route:

From the parking lot the **Ben Tyler Trail** climbs onto a ridge via a series of well-engineered switchbacks. It then makes a long excursion to the southeast,

crossing several drainages, before turning southward and emerging onto the **Lower Meadow**, at 8800 ft. As discussed above, this scenic area is a reasonable destination for many hikers and offers and excellent spot for a picnic lunch; returning to your car from the meadow yields a roundtrip hike of 2.5 miles.

Those who continue along the **Ben Tyler Trail** will soon leave the meadow and enter the streamside forest, paralleling the creek above its west bank. After crossing the stream the trail begins a long, steady climb to the crest of the Platte River Mountains. Entering a dense grove of young aspen, the path makes two jogs to the left and then climbs through a rocky section where numerous springs drain across the trail.

Increasingly distant from Ben Tyler Creek, the route crosses several side streams enroute to the Upper Valley. Four miles from the trailhead you will reach a sign indicating that the **Craig Park Trail** is 1.9 miles ahead. Another .5 mile brings you to a small clearing and, within a few hundred yards the forest begins to open up. Broad views extend back through the valley as several long switchbacks take you into the **Upper Meadow** of Ben Tyler Gulch. Your efforts are rewarded by a magnificent vista to the northeast, flanked by the aspen-cloaked walls of the valley. Black Mountain is the massive block at the left edge of the horizon and Riley Peak (9428 feet) is the rounded pinnacle to the ENE. Further to the right is the jagged silhouette of the Cathedral spires. Those who return to the trailhead from this high meadow will complete a roundtrip hike of 11 miles.

Looking northeast from the Upper Valley Meadow.

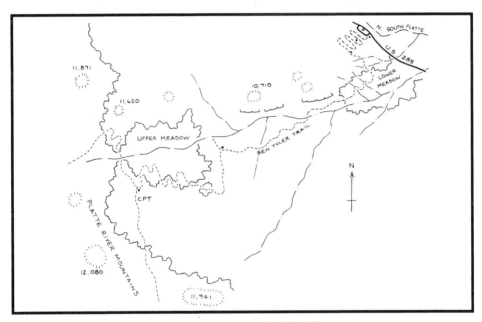

THE BEN TYLER TRAIL

Truly adventurous and conditioned hikers can continue upward along the **Ben Tyler Trail** to the crest of the Platte River Mountains. The trail re-enters the subalpine forest, passes the cutoff to the **Craig Park Trail (CPT)** and soon reaches timberline. Once atop the tundra-covered ridge you are treated to spectacular views to either side of the Range. The Mt. Evans massif rises to the north, its maze of foot-hills and canyons spreading eastward to the Colorado Piedmont. To the southwest is the broad expanse of South Park, backed by the Mosquito Range and the massive Collegiate Peaks of the Upper Arkansas Valley. Thirty-four hundred feet above the North Fork of the South Platte River, your legs must now endure a seven mile descent to the Ben Tyler Trailhead.

191

68 DEVIL'S HEAD

Distance: 2.8 miles roundtrip
Difficulty: Strenuous
Walking Time: 3-3.5 hrs.
Elevation: 8800-9748 ft.

Towering above the Rampart Range, Devil's Head is a familiar landmark for those who travel between Denver and Colorado Springs. Named for the gargoyle-like silhouette imparted by its many outcroppings of granite, the mountain's summit yields a spectacular panorama of the Colorado Piedmont, the Front Range and the Pike's Peak region.

A 1.4 mile interpretive trail winds upward from the access lot, yielding an elevation gain of almost 1000 feet. Designated a National Recreation Trail, the route is named for Helen Dowe, the first woman fire lookout in the U.S. Forest Service, who manned the Devil's Head station from 1919 to 1921. Educational plaques are spaced along the route, illustrating the natural features of this rocky habitat. Though a bit strenuous, the climb is well-engineered with switchbacks and the ascent to the lookout tower is a popular day hike for families.

Directions:
From I-470, south of Denver, exit onto Santa Fe Drive (U.S. 85) and head south. Drive almost 10 miles to Sedalia and turn right (west) onto Colorado 67. Proceed 9.7 miles, knifing into the Rampart Range, and turn left (south) on Rampart Range Rd. This dirt/gravel road is a bit bumpy but can be easily traversed with the family car. Drive 8.8 miles and bear left on the entry road to the Devil's Head Lookout. Snow season visitors may find the entry road closed and will need to park at the junction; this will add .5 mile to your hike in each direction, bringing your total roundtrip hike to 3.8 miles.

Route:
Proceed to the south end of the parking area and pick up the 1.4 mile **Helen Dowe Trail**. Winding further to the south, the route crosses a stream via a footbridge and cuts back to the north. You will soon angle to the east, pass a huge granite monolith and begin a long, gradual climb across the northern flank of Devil's Head. Broad views of the Front Range and the Colorado Piedmont begin to unfold as you traverse a series of switchbacks.

Gradually shifting to the west side of the ridge, the route yields sweeping views of the Mt. Evans massif, the Kenosha Mountains and the Tarryall range. One natural overlook (V) offers an exceptional vista of the Front Range and of numerous rock formations that characterize the Devil's Head region.

Climbing southward, the trail skirts several huge chimneys of pink granite that tower above the pine-fir forest. Nearing the summit, a spur trail cuts eastward to the Zinn Memorial Overlook while the main route climbs toward the southwest and soon enters a clearing where the ranger's cabin is sheltered by towering walls of rock.

The cabin and fire tower were first constructed atop Devil's Head in 1907 but were replaced by newer structures in 1951. A flight of 143 metal stairs provides the final 200 ft. climb to the Lookout Station. From the windy summit you are treated to one of the most spectacular panoramas in all of Colorado. On a clear day you can see over 100 miles in every direction.

To the south, majestic Pike's Peak towers above its surrounding foothills and

*Rock domes and pinnacles adorn the
flanks of Devil's Head.*

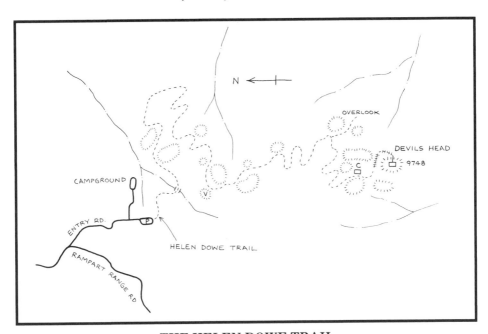

THE HELEN DOWE TRAIL

canyons. Further to the south, and to the west of Pike's Peak, the narrow spine of the Sangre de Cristo Range shimmers above the San Luis Valley. To the west is the jagged ridge of the Tarryall Range and the more rounded peaks of the Kenosha and Platte River Mountains. Mt. Evans looms to the northwest, anchoring the Front Range that sweeps northward to the Wyoming border. Long's Peak and the Mummy Range pinpoint the location of Rocky Mountain National Park. Metro Denver sprawls across the Piedmont to the NNE while the varied mesas of the Castle Rock formation stretch eastward from your perch on the Rampart Range.

After a picnic lunch on the sheltered meadow, return to your car via the same route, completing a day hike of 2.8 miles.

APPENDIX I
A Brief History of the Front Range

An understanding of the natural and human history of the Denver-Boulder region will add to your enjoyment of the walks and hikes in this guide. We thus offer the following chronology of prehistoric and historic events that have culminated in the environment that we find today.

PRECAMBRIAN ERA (4600 to 600 MYA*)

The first 4 billion years of earth history were characterized by cooling of the planet's crust, evolution of the atmosphere and formation of the primordial oceans. Life evolved in the sea about 3.6 billion years ago, protected from the intense solar radiation by the ocean waters. By the end of the era a remarkable diversity of primitive invertebrates had evolved.

PALEOZOIC ERA (600-225 MYA)

Further evolution of marine life and increasing atmospheric oxygen set the stage for colonization of coastal areas by the first land plants. This occurred during the **Silurian Period (440-400 MYA)** when the ozone layer had thickened sufficiently to protect these primitive species from the sun's ultraviolet rays. By the middle of the Paleozoic, sharks and fish had evolved in the ocean and the first amphibians appeared on the continents. Tree-sized ferns, giant horsetails and coniferous woodlands evolved about 300 MYA, later decomposing into the coal seams that lace the globe today.

During the **Pennsylvanian Period (310-270 MYA)** the Ancentral Rocky Mountains pushed skyward across what is now central Colorado. Erosional debris spread out from the flanks of these mountains and would later harden into the Fountain Formation, a red sandstone that is now exposed along the base of the modern Rockies (see Roxborough Park, Red Rocks Park and the Mesa Trail hikes).

Late in the Paleozoic Era, during the **Permian Period**, the earth's continents merged into the land mass of Pangea. Altered ocean currents created a dry, warm climate across much of the landscape, setting the stage for the rise of the dinosaurs. The Lyons Formation, west of the Dakota Hogback, was deposited during the Permian Period.

MESOZOIC ERA (225-65 MYA)

Know as the Age of Reptiles, the Mesozoic is divided into three periods: the Triassic, the Jurassic and the Cretaceous.

The **Triassic Period (225-190 MYA)** was characterized by a warm, dry global climate. Crocodiles, turtles and small, herbivorous dinosaurs appeared during this Period.

The **Jurassic Period (190-135 MYA)** witnessed the split of Pangea into Laurasia (the northern continents) and Gondwanaland (the southern continents).

*MYA - million years ago

194

Large dinosaurs, including allosaurus, stegosaurus, pleisiosaurs and pterysaurs, made their appearance, conifers reached their evolutionary peak and flowering plants began to colonize the earth. By the end of the Period, small, shrew-like creatures appeared — the ancestral mammals.

Jurassic shale, deposited in shallow seas, is rich in dinosaur fossils. The Morrison Formation, named for Morrison, Colorado, is renowned for its wealth of Jurassic fossils. Less resistant to erosion than the overlying (Dakota) and underlying (Lyons) sandstones, the Morrison shale has been shaped into a valley just west of the Hogbacks.

The **Cretaceous Period (135-65 MYA)** dawned when the dinosaurs were reaching their evolutionary peak; Tyrannosaurus rex and the horned dinosaurs appeared early in the Cretaceous. Marsupials evolved in Gondwanaland while primitive eutherians (placental mammals) spread across Laurasia.

Dakota sandstone, the resistant cap of the Front Range Hogbacks, was deposited along the edge of Cretaceous seas. Overlying this sandstone are late-Cretaceous shales (Pierre shale) and sandstones that now underlie the rolling Colorado Piedmont. Seventy million years ago, near the end of the Cretaceous, future-Colorado was a table-top landscape of horizontal Paleozoic and Mesozoic sediments. From top to bottom were: late Cretaceous shales and sandstones, Dakota sandstone, Jurassic shale (the Morrison Formation), Lyons sandstone, the Fountain Formation and early Paleozoic deposits. It was through this layer-cake of sedimentary rock that the ancient, Precambrian core of the modern Rockies pushed skyward (70-60 MYA).

Increasing pressure within the North American craton set in motion the **Laramide Orogeny**, a sequence of uplift, folding and faulting along the corridor that is now the Rocky Mountain chain. Overlying sedimentary rocks were eroded from the crest of the range but their upturned edges can still be seen along the base of the foothills. Even today the uplift and erosion continue, the latter slowly gaining an upper hand; within another 60 million years a flattened landscape may once again characterize Colorado territory.

As the Rockies were forced upward, tremendous pressure developed within the Precambrian, granite core. Cracks and fissures in this ancient rock filled with mineral-rich lava, forced up from the crust-mantle interface. This molten material would later cool to form metamorphic strata within the granite core and veins of precious metal laced the Rockies. These veins are especially concentrated across the **Mineral Belt**, a swath of high country from the Boulder foothills to the San Juan Mountains of southwest Colorado.

CENOZOIC ERA (65 MYA to Present)

The rise of the modern Rockies coincided with cooling of the earth's climate, the demise of the dinosaurs and the onset of the Age of Mammals. Grass evolved in the "rain shadow" of the Rocky Mountains, drawing small, forest-dwelling mammals onto the nutritious, open plains; in doing so they evolved into larger species and developed herding behavior to defend themselves from predators. By the middle of the Era, primitive horses, rhinocerous and camels appeared across North America while ancentral deer, elephants and bison were evolving in Africa and Asia. Further cooling of the climate ushered in periods of glaciation and extensive ice formation at the poles. This resulted in the lowering of sea level and "land bridges" opened between the continents, permitting an interchange of species. Marsupials migrated northward from South America while placental mammals spread to the south across the Isthmus of Panama. Asian and North American species intermingled via the broad expanse of Beringea.

The **Pleistocene Epoch (2-.01 MYA)** is the period of the Cenozoic when glacial activity reached its peak. Known as the "Ice Age," several glacial advances occurred during the Epoch though none penetrated Colorado. However, smaller glaciers did form across the crest of the Rocky Mountain chain, cutting cirques and valleys as they advanced and receded. Meltwater from these ice sheets carved the many canyons that we see along the Front Range today.

It was during the latter half of the Pleistocene that man evolved in eastern Africa. By the end of the Epoch his influence was felt across Europe, Asia and the Americas. Man reached North America via the Bering land bridge late in the Pleistocene Epoch and likely penetrated the center of the continent as the Wisconsin Glaciers were melting back into Canada (10-15,000 years ago). Nomadic **Paleo-hunters** chased herds of bison and mammoths through the "central corridor" and onto the vast grasslands of the Great Plains. Native Americans soon developed an "archaic" lifestyle whereby the various tribes established regional territories and a less-nomadic existence.

Among the earliest known Coloradans were the "Basket Makers" of the Four Corners region, the vanguard of the **Anasazi Civilization**. Best known for their unique pottery and their cliffside dwellings (e.g. Mesa Verde), the Anasazi deserted southwest Colorado by 1276 A.D. The reason for their sudden departure remains a mystery but many anthropologists suspect that a prolonged drought forced them to move into mountainous areas of Colorado, Utah and New Mexico.

By the time the first white explorers reached the Rocky Mountain West, **modern Indian tribes** were encountered. The Utes ruled the mountains of Colorado while the Shoshoni Tribe occupied most of Wyoming. The Arapahoes, Kiowas and Cheyenne Indians hunted across the Colorado Piedmont and eastern plains. To the southeast were the Comanches and the Apaches controlled the high plateaus of northern New Mexico and Arizona.

Historical records of the region began with the explorations of Lewis & Clark, Zebulon Pike, Major Stephen Long and Captain John C. Fremont. The following chronology outlines the history of the Denver-Boulder region; emphasis is placed on events covered in this guide.

1803 - The Louisiana Purchase more than doubles U.S. territory.

1803-1806 - Lewis & Clark are sent to explore the Missouri River headwaters and the Pacific Northwest by President Jefferson.

1806 - Zebulon Pike and his party explore the upper reaches of the Arkansas River.

1820 - Major Stephen Long and his party explore the Front Range region; he is unimpressed with the "Great American Desert".

1833 - Bent's Fort is established along the Arkansas River.

1835-1837 - Increasing fur trade prompts the construction of several Forts along the South Platte River in northeast Colorado.

1842-1844 - Captain John C. Fremont and his party explore Central and Western Colorado.

1848 - The Treaty of Guadelupe-Hidalgo at the end of the Mexican-American War cedes New Mexico and southern Colorado to the U.S.

1849 - The California Gold Rush begins.

1850 - Lewis Ralston finds gold in a tributary of Clear Creek.

196

1858 - Auraria is established by the Russell brothers after they discover gold near the confluence of Cherry Creek and the South Platte; their discovery sets off the "Pike's Peak Gold Rush".
 - William Larimer founds Denver City, naming it for the Governor of the Kansas Territory.
 - Captain Thomas Aikens and his party camp in the Boulder Valley.
1859 - Golden is founded by the Boston Company.
 - Boulder City Town Company is formed.
 - George Jackson discovers gold and hot springs in Grass Valley, the future site of Idaho Springs.
 - John Gregory strikes gold in a gulch above the North Fork of Clear Creek, setting in motion the birth of Central City.
 - George and David Griffith found "George's Town" at the junction of Clear Creek and its southern branch.
 - The town of Mt. Vernon is founded by Dr. Joseph Casto.
 - Four Mile House is built along Cherry Creek.
 - Stagecoach lines reach Denver City.
 - William N. Byers founds the Rocky Mountain News.
 - Jefferson Territory is carved from the Nebraska and Kansas Territories.
1860 - Auraria and Denver City merge to become "Denver".
 - Morrison is founded by George Morrison.
 - The first schoolhouse in the Territory is built in the Boulder Valley.
1861 - Colorado Territory is created and Golden becomes its first capital.
 - Boulder County is established.
 - Sloan's Lake is accidentally created.
1863 - Dr. E. M. Cummings opens his "health baths" along Soda Creek (in present-day Idaho Springs).
 - The Boulder School District is formed.
1864 - A major flood devastates much of the Cherry Creek Valley
 - "The Colorado Seminary," predecessor to the University of Denver, is founded.
1865 - The Squires-Tourtellot House, the first permanent residence in Boulder, is built.
1867 - Smith's Ditch is completed, bringing irrigation waters to southern and eastern sections of Denver.
 - Richard Little builds his Rough & Ready Flour Mill on the South Platte at present-day Littleton.
 - Denver becomes the capital of Colorado Territory.
1868 - Curtis Park becomes Denver's first public park.
 - Georgetown is founded.
1870 - A Board of Trustees for the University of Colorado is appointed.
 - The Kansas-Pacific and Union-Pacific Railroads reach Denver.
 - A plat for the town of Arvada is filed by Benjamin and Mary Wadsworth.
1871 - The town of Boulder is founded.
 - The Zang Brewery begins operation.
 - Rail service reaches Littleton.
1872 - City Cemetery is established at what is now Cheesman Park.
 - Land is donated for the University of Colorado.
 - Richard Little files a plat for the town of Littleton.
 - The Teller House opens in Central City
 - The Colorado & Southern Railroad reaches Black Hawk and Central City.

1873 - George Morrison builds the "Cliff House" in Morrison
     - The Idaho Springs Townsite is registered.
1874 - A fire destroys much of Central City.
     - The Colorado School of Mines is founded in Golden.
     - The Territorial Legislature authorizes funding of the University of Colorado.
1875 - The Hotel de Paris opens in Georgetown.
     - The City of Denver purchases John Smith's Ditch.
     - The Village of Highlands, northwest of downtown Denver, is incorporated.
1876 - Colorado becomes the 38th State.
     - The University of Colorado is founded.
     - The Colorado Brewing Company is established (forerunner of the Tivoli Brewery).
     - Emmanuel-Sherith Israel Temple is built in Auraria.
1877 - The Central Colorado Railroad reaches Idaho Springs and Georgetown.
     - The University of Colorado opens.
1878 - The Colorado Legislature authorizes funding for Denver's Park System.
     - The Central City Opera House is built.
     - The City of Boulder is incorporated.
1880 - The Adolph Coors Brewing Company is founded.
     - Work is begun on the Highline Canal.
     - The University of Denver is founded.
1882 - A Plan for City Park is presented to the Denver City Council.
     - The Walker Ranch is established in the foothills west of Boulder.
     - The Hotel Barth opens in downtown Denver.
1883 - Denver's old City Hall is built at 14th & Larimer.
1886 - Ground is broken for the State Capitol.
1887 - Baron von Richthofen completes his castle in Montclair.
1888 - The Chamberlain Observatory is built.
1889 - The Denver Public Library is established.
     - The Molly Brown House is built.
1890 - The State Capitol is dedicated (though not completely done).
     - Littleton is incorporated.
     - The Castlewood Dam is built.
1891 - Manhattan Beach opens on the north shore of Sloan's Lake.
     - Colorado's first kindergarten opens at Stanley School.
1893 - The Sherman Silver Purchase Act is repealed, triggering a free fall in the price of silver.
     - Charlie Tayler builds his water wheel near Idaho Springs.
     - The "Artists' Club," predecessor of the Denver Art Museum, is founded.
1895 - The Colorado Sanitarium opens at the mouth of Sunshine Canyon.
     - Washington Park becomes Denver's 12th public park.
1896 - St. Elizabeth Church is built near downtown Denver, the first consecrated Catholic Church in Colorado.
1898 - The Texas-Colorado Chautauqua holds its first summer session.
1900 - The Denver Museum of Natural History is incorporated.
1904 - Littleton is named the seat of Arapaho County.
     - The Moffat Railroad is completed across Rollins Pass.
     - The U.S. Mint Building is completed in Denver.
1906 - Flagstaff Road, west of Boulder, is opened.

1907 - The first lookout tower is placed on Devil's Head.
- Cheesman Park is dedicated.
1908 - The Denver Museum of Natural History opens to the public.
- Gold plating of the Capitol dome is completed.
- The Crags Hotel opens in Eldorado Canyon.
1909 - The Daniels & Fisher Tower in downtown Denver is built.
1914 - Union Station opens.
1917 - The Boettcher Mansion is built on Lookout Mountain.
1918 - John Brisben Walker's Mansion burns down on Mt. Falcon.
1923 - Civic Center Park is completed.
1925 - The Arvada Flour Mill is built.
1927 - The Moffat Tunnel is completed.
1932 - The City & County Building is dedicated in Denver.
- The Central City Opera House re-opens.
1934 - Four.Mile House is registered with the Historic American Building Survey.
1942 - Buckley Field is established.
1950 - Cherry Creek Dam is completed.
- The Denver Zoological Foundation is established.
1951 - The Botanical Gardens Foundation of Denver is chartered.
- Rocky Flats opens.
1952 - The Denver-Boulder Turnpike is completed.
1959 - The Denver Botanic Gardens relocates to the old Mt. Calvary Cemetery.
1960 - The Governor's Mansion is donated to the State of Colorado by the Boettcher Family.
1965 - A major flood devastates the South Platte Valley.
1966 - The Georgetown-Silver Plume National Historic District is dedicated.
1969 - The Littleton Historical Museum opens.
- The Tivoli-Union Brewing Company closes.
1971 - The Denver Art Museum opens.
- The Larimer Square Historic District is dedicated.
1973 - Bald Mountain Scenic Area becomes the first Boulder County Open Space Park.
1975 - The Lookout Mountain Nature Center opens.
1976 - The Platte River Greenway Foundation is established.
- Chatfield Dam is completed.
1977 - The Pearl St. Mall opens in Boulder.
1978 - Four Mile Historic Park is dedicated.
1980 - The Mt. Evans Wilderness Area is created.
1982 - The Bear Creek Dam is completed.
1984 - The Georgetown Loop Railroad is dedicated.
1987 - The Colorado Trail, linking Metro Denver with Durango, is completed.
1991 - The Carson Nature Center opens along the South Platte.
- Limited stakes gambling begins in Central City & Black Hawk.
- The Buell Theater opens in Denver.

APPENDIX II
LOCAL CONSERVATION ORGANIZATIONS

Below is a **partial list** of organizations that are devoted to historic preservation, open space protection or wildlife conservation in the Denver-Boulder region. Your active and/or financial support of their efforts will help to ensure the future protection of our natural and cultural heritage.

Adams County Park Department, 9755 Henderson Rd., Brighton, Colorado 80601, 659-4150

Arvada Historical Society, P.O. Box 419, Arvada, Colorado 80001

Aurora Parks & Recreation Department, 1470 S. Havana, Aurora, Colorado 80012, 695-7168

Boulder County Parks & Open Space Department, 2045 13th St., Boulder, Colorado 80302, 441-3950

Boulder Museum of History, 1206 Euclid Ave., Boulder, Colorado 80302, 449-3464

Boulder Parks & Recreation Department, Iris Center, 3198 N. Broadway, Boulder, Colorado 80302, 441-3400

Carson Nature Center, 7301 S. Platte River Parkway, Littleton, Colorado 80120, 730-1022

City of Boulder Open Space Department, 1101 Arapahoe Ave., Boulder, Colorado 80302, 441-3440

Colorado Bird Observatory, Barr Lake State Park, 13401 Picadilly Rd., Brighton, Colorado 80601, 659-4348

Colorado Department of Natural Resources, 1313 Sherman St., Room 718, Denver, Colorado 80203, 866-3311

Colorado Division of Parks & Outdoor Recreation, 1313 Sherman St., Room 618, Denver, Colorado 80203, 866-3437

Colorado Division of Wildlife, 6060 Broadway, Denver, Colorado 80216

Colorado Environmental Coalition, 777 Grant, Suite 606, Denver, Colorado 80203, 837-8701

Colorado Geological Survey, 1313 Sherman St., Room 715, Denver, Colorado 80203, 866-2611

Colorado History Museum, 1300 Broadway, Denver, Colorado 80203, 866-3682

Colorado Mountain Club of Boulder, 900 Baseline Rd., Boulder, Colorado 80302, 449-1135

Colorado Mountain Club of Denver, 2530 W. Alameda Ave., Denver, Colorado 80218, 922-8315

Colorado Open Lands, 1050 Walnut St., Suite 525, Boulder, Colorado 80302, 443-7347

Colorado Parks & Recreation Association, P.O. Box 1037, Wheat Ridge, Colorado 80034, 231-0943

Colorado Trail Foundation, 548 Pine Song Trail, Golden, Colorado 80401

Colorado Waterfowl Association, RD #53, Kiowa, Colorado 80117

Colorado Wildlife Federation, 7475 Dakin, Suite 137, Denver, Colorado 80221, 429-4500

Denver Botanic Gardens, 909 York St., Denver, Colorado 80206, 331-4000

Denver Mountain Parks, 2300 15th, Suite 150, Denver, Colorado 80202, 697-4545

Denver Museum of Natural History, 2001 Colorado Blvd., Denver, Colorado 80205, 322-7009

Denver Parks & Recreation Department, 2300 15th, Suite 150, Denver, Colorado 80202, 964-2500

Denver Zoological Foundation Inc., City Park, Denver, Colorado 80205-4899, 331-4110

Environmental Protection Agency Regional Office, 999 18th, Denver, Colorado 80202-2466, 293-1603

Four Mile Historic Park, 715 S. Forest St., Denver, Colorado 80222, 399-1859

Georgetown Society, P.O. Box 667, Georgetown, Colorado 80444

Highline Canal Preservation Association, c/o C.B.D.A., 2140 S. Ivanhoe #G-7, Denver, Colorado 80222, 756-7925

Historic Boulder Inc., 1733 Canyon Blvd., Boulder, Colorado 80302, 444-5192

Historic Denver Inc., Market Center, 1330 17th, Denver, Colorado 80202, 534-1858

Historical Society of Idaho Springs, P.O. Box 1318, Idaho Springs, Colorado 80452-1318, 567-4709

Jefferson County Open Space Department, 700 Jeffco Parkway, Suite 100, Golden, Colorado 80401, 278-5925

Littleton Historical Museum, 6028 S. Gallup St., Littleton, Colorado 80120, 795-3950

Lookout Mountain Open Space Nature Center, 910 Colorow Rd., Golden, Colorado 80401, 526-0594

National Audubon Society, Rocky Mountain Regional Office, 4150 Darley Ave., Suite 5, Boulder, Colorado 80303, 499-0219

National Park Service, 12795 W. Alameda, Lakewood, Colorado 80228, 969-2000

Nature Conservancy, Colorado Field Office, 1244 Pine St., Boulder, Colorado 80302, 444-2950

The Park People, 715 South Franklin St., Denver, Colorado 80209, 722-6262

Platte River Greenway Foundation, 1666 S. University Blvd., Denver, Colorado 80210, 698-1322

Sierra Club, Rocky Mountain Chapter, 777 Grant St., Suite 606, Denver, Colorado 80203, 861-8819

South Suburban Metropolitan Recreation & Park District, 6315 S. University Blvd., Littleton, Colorado 80121, 798-2493

United States Department of Interior, Geological Survey, Denver Federal Center, Box 25286, Denver, Colorado 80225, 236-7477

University of Colorado Museum, Henderson Building, University of Colorado, Boulder, Colorado, 492-6165

APPENDIX III

TOPOGRAPHIC MAPS

Some who use this guide will want more detailed topographic information for hikes in the foothills and mountains. We have thus listed those **U.S. Geological Survey Maps (7.5 minute series)** that correspond to the Foothill and High Country hikes in this book. These maps can be obtained at the Federal Center, in Lakewood, or at many of the map stores in the Denver-Boulder area.

FOOTHILL HIKES	U.S.G.S. 7.5' MAP(S)
Bald Mountain Scenic Area (#34)	Boulder
Mount Sanitas (#35)	Boulder
Betasso Preserve (#36)	Boulder
Gregory Canyon/Saddle Rock Trail (#37)	Eldorado Springs
Green Mountain/West Ridge Trail (#38)	Eldorado Springs
Walker Ranch (#39)	Eldorado Springs
Eldorado Canyon State Park (#40)	Eldorado Springs
Mesa Trail/Shadow Canyon (#41)	Eldorado Springs
Golden Gate Canyon State Park (#42)	Black Hawk, Ralston Buttes, and Tungsten
White Ranch Park (#43)	Ralston Buttes
Beaver Brook Trail (#46)	Morrison and Evergreen
Jefferson Co. Conference & Nature Center (#47)	Morrison

FOOTHILL HIKES	U.S.G.S. 7.5′ MAP(S)
Matthews/Winter Park-Red-Rocks-Hogback Park (#48)	Morrison
Lair O' The Bear Park (#49)	Evergreen
Mount Falcon Park (#50)	Morrison
Elk Meadow Park/Bergen Peak (#51)	Evergreen and Squaw Pass
Alderfer/Three Sisters Park (#52)	Conifer and Evergreen
Meyer Ranch Park (#53)	Conifer
Reynolds Park (#54)	Platte Canyon and Pine
Waterton Canyon (#55)	Kassler and Platte Canyon
Roxborough State Park (#56)	Kassler

HIGH COUNTRY HIKES

Indian Peaks Wilderness (#57)	Ward
East Portal/Crater Lakes (#58)	East Portal
St. Mary's Glacier (#59)	Empire
The Continental Divide/Berthoud Pass (#60)	Berthoud Pass
Chicago Lakes Trail (#62)	Idaho Springs, Georgetown and Mount Evans
Chief Mountain (#63)	Idaho Springs
Abyss Lake Trail (#64)	Mount Evans
Three-Mile Trail (#65)	Mount Logan and Mount Evans
Tanglewood Trail (#66)	Harris Park
Ben Tyler Trail (#67)	Shawnee and Mount Logan
Devil's Head (#68)	Devil's Head

BIBLIOGRAPHY

1. Arvada Historical Society, **Waters of Gold, A History of Arvada, Colorado, During the Period 1850-1870**, 1973

2. Arvada Regional Library, **Historic Walking Tour of Olde Downtown Arvada**, September, 1978

3. Barker, Jane Valentine, **76 Historic Homes of Boulder, Colorado**, Pruett Publishing Company, 1976

4. Barrett, Marjorie, **"Hill Comes of Age,"** Rocky Mountain News, September 4, 1973

5. Boulder Mountain Park Rangers, **Boulder's Historic Highlights**

6. Brettell, Richard R., **Historic Denver, The Architects & The Architecture 1858-1893**, Historic Denver Inc., 1973

7. **A Centennial Celebration, Highlands Lodge No. 86, 1891-1991**

8. City of Littleton, City Managers Office, **Littleton, A Special Spirit**, 1987

9. Coel, Margaret, Gladys Doty & Karen Gilleland, **Under the Golden Dome**, Colorado & West, 1985

10. Colorado State Parks, **The Trails of Golden Gate Canyon State Park**

11. Colorado Yesterday & Today, **A Walking Tour of Idaho Springs' Newly Renovated Downtown Historic District**, Summer, 1991

12. Denerstein, Robert, **"Country Club Area becomes Denver's largest historic district,"** Rocky Mountain News, August 4, 1979, 38-68

13. Ditmer, Joanne, **"Happy Endings,"** Denver Post, December 30, 1990, pg. 13

14. Dorsett, Lyle W. and Michael McCarthy, **The Queen City, A History of Denver**, Second Edition, Pruett Publishing Company, 1986

15. Etter, Don, **Auraria, Where Denver Began**, Colorado Assoc., 1972

16. Etter, Don, **University Park/Denver, Four Walking Tours**, Graphic Impressions Inc., 1974

17. Frink, Maurice, **The Boulder Story**, Pruett Publishing Company, 1965

18. **Georgetown, Colorado, Historic Buildings Tour**

19. Georgetown Society Inc. & the People for Silver Plume Inc., **Georgetown-Silver Plume, Guide to the Historic District**, Cordillera Press Inc., 1990

20. Goodstein, Phil, **Denver's Capitol Hill**, Stuart MacPhail Publisher, Life Publications, 1988

21. Hicks, Dave, **Aurora From the Beginning**, Egan Printing & A-T-P Publishing Co., 1977

22. Hillestad, Charles, **Denver Historic, A Self-Guided Walking Tour**, 1988

23. Historical Society of Idaho Springs, **"A Walking Tour of Idaho Springs,"** The Idahoe, Summer, 1991

24. **Historic Central City, Colorado: A Walk Through Colorado's History**

25. Horton, Lorene, **Morrison Historical Guide**, 1975

26. Krueger, Mary G., Pam Phipps and Arlie M. Clark, **Historical Walking Tour of Idaho Springs, Colorado; A Victorian Mining Town, Past & Present**, Published by Les and Arlie Clark, for Historical Society of Idaho Springs Inc., 1987

27. McQuarie, Robert J. and C.W. Buchholtz, **Littleton, Colorado, Settlement to Centennial**, Littleton Historical Museum & Friends of the Littleton Library & Museum, 1990

28. Mehls, Steven F., Carol J. Drake and James E. Fell Jr., **Aurora, Gateway to the Rockies**, Cordillera Press Inc., 1985

29. Morris Jr., Langdon E., **Denver Landmarks**, Charles W. Cleworth Publisher, Denver, Colorado, 1979

30. Muntz, Geoffrey L. and Alan S. Wuth, **A Path Through Time, A Guide to the Platte River Greenway**, Frederick, Colorado: Jende-Hagan, 1983

31. Noel, Thomas J., **Richthofen's Montclair, A Pioneer Denver Suburb**, Pruett Publishing Company, 1976

32. Peters, Bette D., **Denver's City Park**, University of Colorado at Denver, Historical Studies Vol. II, No. 2, Special Issue, 1985

33. Peters, Bette D., **Denver's Four Mile House**, The Junior League of Denver, Inc., for Four Mile Historic Park, Inc., 1980

34. Pritchett, Bryan, **"Urban Wildlife Management at Crown Hill Park Wildlife Refuge,"** Colorado Outdoors, March/April 1990

35. Repplier, F.O., **A History of St. John's Episcopal Church, Boulder, Colorado, 1873-1963**

36. Seiden, O.J., **Denver's Richthofen Castle**, Stonehenge Books, 1980

37. Simmons, R. Laurie and Thomas H. Simmons, **"Historic Research on 1015 Ford St., Golden, Colorado,"** Front Range Research Associates, Inc., August 9, 1991

38. Smith, Phyllis, **A History of Mapleton School, Boulder, Colorado**, Boulder Valley Public Schools Print Shop, 1975, Revised 1986

39. Smith, Phyllis, **A Look at Boulder, From Settlement to City**, Pruett Publishing Company, 1981

40. Town of Morrison, **A Tour of Morrision Historic Sites**

41. University of Colorado, Boulder, **A Visitors Guide to the Norlin Quadrangle Historic District**, funded in part by First National Bank of Boulder

42. West, William A., **Curtis Park, A Denver Neighborhood**, Colorado Associated University Press in cooperation with Historic Denver Inc., 1980

43. Wiberg, Ruth E., **Rediscovering Northwest Denver, Its History, Its Landmarks**, Northwest Denver Books, 1976

44. Writers' Program of the W.P.A., **The W.P.A. Guide to 1930s Colorado**, University Press of Kansas, 1987; originally published in 1941 by Colorado State Planning Commission, Hastings House, as **Colorado: A Guide to the Highest State**

Index